THE
ANXIOUS BENCH
(Second Edition)

ANTICHRIST

AND THE SERMON
CATHOLIC UNITY

by

John Williamson Nevin

Edited by
Augustine Thompson, O.P.

Wipf and Stock Publishers
150 West Broadway • Eugene OR 97401

Wipf and Stock Publishers
150 West Broadway • Eugene OR 97401

(541) 485-5745 or 344-1528
WSPub@academicbooks.com

Originally published:

John W. Nevin, "Letter to Dr. Henry Harbaugh," in *Catholic and Reformed: Selected Theological Writings of John Williamson Nevin*, ed. Charles Yrigoyen, Jr., and George H. Bricker (Pittsburgh, PA: Pickwick Press, 1978), pp. 407–11, USED WITH PERMISSION;

John W. Nevin, *The Anxious Bench*, 2d. ed. (Chambersburg, PA: Publication Office of the German Reformed Church, 1844);

John W. Nevin, "Catholic Unity," in Philip Schaff, *The Principle of Protestantism as Related to the Present State of the Church* (Chambersburg, PA: Publication Office of the German Reformed Church, 1845), pp. 193–215;

John W. Nevin, *Antichrist; or the Spirit of Sect and Schism* (New York: John S. Taylor, 1848).

Texts are reproduced as they appear in the original editions,
but obvious typographical errors are silently corrected,
as are missing Greek diacritical marks and punctuation.

THE MERCERSBURG THEOLOGY

This small treatise prepared by John W. Nevin for his student, Henry Harbaugh (1817–1867), later pastor at Lancaster and Lebanon and finally elected to the Chair of Didactic and Practical Theology at Mercersburg, is found in the archives of the Evangelical and Reformed Historical Society. Harbaugh was on the committee that drafted the German Reformed Church's Provisional Liturgy *of 1857 and the* Order of Worship *of 1866. Although undated, the text was written after 1860 and has attached a short note to Harbaugh indicating that Nevin wrote it at his request. The essay contains Nevin's summary of the* Mercersburg Theology, *of which he was the great exponent. In the essay Nevin describes four of his works as seminal in the development of the Mercersburg Theology. Three of these,* The Anxious Bench, Catholic Unity, *and* Antichrist *are gathered in this volume. A new edition of the fourth,* The Mystical Presence, *will follow in a second volume.*

THE MERCERSBURG THEOLOGY.

What is called the "Mercersburg System of Theology" grew into shape without calculation or plan. It owes its existence properly not to any spirit of philosophical speculation as has been sometimes imagined, but to an active interest in practical Christianity. Questions of religious life have governed in succession the course of its history. Still those have moved, with more or less insight always, round a common centre; and the system is found to be accordingly in the end sufficiently scientific, and in full harmony with itself throughout.

Historically it may be said to have commenced with the publication in 1843 of the *Anxious Bench*—a tract, which found wide favor, but drew upon its author at the same time in certain quarters a perfect hurricane of reproach. Then came the sermon on *Church Unity* preached by Dr. Nevin at the opening of the Triennial Convention of the Reformed Dutch and German Reformed Churches held at Harrisburg in the year 1844; a discourse sanctioned by the full approbation of the worthy representatives of both Churches at the time, the positions of which, however, on the subject of the Mystical Union and in opposition to the sect system, were felt by many afterwards to involve a dangerous *tendency*. Dr. Schaff's memorable *Principle of Protestantism*, published in 1845, brought out the tendency, in the apprehension of such persons, under still more alarming proportions. This was followed, the next year, by the *Mystical Presence*, with a translation of Dr. Ullmann's most masterly tract on *The Distinctive Character of Christianity* prefixed in the form of a Preliminary Essay. The work was a vindication at large of the old Calvinistic Doctrine of the Lord's Supper, conveying against the general Protestantism of the present time a charge of wholesale defection from the Protestant sacramental faith of the sixteenth century. The tract *Antichrist* was a regular assault upon the sect system, as being in full antagonism to the true idea of the Church, and such a heresy as draws after it virtually in the end a Gnostic denial of the proper mystery of the Incarnation itself. As the occasions of Theological discussion were multiplied, it was felt necessary to establish a special organ for carrying it forward; the more so as it seemed altogether impractical to gain a fair hearing in any other quarter. Hence, the *Mercersburg Review*, the pages of which for some years form a sort of progressive picture of the system to whose exposition and defence it has been all along devoted. So much for the general history of the movement.

We come now to what is more important, the organization of inward structure of the Mercersburg System regarded as a whole.

Its cardinal principle is the fact of the Incarnation. This viewed not as a doctrine or speculation but as a real transaction of God in the world, is regarded as being necessarily itself the essence of Christianity, the sum and substance of the whole Christian redemption. Christ saves the world, not ultimately by what he teaches or by what he does, but by what he *is* in the constitution of his own person. His person in its relations to the world carries in it the power of victory over sin, death, and hell, the force thus of a real atonement or reconciliation between God and man, the triumph of a glorious resurrection from the dead, and all the consequences for faith which are attributed to this in the grand old symbol called the Apostles' Creed. In the most literal sense accordingly Christ is here held to be the "way, the truth and the life," the "resurrection and the life," the principle of "life and immortality"—the "light" of the world, its "righteousness," and its "peace." The "grace which brings salvation" in this view is of course always a real affluence from the new order of existence, which has been thus made to be by the exaltation of the Word made flesh at the right hand of God. It must be supernatural as well as natural, and the organs and agencies by which it works must in the nature of the case carry with them objectively some thing of the same character and force. To resolve all into the opinions and feelings of those who call themselves believers, is to do away with the proper objects of faith altogether; for these must be apprehended as actually at hand under a supernatural form. They are all mysteries, holding in them objectively some measure of what belongs to the mystery of Christ's glorification. In this way the Church is an object of faith—the presence of a new creation in the old world of nature—the body of Christ through which as a medium and organ he reveals himself and works till the end of time. Its ministers hold a divine power from him by apostolical succession. Its sacraments are not signs merely, but goals of the grace they represent. Baptism is for the remission of sins. The Eucharist includes the real presence of Christ's whole glorified life, in a mystery, by the power of the Holy Ghost. The idea of the Church, so sound, it is made to be in this way an object of faith, involves necessarily the attributes which were always ascribed to it in the beginning, unity, sanctity, catholicity, and apostolicity. The spirit of sect, as it cleaves to Protestantism at the present time, is a very great evil, which is of itself sufficient to show that if Protestantism had any historical justification in the beginning, its mission thus far has been only half fulfilled, and that it can be rationally approved only as it is taken to be an interimistic preparation for some higher and better form of Christianity hereafter.

The distinguishing character of the Mercersburg Theology, in one word, is its Christological interest, its way of looking at all things through the Person of the crucified and risen Saviour. This, as the world now stands, embraces necessarily all that enters into the conception of the Church Question—the problem of problems for the Christianity of the present time. That the system has been able to solve in full the difficulties belonging to this great subject, its friends have never pretended for one moment to imagine. On the contrary, they have always confessed their sense of vast practical embarrassment confronting their views. But they have not considered this a sufficient reason for refusing to affirm what has appeared to them to be biblically or historically true, in spite of such inconvenience. Facts and principles have a right to challenge attention at times, even if no satisfactory scheme can be offered for their application. The Mercersburg Theology claims the advantage of standing here, in its main positions, on the same ground with the faith of the early Church. Its Christology is that of the ancient Creeds. It insists on casting the Christian belief of the world still in the same primitive mould; and the burden of its controversy with those who stand opposed to it is that they either ignore the Apostles' Creed altogether or else make no earnest with its proper historical sense, but vainly imagine that it may be superseded or mended by other modern forms of confession, more suited to their own unchurch ly sense.

In thus agreeing with the Creed, the system of course holds itself to be to the same extent in full agreement with the proper sense of the Scriptures; where in truth all stress is laid on the Person of Christ, on his resurrection from the dead, on his glorification at the right hand of God, on the sending of the Holy Ghost, and on his presence and work-ing through all time in the Church which is his body, the fulness of Him that filleth all in all.

A TRACT FOR THE TIMES.

THE
ANXIOUS BENCH,

BY

John W. Nevin, D.D.,

PROFESSOR OF THEOLOGY IN THE SEMINARY OF THE GER. REF. CHURCH.

SECOND EDITION,

REVISED AND ENLARGED.

TECKEL.—*Daniel* v. 27.

CHAMBERSBURG, Pa.

PRINTED AT THE PUBLICATION OFFICE OF THE GERMAN REF. CHURCH.

....

1844.

Copy right secured according to Law.

PREFACE.

In coming before the public with a *Second edition* of The Anxious Bench, it seems proper to introduce it with a short preface.

The publication, as was to be expected, has produced considerable excitement. At least half a dozen of replies to it, shorter or longer, have been announced in different quarters, proceeding from no less than five different religious denominations. Various assaults, in addition to this, have been made upon it from the pulpit; to say nothing of the innumerable reproaches it has been required to suffer in a more private way.

All this, however, calls for no very special notice in return. I am sorry to say that of all the published replies to the tract, which have come under my observation, not one is entitled to any respect, as an honest and intelligent argument on the other side. In no case has the question at issue been fairly accepted and candidly met. I do not feel myself required at all, then, to enter into a formal vindication of the tract, as assailed in those publications. I consider it to be in itself a full and triumphant answer to all they contain against it, in the way of objection or reproach. If permitted to speak for itself, by being seriously and attentively read, it may safely be left to plead its own cause. In such circumstances it would be idle to enter into a controversial review of the manifold misrepresentations to which it has been subjected. The only proper reply to them is a republication of the tract itself.

With the reproaches that have been showered upon me personally, in different quarters, I have not allowed myself to be much disturbed. I had looked for it all beforehand; knowing well the spirit of the system with which I was called to deal. I knew of course that I should be calumniated as an enemy to revivals, and as an opposer of vital godliness. But I felt satisfied at the same time that the calumny would, in due season, correct itself, and recoil with disgrace on the heads of those from whom it might proceed. It has begun to do so already, and will continue to do so, no doubt, more and more.

Some have wondered that I did not take more pains to define my position with regard to revivals, by writing a chapter on the subject, so as to cut off occasion for the reproach now mentioned. But this would have been, in some measure, to justify and invite the wrong, which it was proposed to prevent. There is gross insolence in the assumption that a man should at all *need* to vindicate himself in this way, in venturing to speak against the system of New Measures. And then, it is not by formal protestations, when all is done, that the point, in any such case, can be fully settled. A chapter on revivals would be of little account in my tract if my own character, and the whole spirit of the tract itself, were not such as to show an honest zeal in favor of serious religion. The publications which have come out in reply to it all affect an extraordinary interest in the subject of revivals, exhibited often with a very blustering air; but in the case of some of them, this pretension is utterly belied, to all who have the least amount of spiritual discernment, by the tone of feeling with which they are characterized throughout. They carry in them no savor at all of the wisdom that cometh from above, no sympathy whatever with the mind of Jesus Christ. The remark is made of *some* of these publications, not of the whole of them indiscriminately.

Nor would any special protestation in favor of revivals be of much account to guard the tract from being perversely used by those who are in fact opposed to this precious interest. The only true and proper provision against such abuse must be found, if it exists at all, in the general spirit of the tract itself. Let this be right, and it must be considered enough. It may be perverted still; but men can pervert the Bible, too, if they please.

Fears have been expressed that in the present position of the German Churches particularly, the publication may operate disastrously upon the interests of vital godliness. But in my own view there is no good reason for any such fears. I believe its operation has been salutary already, and trust it will be found more salutary still in time to come. It has engaged attention extensively to the subject of which it treats, and is likely to go farther than anything that has appeared before, in correcting the confusion and mystification in which it has been so unhappily involved, in certain parts of the country, to the great prejudice of religion. It may be hoped now that the subject of New Measures will be so examined and understood, that all shall come to make a proper distinction between the system of the Anxious Bench and the power of evangelical godliness, working in its true forms. In the case of the German Churches, this would be a result of the very highest consequence. If the present tract may open the way for its accomplishment, its mission will be one in which all the friends of true religion in these Churches will have occasion to rejoice.

But instead of lending their help to secure this most desirable object, the friends of the Anxious Bench seem concerned to maintain as long as possible the very mystification that stands in its way. They tell us we must not speak against New Measures, because this term is made to include, in some parts of the country, revivals and other kindred interests; and then, when we propose to correct this gross mistake by proper instruction, they set themselves with all their might to counteract the attempt, and insist that the people shall be suffered to confound these different forms of religion as before. Those who act thus are themselves enemies in fact to the cause of revivals. From no other quarter has it been made to suffer so seriously. Its greatest misfortune is that it should lie at the mercy of such hands.

It is with a very bad grace that reference is made occasionally by some to the idea of a *foreign* spirit in the tract, as related to the German Churches. It is in full sympathy with the true life of these Churches, as it stood in the beginning. The charge of seeking to force a foreign spirit on them lies with clear right against the other side. The system of New Measures has no affinity whatever with the life of the Reformation, as embodied in the *Augsburgh Confession* and the *Heidelbergh Catechism*. It could not have found any favor in the eyes of Zwingli or Calvin. Luther would have denounced it in the most unmerciful terms. His soul was too large, too deep, too free, to hold communion with a style of religion so mechanical and shallow. Those who are actively laboring to bring the Church of Luther, in this country, into subjection to the system, cannot be said to be true to his memory or name. The challenge, *Why are you a Lutheran?* is one which they would do well seriously to consider. It is most certain that the interest they are pushing forward, in this view, is not Lutheranism in any sense that agrees with the true historical life of the Church. It involves a different theory of religion, that stands in no fellowship with the views, either of the fathers and founders of the Church, or of its most evangelical representatives in modern Germany. It is another element altogether that surrounds us, in the writings of such men as Olshausen, Tholuck, Sartorius, and Neander. The system in question is in its principle and soul neither Calvinism nor Lutheranism, but Wesleyan *Methodism*. Those who are urging it upon the old German Churches are in fact doing as much as they can to turn them over into the arms of Methodism. This may be done without any change of denominational name. Already the *life* of Methodism, in this country, is actively at work among other sects, which owe no fellowship with it in form. So in the present case, names may continue to stand as before; but they will be only as the garnished sepulchres of a glory that belonged to other days.

But is not Methodism Christianity? And is it not better that the German Churches should rise in this form than not rise at all? Most certainly so, I reply, if that be the only alternative. But that is *not* the only alternative. Their resurrection may just as well take place, in the type of their own true, original, glorious life, as it is still to be found enshrined in their symbolical books. And whatever there may be that is good in Methodism, this life of the Reformation I affirm to be immeasurably more excellent and sound. Wesley was a small man as compared with Melancthon. Olshausen, with all his mysticism, is a commentator of the inmost sanctuary in comparison with Adam Clark. If the original, distinctive life of the Churches of the Reformation be not the object to be reached after, in the efforts that are made to build up the interests of German Christianity in this country, it were better to say so at once openly and plainly.

If we *must* have Methodism, let us have it under its own proper title, and in its own proper shape. Why keep up the walls of denominational partition in such a case, with no distinctive spiritual being to uphold or protect? A sect without a soul has no right to live. Zeal for a separate denominational name that utters no separate religious *idea* is the very essence of sectarian bigotry and schism.

In opposing the Anxious Bench, I mean no disrespect, of course, to the many excellent men, in different Churches, who have given it their countenance. This has been done by some of the best ministers in the land, for whom I entertain the very highest regard. Not a few are to be found who themselves condemn their own former judgment in so doing; which does not imply surely any want of proper *self*-respect. The *system* of the Anxious Bench, in its full development, is one which these persons have always disapproved; only they have not considered this particular measure to be a part of the system. That this should be the case need not seem strange; for in the view of the measure here taken, it is supposed to be in its simple form, on the bright side of this system, and close upon the boundary that separates it from the territory of the truth. The tract exhibits the measure in this view, not as the origin of the system historically, not as necessarily conducting in all cases to worse things that lie beyond; but as constitutionally involving the principle of those worse things, under the least startling form, and legitimately opening the way for their introduction, if circumstances should permit. It would seem to show the correctness of this view, that while the answers to the tract protest against it, as a false and arbitrary classification, they all conform to it notwithstanding, in spite of themselves, in a practical way. They defend the use of the bench as the Thermopylae of New Measures; and their argument, such as it is, has just as much force to justify the system in full, as it has to justify this measure in particular. An effort is made, indeed, to mystify the subject, by dragging into connection with it interests of a different order altogether; but still it is plain enough that this is done with violence, and the controversy falls back always in the end to its proper limits.

The abuse of a thing, it is said, is no argument against its proper use; and therefore the object, in the present case, should be to reform and regulate rather than to abolish. To this I reply, the whole system contemplated in the tract is an abuse, from which it is of the utmost importance that the worship of the sanctuary, and the cause of revivals, should be rescued. Belonging as it does to this system, then, and contributing to its support, the Anxious Bench is a nuisance that can never be fully abated except by its entire removal. Its tendencies, as shown in the tract, are decidedly bad, without any compensation of a solid kind. It may be used with moderation; but it will stand still in the same relation to the system it represents, that moderate drinking holds to intemperance in its more advanced forms. Popery started, in the beginning, under forms apparently the most innocent and safe. What might seem to be, for instance, more rational and becoming than the *sign of the cross*, as used by Christians, on all occasions in the early Church? And yet, when the corruptions of Rome were thrown off by the Protestant world, in the sixteenth century, this and other similar forms were required to pass away with the general mass. And why is it that the sign of the cross, as once used, is now counted a dangerous superstition, not to be permitted among Protestants? Simply because it falls naturally over to that vast system of abuses, of which it forms a part in the Romish Church. Thus it *represents* that system, and furnishes a specimen of it constitutionally, under the most plausible shape. Such is the position of the Anxious Bench, as a particular measure, in the general case now under consideration. It is just as easy to conceive of a judicious and salutary use of the Anxious Bench; and I have no doubt at all but that the first has been owned and blessed of God full as extensively, to say the least, as this has ever been the case with the last.

J. W. N.

Mercersburg, *Jan.* 1844

CHAPTER I.

Design of the Tract.—Occasion for inquiry.—Importance and solemnity of the subject.

It is proposed to institute a free inquiry into the merits of the *Anxious Bench*, as it has been enlisted extensively of late years in the service of religion. My object will be to show that the measure is adapted to obstruct rather than to promote the progress of true godliness, and that it deserves to be discouraged on this account.

No one needs to be informed what is meant by the *Anxious Bench*. Its nature and design have come to be as familiar to most people as the nature and design of the pulpit itself. Even among those who dislike it there are few perhaps who have not had the opportunity at one time or another of witnessing its operation, while all are well acquainted with it at least in the way of description and report.

It will be understood that the Anxious Bench is made to stand, in this case, as the type and representative of the entire system of what are technically denominated in our day "*New Measures.*" It is not meant by this, of course, that it is so bound to the system as never to be separated from other parts of it in actual practice. It may be in use where no new measures besides are tolerated; and it is possible, on the other hand, that it may not be employed by some who in other respects are wholly in this interest. But still it may very fairly be exhibited as a type of the system at large. These measures form properly a *system*; and it is only in this view that it is possible to estimate rightly their nature and character. It is not uncommon to class with them things of a different nature altogether; and then advantage is taken of the confusion thus produced to evade the point of objections urged against new measures in the proper sense. This, however, is sophistry of a very shallow order. The idea of *New Measures* is just as well defined in itself and as generally intelligible in the American Church as the idea of popery, Methodism, Presbyterianism, or almost anything else of the same general character that might be named. It is only by a gross and palpable abuse that some wish to make it include the best things in the Church. New measures, in the technical modern sense, form a particular system, involving a certain theory of religious action, and characterized by a distinctive life, which is by no means difficult to understand. Of this system the Anxious Bench is a proper representative. It opens the way naturally to other forms of aberration in the same direction, and may be regarded in this view as the threshold of all that is found to follow, quite out to the extreme verge of fanaticism and rant. The measure belongs to the system, not in the name simply, but in its life and spirit. At the same time, it is the most favorable aspect in which the cause of New Measures can be presented to our view. The simple Anxious Bench, as it is often used in a sober way, is the most moderate and plausible shape the system can well take. If this then be found unworthy of confidence, the whole system will be shorn of its title to confidence at the same time. If the Anxious Bench can claim no indulgence, it must be idle to put in a plea for its kindred measures. All *beyond* this is only something worse.

It is well too that we can thus deal with our subject. If there be no room, as some pretend, for treating it in a clear and satisfactory way under the title of New Measures, by reason of the confusion with which that term is used, it is so much the more important that we should substitute the particular for the general; and we have reason to congratulate ourselves on finding a single, well known form of action that can be taken fairly as the representative of the whole system. In this way our argument will not be abstract and vague, but pointed and clear. Whatever dust it might be contrived to raise with regard to the proper sense of the term *New Measures*, all know at least the meaning of the *Anxious Bench*. Here then we have a tangible, concrete subject with which to deal. Let it serve as a specimen of the system to which it belongs. In this way the system is characterized and distinguished. It includes things of the same general constitution and spirit with the Anxious Bench. In trying the merits of this, we try at the same time all these kindred practices and nothing more.* If any choose to incorporate with *their* idea of New Measures, things of a different constitution and spirit entirely, it cannot be helped. But they can have no right to force any view of this sort upon the present argument. Our business is with New Measures in the proper sense; and that we may not seem to run uncertainly, or beat the air, we characterize the system by one of its most familiar exhibitions. It stands before us in the type of the Anxious Bench.

Here too is the proper point for grappling with the heresy of New Measures. It can answer no purpose to discountenance the system in general, if we lend our influence theoretically or practically to uphold a measure forming like this a legitimate stepping stone to all the system is found to embrace. No satisfactory line can be drawn between this and the more advanced forms of extravagance for which it prepares the way. They

---

*"How can the import of this measure exhibit the character of protracted meetings, both which in many German churches are well known to be included in their idea of New Measures?"—*Luth. Obs.*, Nov. 17, 1843. Of a truth, it may be replied, not very well; and for this reason precisely it is made to stand here as the representative of the system to which it of right belongs, that every body may be able at once to see and understand that prayer meetings, protracted meetings, and other interests of the same complexion come not in any sense within the scope of the present inquiry.

will be found to involve in the end the same principle. That is a false position, therefore, by which some excellent men allow themselves to speak freely against noise and disorder and bodily exercises in public worship under other forms, while at the same time the Anxious Bench is not only spared, but treated with honor and confidence, as though it had come to form part of the accredited and regular service of God's House. Men who occupy this position may preach or write an abundance of wholesome advice on the subject of false excitement in religion; but their advice is not likely to carry much weight with it in the end, as not going after all to the ground of the error against which it is directed. If we would utter an intelligible and consistent testimony against New Measures, we must make no exception, openly or tacitly, in favor of the Anxious Bench. Here precisely is the proper point at which to grapple with the whole system.

There is occasion for the inquiry here proposed. It is true, indeed, that throughout a large portion of the country the Anxious Bench, after having enjoyed a brief reputation, has fallen into discredit. It has been tried, and found wanting; and it might have been trusted that this experiment would be sufficient to drive it completely out of use. But unfortunately this has not been the case. Over a wide section of the land we find it still holding its ground, without any regard to the disgrace with which it has been overtaken in the North and East. Peculiar circumstances have conspired to promote its credit on this field.

It is within the range particularly of the German Churches that a new life may be said to have been communicated latterly to the system of New Measures. No field is more interesting at this time than that which is comprehended within these limits. A vast moral change is going forward upon it, involving consequences that no man can properly calculate. From various causes a new feeling is at work everywhere on the subject of religion. As usual, the old struggles to maintain itself in opposition to the new, and a strong tendency to become extreme is created on both sides. The general mind unhappily has not been furnished thus far with proper protection and guidance in the way of full religious teaching; and the result is that in these interesting circumstances it has become exposed more or less at almost every point to those wild fanatical influences which in this country are sure to come in like a desolating flood wherever they can find room. Upstart sects have set themselves to take possession, if possible, of the entire field in this way, on the principle that the old organizations are corrupt and deserve to be destroyed. Their reliance, of course, in this work of reformation, is placed largely on New Measures! Thus a whole Babel of extravagance has been let loose upon the community far and wide in the name of religion, one sect vying with another in the measure of its irregularities. In these circumstances it has not been easy for the friends of earnest piety always in the regular churches to abide by the ancient landmarks of truth and order. The temptation has been strong to fall in, at least to some extent, with the tide of fanaticism as the only way of making war successfully on the dead formality that stared them in the face in one direction, and the only way of counteracting the proselyting zeal of these noisy sects in the other.

This and other considerations have had the effect of opening the way for the use of New Measures to some extent in the German Reformed Church, and to a much greater in the Lutheran. It is well known that a large division of this last denomination has identified itself openly and zealously with the system, both in doctrine and practice. The *Lutheran Observer*, which has a wide circulation and great influence, has lent all its authority to recommend and support the Anxious Bench with its accompaniments, taking every occasion to speak in its favor and making continually the most of its results. The "revivals" of the Church latterly have been very generally carried forward with the use of New Measures, as may be perceived from the reports of them published from time to time in the *Observer*. The great awakening of last winter, pronounced by the editor of that paper to have been probably the greatest since the days of the Apostles, seems almost everywhere to have involved the free use of this method. Thus ministers and congregations have became extensively committed in its favor; so that with many the use of the Anxious Bench, and a zeal for evangelical godliness, are considered to be very much the same thing. It might seem indeed as though all the interests of religion, in the case of the German community, were to the view of a large class suspended on the triumphant progress of New Measures.* These are with them emphatically the "great power of God," which may be expected to turn and overturn, till old things shall fairly pass away and all things become new. And it must be acknowledged that the system bids fair at present to go on conquering and to conquer in its own style within the limits at least of this widely extended and venerable denomination. It seems to bear down more and more all opposition. It has become an interest too strong to be resisted or controlled. What are to be its ultimate issues and results, time only can reveal.

All this is within the reach of the most common observation. And no one reflecting on the actual state of things at this time on the field

---

*"And let me tell you, Sir, that whatever Prof. NEVIN may (in the abstraction of his study) have written to the contrary, I am nevertheless strongly convinced, as a pastor, that the so-called '*Anxious bench*' is the lever of Archimedes, which by the blessing of God can raise our German churches to that degree of respectability and prosperity in the religious world which they ought to enjoy."—*Correspondence of the Luth. Obs., Nov.* 17, 1843.

"Such measures are usually inseparable from great revivals, and if the great luminaries in the Church set themselves up against them, why they must be content to abide the consequences. By the judicious use of such measures, the millennium must be accelerated and introduced; &c.—*Luth. Obs., Jan.* 26, 1844.

occupied by the German Churches can well fail to perceive that there is full occasion for calling attention to the subject which it is here proposed to consider. An inquiry into the merits of the Anxious Bench and the system to which it belongs is not only seasonable and fit in the circumstances of the time, but loudly called for on every side. It is no small question that is involved in the case. The bearing of it upon the interests of religion in the German Churches is of fundamental and vital importance. A crisis has evidently been reached in the history of these Churches; and one of the most serious points involved in it is precisely this question of New Measures. Let this system prevail and rule with permanent sway, and the result of the religious movement which is now in progress will be something widely different from what it would have been under other auspices. The old regular organizations, if they continue to exist at all, will not be the same Churches. Their entire complexion and history in time to come will be shaped by the course of things with regard to this point. In this view the march of New Measures at the present time may well challenge our anxious and solemn regard. It is an interest of no common magnitude, portentous in its aspect, and pregnant with consequences of vast account. The system is moving forward in full strength, and putting forth its pretensions in the boldest style on all sides. Surely we have a right, and may well feel it a duty, in such a case, to institute an examination into its merits.

Nor is it any reason for silence in the case that we may have suffered as yet comparatively little in our own denomination from the use of New Measures. We may congratulate ourselves that we have been thus favored, and that the impression seems to be steadily growing that they ought not to be encouraged in our communion. Still, linked together as the German Churches are throughout the land, we have reason to be jealous here of influences that must in the nature of the case act upon us from without. In such circumstances there is occasion, and at the same time room, for consideration. It might answer little purpose to interpose remonstrance or inquiry if the rage for New Measures were fairly let loose, as a sweeping wind, within our borders. It were idle to bespeak attention from the rolling whirlwind. But with the whirlwind in full view, we may be exhorted reasonably to consider and stand back from its destructive path. We are not yet committed to the cause of New Measures in any respect. We are still free to reject or embrace them as the interests of the Church, on calm reflection, may be found to require. In such circumstances precisely may it be counted in all respects proper to subject the system to a serious examination.

It has been sometimes intimated that it is not safe to oppose and condemn the use of New Measures, because of their connections and purpose. Their relation to the cause of revivals is supposed to invest them with a sort of sacred character which the friends of religion should at least respect, even if they may not be able in all cases to approve. The system has taken hold of the "horns of the altar," and it seems to some like sacrilege to fall upon it there, or to force it away for the purposes of justice to any other place. It is a serious thing, we are told, to find fault with any movement that claims to be animated by the Spirit of God. By so doing we render it questionable whether we have ourselves any proper sympathy with revivals, and furnish occasion to the world also to blaspheme and oppose everything of the kind. But this is tyrannical enough to take for granted the main point in dispute, and then employ it as a consideration to repress inquiry or to silence objection. If New Measures can be shown to proceed from the Holy Ghost, or to be identified in any view with the cause of revivals, they may well demand our reverence and respect. If they can be shown even to be of *adiaphorous* character with regard to religion, harmless at least if not positively helpful to the Spirit's work, they may then put in a reasonable plea to be tolerated in silence, if not absolutely approved. But neither the one nor the other of these positions can be successfully maintained. It is a mere trick unworthy of the gospel for any one to confound with the sacred idea of a revival things that do not belong to it in truth at all for the purpose of compelling a judgment in their favor. The very design of the inquiry now proposed is to show that the Anxious Bench, and the system to which it belongs, have no claim to be considered either salutary or safe in the service of religion. It is believed that instead of promoting the cause of true vital godliness, they are adapted to hinder its progress. The whole system is considered to be full of peril for the most precious interests of the Church. And why then should there be any reserve in treating the subject with such freedom as it may seem to require? We may well feel indeed that the subject is solemn. All that relates to the interests of revivals, and the welfare of souls, is solemn; and it becomes us to approach it in a serious way. But this is no reason why we should close our eyes against the truth, or refuse to call things by their proper names. This would be to trifle with sacred things truly.

And it should be born in mind that the danger against which we need to be warned in this case is not confined by any means to one side. It is a serious thing to profane the worship of God by offering upon His altar strange fire. Those who recommend and practice New Measures should see well to it that they be not themselves chargeable with the very sin which they are too prone to charge upon such as withstand their views. It is surely not a case in which men can be justified in taking up a judgment lightly and with little or no reflection. Mighty interests are concerned in the question whether such means should be employed in the service of God's sanctuary or not. A great responsibility is involved in urging the system upon a congregation, or in trying to give it currency and authority in a religious community. If it should be found after all to be *not* the wisdom and power of God unto salvation, but the fruitful source of error and confusion in religion, an occasion of reproach to the gospel and of ruin to the souls of men, it would be a heavy account surely to answer for any part taken in its favor.

It is truly strange how one-sided the patrons of this system show themselves, as a general thing, in their views and feelings with regard to the point now presented. They affect an extraordinary interest in the cause of revivals, and seem to have a pious dread of sinning against it in any way. But the danger of doing so is all, to their view, in one direction. The idea of opposing the work of God is terrible. Whatever claims to be His work, then, must be respected and reverenced. No matter what irregularities are attached to it, so long as it stands before us in the holy garb of a revival, it is counted unsafe to call it to account. The maxim *Prove all things*, must be discarded, as well as the caution, *Believe not every spirit*. No room must be allowed to criticism where the object proposed is to rescue souls from hell. To stand upon points of order in such a case is to clog the chariot wheels of salvation. Meanwhile the disastrous consequences of false excitement, in the name of religion, are entirely overlooked. No account is made comparatively of the danger of bringing both the truth and power of God into discredit by countenancing pretentions to the name of a revival where the thing itself is not present. The danger itself is by no means imaginary. Spurious excitements are natural and common. Gross irregularity and extravagance, carried often to the point of downright profanity, are actually at work in connection with such excitements on all sides. The whole interest of revivals is endangered by the assumption impudently put forward that these revolting excesses belong to the system. False and ruinous views of religion are widely disseminated. Thousands of souls are deceived into a false hope. Vast obstructions are thrown in the way of true godliness. But of all this no account is made by those who are so sensitively jealous of danger on the other side. The only alternative they seem to see is *Action* or *No action*. But the difference between *right* action and *wrong* action, one would think, is fully as important, to say the least, as the difference between action and no action.

We are told however that the term "*New Measures*" is vague, covering in the view of some more than it covers in the view of others; so that there is danger of encouraging prejudice and opposition against the best things as well as the worst in venturing to criticize and censure the general system. In the German community in particular it is well known that great confusion prevails with regard to the subject in this view. With many all active efforts in favor of serious evangelical piety are branded with the reproach of new measures. Protracted meetings, prayer meetings, the doctrine of the new birth, special efforts for the salvation of sinners, revivals in the true and proper sense, tract societies, missionary societies, and benevolent operations, generally, all are regarded with suspicion, or it may be actually opposed as belonging to the same system of extravagance that includes the Anxious Bench and its natural connections. To oppose the latter, then, we are told is virtually to oppose the former. People will not distinguish. By exposing the nakedness of the Anxious Bench, we must expect to strengthen the hands of those who cry out against all active religion. Better to be silent than to incur so heavy a responsibility. Especially at this juncture should we observe such sacred caution, it is intimated, when the German Churches are waking from the sleep of years and passing the crisis of a great spiritual revolution whose consequences no one can measure.

Most certainly in such circumstances caution does become us all. We should tremble to touch the ark of God with unhallowed hand. It were only to be wished that this might be seriously laid to heart by the champions of the Anxious Bench themselves, as well as by others.

It has been already stated that the Anxious Bench is made the direct object of regard in this tract rather than New Measures in general for the very purpose of cutting off occasion, as much as may be from those who seek occasion, for confounding in this way things that are entirely distinct. The particular is made to stand for the general in the way of specimen or type, so as to exclude all that is not of the same complexion and spirit. If any choose notwithstanding to take the idea of New Measures in a wider sense, they have a right to please themselves in so doing if they see proper; but they can have no right surely to obtrude their own arbitrary view on the present discussion. There is a broad difference between New Measures in the one sense, and the New Measures in the other sense. It is overbearing impudence to pretend that a protracted meeting or a meeting for social prayer is of the same character with the anxious bench, or the various devices for theatrical effect with which this is so frequently linked. Such meetings lie in the very conception of Christian worship and are as old as the Church. The assertion sometimes heard that the idea of protracted meetings now so familiar and so generally approved is one of recent origin for which we are indebted to the system of New Measures, serves only to expose the ignorance of those by whom it is made. It is no less an abuse of terms as well as of common sense to include in this system tract societies, the cause of missions, and the benevolent agencies in general, by which the Church is endeavoring to diffuse the knowledge of the truth throughout the world. All these things are natural, direct utterances of the spirit of Christianity itself, and have no affinity whatever with the order of action represented by the Anxious Bench. The same thing may be said of revivals. They are as old as the gospel itself. Special effusions of the Spirit the Church has a right to expect in every age, in proportion as she is found faithful to God's covenant; and where such effusions take place, an extraordinary use of the ordinary means of grace will appear, as a matter of course. But still a revival is one thing, and a Phrygian dance another; even though the Phrygian dance should be baptized into Christian Montanism. Life implies action, but all action is not life. It is sheer impudence to say that new measures and revival measures are the same thing.

And there is good reason to believe that the confusion which is said to prevail with regard to the whole subject is much less in fact than is sometimes represented. As a general thing, people know very well that there is no affinity or connection between the system represented by the Anxious Bench and such evangelical interests as have now been mentioned. Even in those sections where it has been found convenient to stretch the idea of New Measures over this hallowed territory, there is a better knowledge of the true state of the case probably than is often supposed.

But allowing the confusion to be as complete among the German Churches as it is represented, shall no effort be made to correct it and put things in their proper light? Admit that the best practices and most important interests are in the eyes of many identified with the system of New Measures in the proper sense, so that to assault the latter is considered an assault at the same time upon the former; still, is that a reason for sparing and sheltering the system under its own bad form? Is there no help for the German Churches in this predicament? Must they have revivals in the way of the Anxious Bench, or no revivals at all? Must it be with them Finneyism, Methodism, Winebrennerism, or open war with serious religion, and the spirit of missions, under every form? Is the necessary alternative in their case quackery or death? Rather, in these circumstances, it becomes a solemn duty to take the difficulty by the horns, and reduce it to its proper posture. We owe it to the German Churches not to suffer things so different in a case of such vast moment to be so deplorably confounded. The case is one that calls loudly for light, and it is high time that light should be extended to it without reserve. If it be a reigning error to involve light and darkness in this way, under a common term, in the same sweeping censure, that is not a reason surely why we should try to uphold the darkness for the sake of the light, but a sacred requisition upon us rather to insist on a clear, full discrimination of the one element from the other. If Finneyism and Winebrennerism, the anxious bench, revival machinery, solemn tricks for effect, decision displays at the bidding of the preacher, genuflections and prostrations in the aisle or around the altar, noise and disorder, extravagance and rant, mechanical conversions, justification by feeling rather than faith, and encouragement ministered to all fanatical impressions; if these things, and things in the same line indefinitely, have no connection in fact with true serious religion and the cause of revivals, but tend only to bring them into discredit, let the fact be openly proclaimed. Only in this way may it be hoped that the reproach put upon revivals and other evangelical interests by same, under cover of their pretended connection with this system of New Measures in the true sense, will be in due time fairly rolled away.

The fact, that a crisis has come in the history of the German Churches, and that they are waking to the consciousness of a new life with regard to religion, only makes it the more important that this subject should *not* be suffered to rest in vague confusion. It is a popish maxim by which ignorance is made to be the mother of devotion. We say rather, Let there be light. The cause of the Reformation was more endangered by its own caricature, in the wild fanaticism of the Anabaptists, than by all the opposition of Rome. Luther saved it, not by truckling compromise, but by boldly facing and unmasking the false spirit, so that all the world might see that *Lutheran* Christianity was one thing, and wild Phrygian Montanism, with its pretended inspiration, quite another. So in the present crisis, the salvation of the old German Churches in this country is to be accomplished, not by encouraging them to "believe every spirit," but by engaging them, if possible, to "try the spirits, whether they be of God." Let things that are wrong be called by their right names, and separated from things that are right.

A heavy responsibility, in this case, rests upon the friends of New Measures. The circulation of spurious coin, in the name of money, brings the genuine currency into discredit. So also the surest way to create and cherish prejudice against true piety is to identify it with counterfeit pretences to its name. Popery, in popish countries, is the fruitful source of infidelity. So in the case before us it is sufficiently clear that the zeal which the sticklers for the system of the Anxious Bench display, in pressing their irregularities on the Church as a necessary part of the life and power of Christianity, is doing more at present than any other cause to promote the unhappy prejudice that is found to prevail in certain quarters against this interest in its true form. Many are led honestly to confound the one order of things with the other; and still more, no doubt, willingly accept the opportunity thus furnished to strengthen themselves in their opposition to evangelical interests, under a plausible plea, against their own better knowledge. In either case we see the mischievous force of the false issue which the question of New Measures has been made to involve. The Anxious Bench and its kindred extravagances may be held justly responsible for a vast amount of evil in this view. As a caricature always wrongs the original it is made falsely to represent, so has this spurious system, officiously usurping a name and place not properly its own, contributed in no small degree to bring serious religion itself into discredit, obscuring its true form, and inviting towards it prejudices that might otherwise have had no place. It has much to answer for, in the occasion it has given, and is giving still, for the name of God to be blasphemed, and the sacred cause of revivals to be vilified and opposed.

CHAPTER II.

The merits of the Anxious Bench not to be measured by its popularity; nor by its seeming success.—Circumstances in which it is found to prevail.—No spiritual force required to give it effect.

The *Popularity* of the Anxious Bench proves nothing in its favor.*
We find it, to be sure, extensively in vogue, and with a large portion of the community in high honor. There are whole sects that seem to have no conception of any thing like a vigorous life in the Church without its presence. And beyond the range of these, scores of ministers and congregations are found who glory in it as the very "gate of heaven," and consider it no less essential than the pulpit itself to the progress of any considerable revival. During the last winter, as already mentioned, there were places where the spirit of the Anxious Bench might be said to carry all before it, and it is likely that it will be so again during the winter that is to come.

But all who are at all acquainted with the world know that the worst things *may* thus run for a season and be glorified in the popular mind. And especially is this the case, where they hold their existence in the element of excitement, and connect themselves with religion, the deepest and most universal of all human interests. No weight of fashion enlisted in favor of the Anxious Bench can deserve to be much respected in such a trial of its merits as we are here called to make.

It should be remembered, however, that this popularity, such as it is, is in a certain sense but the echo of a sound which has already ceased to be heard. Whatever may be the pretensions of the Anxious Bench, on the field we are now contemplating, it is after all a stale interest, so far as the

---

*"It proves nothing *against* it," we are told from the other side. The remark is most true; but most foreign at the same time from the point, so far as the position of the tract is concerned. The object of this chapter is, not to present any positive argument against the Bench, but simply to undermine certain presumptions in its favor, which are known to stand in the way of a calm and dispassionate consideration of its merits, as afterwards examined. The argument here is *negative*, not positive. The patrons of the system, it is plain, make much account of its popularity, of the success with which it seems to be attended, and of the power it is supposed to manifest on the part of those who can use it with effect. In the present chapter it is attempted to show simply that opportunity and apparent success prove nothing, and that the measure is of such a character as to call for no particular moral force to give it effect. In the following chapter the argument becomes *positive*, showing that there is actual weakness and quackery at the bottom of the whole system.

Church at large is concerned. Not many years since it stood in very considerable credit in different parts of the Presbyterian Church and over a large portion of New England. But on this ground the thing has fairly exploded. It has been tried and found wanting. Here and there, it may still be held in honor. But in a general view even those who were formerly its friends have come to look upon it with distrust, and are no longer willing to give it their countenance. As with general consent, throughout New England and New York, the Congregational and Presbyterian Churches have abandoned the use of the Anxious Bench for "a more excellent way."* With all its popularity then where it now prevails, it is after all a stale interest, worn threadbare and flung aside in a different quarter of the religious world. In these circumstances no great account is to be made of its present credit in any view.

Nothing can be argued again in favor of the Anxious Bench, from the *Success* with which it may appear to be employed in the service of religion. This is often appealed to for this purpose. We are referred triumphantly to the actual results of the system as tried in different places. We are told of hundreds awakened and converted in connection with its use. God, it is said, has owned it, and impressed His seal upon it by working through it mightily as a means of salvation; and if He choose to honor it in this way, who are we that we should find fault or condemn?† We should rejoice to see souls brought into the kingdom in any way. We should be willing to make room in such a case for the manifold grace of God, allowing it to have free course in any channel through which it is found to flow, and not seeking to force it into conformity with our own narrow views. All this carries with it a plausible sound. But after all the representation is entitled to no respect.

---

*This has been contradicted; with more courage, however, than wisdom. It is notorious to all who know anything about the subject that the system of New Measures, in the sense of the present tract, as represented some years since in the north by such men as Burchard and Finney, has latterly fallen into discredit and general disuse throughout the Congregational and Presbyterian Churches. They still cherish of course prayer meetings, protracted meetings, and revivals; and it is quite possible that a number of ministers may still have recourse to the anxious bench as a particular measure at certain times; but the *system*, to which this measure of right belongs, is no longer in vogue. By general consent the churches have fallen back upon the evangelical method to which the use of the anxious bench can adhere only as an accident, if it adhere at all. The revivals of last winter in the North, according to the testimony furnished concerning them in the *New York Observer*, were of a wholly different stamp from those of Mr. Finney's school in former years. These last had strength; but it was such as a wasting fever imparts to a sick man, opening the way for a long prostration afterwards. The revivals of the past winter, it may be trusted, have been the first fruits only of the quiet and enduring vigor that springs from renovated health.

†"Who can behold a congregation of Christians wrestling for an altar full of penitent, anxious sinners, and witness the success of such instrumentality, and say, this is ignorance or fanaticism? God blesses only one way, which is the right way; He has blessed this way, therefore it is the right way"—*Correspondence of the Lutheran Observer, Feb.* 17, 1843.

In the first place, to draw an argument for the Anxious Bench from its immediate visible effects, is to take for granted that these are worth all they claim to be worth. We are pointed to powerful awakenings, of which it is considered to be the very soul. We are referred to scores and hundreds of conversions effected directly or indirectly by its means. But who shall assure us that all this deserves to be regarded with confidence as the genuine fruit of religion? It is marvellous credulity to take every excitement in the name of religion for the work of God's Spirit. It is an enormous demand on our charity when we are asked to accept in mass, as true and solid, the wholesale conversions that are made in this way. It will soon be made to appear that there is the greatest reason for caution and distrust with regard to this point. No doubt the use of the Anxious Bench may be found associated, in certain cases, with revivals, the fruits of which are worthy of all confidence. But this character they will have, through the force of a different system, that would have been just as complete without any such accompaniment. In such cases the revival may be said to prevail *in spite* of the new measures with which it is encumbered. On the other hand, in proportion as the spirit of such measures is found to animate and rule the occasion, there will be reason to regard the whole course of things with doubt. One thing is most certain. Spurious revivals are common, and as the fruit of them false conversions lamentably abound. An Anxious Bench may be crowded where no divine influence whatever is felt. A whole congregation may be moved with excitement, and yet be losing at the very time more than is gained in a religious point of view. Hundreds may be carried *through* the process of anxious bench conversion, and yet their last state may be worse than the first. It will not do to point us to immediate visible effects, to appearances on the spot, or to glowing reports struck off from some heated imagination immediately after. Piles of copper, fresh from the mint, are after all something very different from piles of gold.

Again, it does not follow by any means that a thing is right and good because it may be made subservient occasionally in the hands of God to a good end. Allow that the system represented by the Anxious Bench has often had the effect of bringing souls by a true and saving change to Christ, and still it may deserve to be opposed and banished from the Church. God can cause the wrath and folly of man both to praise Him in such ways as to Himself may seem best. And so, under the influence of His Spirit, He can make almost any occasion subservient to the awakening and conversion of a soul. But it would be wretched logic to infer from this the propriety of employing every such occasion, with preparation and design, as a part of the regular work of the gospel. It is sometimes said indeed that if only *some* souls are saved by the use of new measures, we ought thankfully to own their power, and give them our countenance; since even one soul is worth more than a world. But it should be remembered that the salvation of a sinner may not withstanding cost *too much!* If truth and righteousness are made to suffer for the purpose, more is lost than won by the result. We must not do *wrong*, even to gain a soul for heaven. And if for one thus gained, ten should be virtually destroyed by the very process employed to reach the point, who will say that such a method of promoting Christianity would deserve to be approved? There may be movements in the name of religion, and under the form of religion, and yielding to some extent the fruits of religion, which after all come from beneath and not from above. The history of the Church is full of instances illustrating the truth of this remark.

Simeon, the Stylite, distinguished himself, in the fifth century, by taking his station on the top of a pillar, for the glory of God and the benefit of his own soul. This whimsical discipline he continued to observe for thirty-seven years. Meanwhile he became an object of wide-spread veneration. Vast crowds came from a distance to gaze upon him, and hear him preach. The *measure* took with the people wonderfully. Thousands of heathen were converted, and baptized by his hand. Among these, it may be charitably trusted, were some whose conversion was inward and solid. God made use of Simeon's Pillar to bring them to Himself. The seal of His approbation might seem to have rested upon it to an extraordinary extent. No wonder the device became popular. The quackery of the Pillar took possession of the Eastern world, and stood for centuries a monument of the folly that gave it birth. We laugh at it now; and yet it seemed a good thing in its time, and carried with it a weight of popularity such as no New Measure can boast of in the present day.

But why speak of Stylitism in particular? The whole system of monkery may be taken as an example, of the same force, on a larger scale. What a world of abominations has it not been found to embrace? And yet, under what plausible pretences, it sought the confidence of the Church in the beginning! There were not wanting powerful reasons to give it recommendation. The whole Christian world in fact fell into the snare. The interest became a torrent, before which no man was found able to stand. Most assuredly, too, there was the life and power of religion, to some extent, at work in the movement. Monkery was to many in fact the means of conversion and salvation. And to this hour an argument might be framed in its favor, under this view, not less plausible, to say the least, than any that can be presented for the use of the Anxious Bench.

The Romish Church has always delighted in arrangements and services animated with the same false spirit. In her penitential system all pains have been taken to produce *effect* by means of outward postures and dress, till in the end, amid the solemn mummery, no room has been left for genuine penitence at all. Yet not a ceremony was ever introduced into the system that did not seem to be recommended by some sound religious reason at the time. The same thing may be said for the Services of that Church generally.

In another sphere, look at *Millerism*. The error, as it has been zealously preached within the past year (1843), has no doubt had an awakening effect on the minds of many; and some, it may be trusted, have been actually conducted by means of it into the kingdom of God. But will any pretend to say that it deserves to be encouraged on this account? It is said, indeed, that such an idea has been occasionally thrown out. Only, however, where the judgment had been in some measure corrupted by the spirit of quackery previously at work, No morally sane man could be willing for a moment to patronize such a lie, on account of any apparently salutary effects it might be found to have in particular cases.

Let us not be told, then, that the Anxious Bench is a godly interest, because many *seem* to be convicted by its means, and some are converted in fact. All this may be, and the general operation of the system remain notwithstanding intrinsically and permanently bad.

As a general thing, the movement of coming to the Anxious Bench gives no proper representation of the religious feeling that may be actually at work in the congregation at the time. It is always more or less theatrical, and often has no other character whatever. A sermon usually goes before. But frequently this has no felt relation at all to the subsequent excitement, so far as its actual contents are concerned. The writer was present, not a great while ago, as a stranger in a church, where a preacher of some little note in connection with the subject of revivals had been introduced under the expectation and hope that something of the kind might be secured at the time by his instrumentality. The congregation had but little appearance of life at the beginning, and still less as the sermon drew towards a close. The truth is, it was a very dull discourse at the best. The preacher was not well, and altogether he failed to make the least impression on the great body of his audience. A number were fairly asleep, and others were bordering on the same state. The preacher saw and felt that he had preached without effect; and took occasion, after the sermon was properly ended, to express his regret in view of the fact, and to add a few valedictory remarks in the prospect of his leaving the place the next day, without any thought evidently of calling out the anxious, where not a trace of feeling had been discerned. But the new strain adopted at the close, served to rouse attention and create interest. The congregation put on a more wakeful aspect, and something like emotion could be perceived in the countenances of a few. The preacher took courage, and after a few minutes dared to try the Anxious Bench. As usual, the hymn was started, "*Come, humble sinner,*" etc., and carried through, with pauses, in which sinners present were urged and pressed to seek their salvation by coming forward. Soon a female was seen going to the place, then another, and another—till at last a whole seat was filled.

One old lady rose and moved around, trying to induce others to go forward. At the close of the meeting I retired, wondering within myself that educated men, as were both the preacher in this case and the pastor at his side, could so impose upon themselves as to attach any importance to such a demonstration in such circumstances. It was attempted to carry forward the work by an appointment for the next evening. But on coming together at the time, it was found that it *would* not go forward, and so it was dropped altogether.

Commonly indeed those who deal in the anxious seat rely far less upon the presentation of truth to the understanding than they do upon other influences to bring persons forward. Pains are taken rather to raise the imagination, and confound the judgment. Exciting appeals are made to the principle of fear. Advantage is taken in every way of the senses and nerves. Especially the mysterious force of sympathy is enlisted in support of the measure, and made to tell in many cases with immense effect.

As might be expected accordingly, the most favorable subjects for the operation of the system are persons in whom feelings prevail over judgment, and who are swayed by impulse more than reflection. In an enlightened, well instructed congregation the anxious bench can never be generally popular. Where it is in full favor, a large proportion of those who are brought out by it are females and persons who are quite young.* It often happens that the "bench" is filled altogether with such cases, the greater part of them perhaps mere girls and boys. So, where a community is characterized by a general ignorance with regard to the nature of true religion, the measure is frequently applied with great effect; and those precisely who are the most rude and uncultivated, are the most likely in such circumstances to come under its power.

It requires then no spiritual power to use the Anxious Bench with effect. To preach the truth effectually, a man must have a certain spiritual force in himself which others are made to feel. But nothing of this sort is needed to secure success here. The object sought is a mere outward demonstration on the subject of religion, which may be gained by other forms of influence just as well. It shows no inward power whatever to be

---

*"Females and persons who are quite young have souls to be saved, as well as males and persons who are advanced in life; nay 'mere girls and boys' have an eternal interest pending."—*Luth. Obs.,* Dec. 29, 1843.

"And was not woman last at the cross, and first at the tomb of the Son of God?" —*Davis' Plea,* p. 45.

"Low and jejune indeed must be the conception of a religion which can allow a *divine* to attempt to destroy a 'measure,' through which '*females, girls and boys,*' run to as a means to enable them to flee the wrath to come." —*Denig's Strictures,* p. 26.

What a coincidence of judgment, among the critics of the tract, at this point! And what shall we say of the relevancy and honesty of the criticism itself, in view of the passage thus censured, as it actually stands, and taken in its plain sense? This is a fair specimen, however, of a large part of all that has been *argued* against the tract in these publications.

able to move a congregation in this way. It can be done without eloquence, and calls for no particular earnestness or depth of thought. It is truly wonderful, indeed, with how little qualification of intellect and soul a man may be fitted to carry all before him at certain times, and to show himself off to the eyes of a bewitched multitude as "the great power of God," by having recourse to new measures. He may be vulgar, coarse and dull, and so pointless and sapless in his ordinary pulpit services that it will be a weariness to hear him; and yet you shall find him, from time to time, throwing a whole community into excitement, gathering around him crowded houses night after night, and exercising as it might seem, for the space of three or four weeks, an irresistible sway in favor of religion. Such cases are by no means uncommon. Some of the most successful practitioners in the art of the Anxious Bench show themselves lamentably defective in the power of serious godliness, as well as in mental cultivation generally. The general habit of their lives is worldly and vain, and their religion, apart from the occasional whirlwinds of excitement in which they are allowed to figure in their favorite way, may be said to be characteristically superficial and cold. Nay, the evidence may be palpable that religion has nothing at all to do with the system in cases where it is employed with the greatest apparent effect. Nothing is more common than for those even who glory in the power of the Anxious Bench, as employed within their own communion, to look with entire distrust on its results as exhibited in the practice of other sects. What is trumpeted in the one case as a glorious revival, is allowed to pass in the other without notice as at best a questionable excitement. In this way it is practically acknowledged that the system does not necessarily involve spiritual power. It can be made to work as well in connection with error, as in connection with truth. It is as fully at the service of quackery and imposture, as it can be available in the cause of genuine religion. It is well adapted, indeed, to become the sport of quacks under every name. All wild and fanatical sects employ it with equal success. Campbellites, Winebrennerians and Universalists show the same power, when necessary, in producing revivals under this form. Millerism, and Mormonism, it may be added, are just as capable of doing wonders in the same way; though the last has declared itself not favorable to the Anxious Bench as interfering with regular and rational worship.

Nothing can be more precarious, then, than the argument for this system, as drawn from its apparent effects and results. In the sphere of religion, as indeed in the world of life generally, the outward can have no value, except as it stands continually in the power of the inward. To estimate the force of appearances, we must try their moral constitution; and this always involves a reference to the source from which they spring. A miracle, in the true sense, is not simply a prodigy, nakedly and separately considered. It must include a certain moral character.

Especially there must be inward freedom and divine strength in the person from whom it proceeds. No wonder-works could authenticate the mission of a man pretending to come from God who should display in all his movements an inward habit at war with the idea of religion. And just as little are we bound to respect, in the present case, the mere show of force, without regard to the agency by which it is exhibited. Those who deal in the Anxious Bench are accustomed to please themselves with the idea that it is an argument of power on the part of their ministry, to be able in this way to produce a great outward effect.* This is considered sufficient, it might seem, apart from the personality of the preacher altogether, to authenticate his strength. But no judgment can be more superficial. The personality of the preacher must ever condition and determine the character of his work. It were easy to give a score of living examples in which the semblance of success on a large scale, in the use of this system at the present time, is at once belied by palpable defect here. The men are of such a spirit that it is not possible to confide intelligently in any results it may seem to reach by their ministry. We are authorized before all examination to pronounce them valueless and vain. So utterly weak, in this argument, is the appeal to *facts*, as managed frequently by superficial thinkers. In every view of the case, the fruits of the Anxious Bench must be received with great caution, while to a great extent they are entitled to no confidence whatever.

---

*"Who ever dreamed that a single invitation to penitents to come forward, and a personal conversation with them on their spiritual condition and duties, demanded uncommon inward spiritual force?" Thus the editor of the *Luth. Obs., Nov.* 17, 1843, mystifying the point as usual. His colleague of Pittsburgh, however, comes up boldly to the mark, "A quack may preach a sermon and make a long prayer," he tells us; "but it takes something more than a quack *so* to preach the truth that sinners will *immediately* come forward to the anxious bench."—*Davis' Plea*, p. 32. Right bravely spoken; but the very dialect of quackdom itself.

CHAPTER III.

Nature of Quackery.—To rely on forms or measures shows inward weakness.—"New Measures" a substitute for true strength.—Where they are in honor, ample space is found for novices and quacks.

It has been shown that the successful use of the Anxious Bench calls for no spiritual power. It is within the reach of fanaticism and error to be employed in their service, with as much facility as it may be enlisted in the service of truth. It is no argument of strength, as is often imagined, that a preacher is able to use such an agency with effect. I now go to a step farther and pronounce it an argument of *spiritual weakness* that he should find it either necessary or desirable to call in such help. There is a measure of quackery in the expedient, which always implies the want of strength, so far as it may be relied on at all, as being of material account in carrying on the work of God.*

Quackery consists in pretension to an inward virtue or power, which is not possessed in fact, on the ground of a mere show of the strength which such power or virtue is supposed to include. The self-styled physician who, without any knowledge of the human frame, undertakes to cure diseases by a sovereign panacea in the shape of fluid, powder, or pill, is a quack; and there is no doubt abundance of quackery in the medical profession, under more professional forms, where practice is conducted without any true professional insight and power. Such practice may at

---

*It has I been found convenient with some, it would seem, to misunderstand what is said of spiritual weakness and spiritual strength in this part of the tract. They affect to take it as having respect to intellect, learning, eloquence, &c.; as though it implied that men of ordinary or small abilities are entitled to no respect in the Church; and so we are referred to Paul's *Not many wise men after the flesh, not many mighty,* &c. 1 Cor. I. 26–28, as a scriptural rebuke upon every such judgment. Thus also the editor of the *Lutheran Observer,* Jan. 5, 1844, lugs in by the neck a passage to the same purpose by President Edwards to show that this "great master-spirit did not look upon the *inward weakness* of his co-workers as a matter of reproach." At the close of it he gravely adds; "This quotation needs no comment from us; it speaks for itself. All we ask is to compare it with Dr. N.'s labored effort about the oft-repeated 'inward weakness' of revival preachers in the present day." Now if there be anything plain in the whole tract, it is that the inward weakness attributed by it, not to *revival* preachers, but to such as glory in the system of the Bench, is that of the "flesh" mainly as opposed to the strength which is from God's Spirit. When I am weak, says Paul, then am I strong. Quackery affects to be strong, but is weak in fact. Its weakness does not stand in the measure of its own resources so much as in its separation from the ground of all strength in God.

times seem eminently successful, and yet it is quackery notwithstanding. The same false show of power may, of course, come into view in every department of life. It makes up in fact a large part of the action and business of the world. Quack lawyers, quack statesmen, quack scholars, quack teachers, quack *gentlemen*, quacks in a word of every name and shape, meet us plentifully in every direction. We need not be surprised, then, to find the evil fully at home also in the sphere of religion. Indeed it might seem to be more at home here than anywhere else. Here especially the heart of man, "deceitful above all things and desperately wicked," has shown itself most ingenious in all ages in substituting the shadow for the reality, the form for the substance, the outward for the inward. The religion of the world has always been, for the most part, arrant quackery. Paganism can exist under no other form. The mummery of Rome, as aping powers of a higher order, is the most stupendous system of quackery the world has ever witnessed. But quackery in the Church is not confined of course to Rome. Christianity, in its very nature, must ever act on the corrupt nature of man as a powerful stimulus to the evil. No system embraces such powers, inward, deep and everlasting. These man would fain appropriate and make his own, in an external way, without relinquishing himself, and entering soul and body that sphere of the Spirit in which alone they can be understood and felt. So Simon Magus dreamed of purchasing the gift of God, and clothing himself with it in the way of outward possession. *He* was a quack; the prototype and prince of evangelical quacks. The second century shows us the whole Christian world brilliantly illuminated with rival systems of quackery under the name of Gnosticism, which for a time seemed to darken the sun of truth itself by their false but powerful glare. Afterwards, under a less idealistic garb, the evil fairly enthroned itself in the Church. The Reformation was the resurrection of the Truth once more, in its genuine and original life. Luther was no quack. But Protestantism itself soon had its quacks again in plentiful profusion, and has them all the world over at the present day. Christianity, as of old, serves to call the false spirit continually into action. Some whole sects stand only in the element of quackery. And among all sects it is easy to find the same element to some extent actively at work; sometimes under one form, and sometimes under another; but always exalting the outward at the cost of the inward and promising in the power of the flesh what can never be accomplished except in the power of the spirit.

Wherever *forms* in religion are taken to be—we will not say the spiritual realities themselves with which the soul is concerned, for the error in that shape would be too gross—but the power and force at least by which these realities are to be apprehended, without regard to their own invisible virtue, there we have quackery in the full sense of the term. Religion must have forms, as well as an inward living force. But these can have no value, no proper reality, except as they spring perpetually from the presence of that living force itself. The inward must be the bearer of the outward. Quackery, however, reverses the case. The outward is made to bear the inward. The shrine, consecrated with the proper ceremonies, *must* become a shechinah. Forms have a virtue in them to bind and rule the force of things. Such forms may be exhibited in a ritual, or in a creed, or in a scheme of a religious experience mechanically apprehended; but in the end the case is substantially the same. It is quackery in the garb of religion without its inward life and power.

That *old* forms are liable to be thus abused, and have been extensively thus abused in fact, is easily admitted. But it is not always recollected that *new* forms furnish precisely the same opportunity for the same error. It is marvellous indeed how far this seems to be overlooked by the zealous advocates of the system of New Measures in our own day. They propose to rouse the Church from its dead formalism. And to do this effectually, they strike off from the old ways of worship, and bring in new and strange practices that are adapted to excite attention. These naturally produce a theatrical effect, and this is taken at once for an evidence of waking life in the congregation. One measure, losing its power in proportion as it becomes familiar, leads to the introduction of another. A few years since a sermon was preached and published by a somewhat distinguished revivalist, in which the ground was openly taken that there must be a constant succession of new measures in the Church, to keep it alive and awake; since only in this way could we hope to counteract permanently the force of that spiritual gravitation, by which the minds of men are so prone continually to sink towards the earth in the sphere of religion. The philosophy this precisely by which the Church of Rome, from the fourth century downward, was actuated in all her innovations. Her worship was designed to make up through the flesh what was wanting in the spirit. The friends of new measures affect to be more free than others from the authority of mere forms. They wish not to be fettered and cramped by ordinary methods. And yet none make more account in fact of forms. They discard old forms, only to trust the more blindly in such as are new. Their methods are held to be all-sufficient for awakening sinners and effecting their conversion! They have no faith in ordinary pastoral ministrations, comparatively speaking; no faith in the Catechism. Converts made in this way are regarded with suspicion. But they have great faith in the Anxious Bench and its accompaniments. Old measures they hold to be in their very nature unfriendly to the spirit of revivals; they are the "letter that killeth." But new measures "make alive." And yet they are *measures* when all is done; and it is only by losing sight of the inward power of truth that any can be led to attach to them any such importance.

To rely upon the Anxious Bench, to be under the necessity of having recourse to new measures of any sort to enlist attention or produce effect in the work of the gospel, shows a want of inward spiritual force. If it be true that old forms are dead and powerless in a minister's hands, the fault is not in the forms, but in the minister himself; and it is the very impotence of quackery to think of mending the case essentially by the introduction of new forms. The man who had no power to make himself felt in the catechetical class is deceived most assuredly and deceives others when he seems to be strong in the use of the anxious bench. Let the power of religion be present in the soul of him who is called to serve at the altar, and no strange fire will be needed to kindle the sacrifice. He will require no new measures. His strength will appear rather in resuscitating, and clothing with their ancient force the institutions and services already established for his use. The freshness of a divine life, always young and always new, will stand forth to view in forms that before seemed sapless and dead. Attention will be engaged; interest excited; souls drawn to the sanctuary. Sinners will be awakened and born into the family of God. Christians will be builded up in faith, and made meet for the inheritance of the saints in light. Religion will grow and prosper. This is the true idea of evangelical power. But let a preacher be inwardly weak, though ambitious at the same time of making an impression in the name of religion, and he will find it necessary to go to work in a different way. Old forms must needs be dull and spiritless in his hands. His sermons have neither edge nor point. The services of the sanctuary are lean and barren. He can throw no interest into the catechism. He has no heart for family visitation and no skill to make it of any account. Still he desires to be doing something in his spiritual vocation, to convince others and to satisfy himself that he is not without strength. What then is to be done? He must resort to quackery; not with clear consciousness, of course; but instinctively, as it were, by the pressure of inward want. He will seek to do by the flesh what he finds himself too weak to effect by the spirit. Thus it becomes possible for him to make himself felt. New measures fall in exactly with his taste, and are turned to fruitful account by his zeal. He becomes theatrical; has recourse to solemn tricks; cries aloud; takes strange attitudes; tells exciting stories; calls out the anxious, &c. In this way possibly he comes to be known as a revivalist, and is counted among those who preach the Gospel "with the demonstration of the Spirit and with power." And yet when all is done he remains as before without true spiritual strength. New measures are the refuge of weakness.

There may be cases indeed in which genuine power will express itself in new forms. But when this occurs it will always be without ostentation or effort. Miracles are ever natural, as distinguished from mere wonderworks and feats of legerdemain. The form is the simple product of the power it represents, growing forth from it, and filled with it at every point. Where this is the case, what is new is at the same time free and entitled to our respect. But such instances can never authorize imitation where the same inward power is not present. Such imitation is quackery and an argument of weakness. Paul had power to wield the name of Jesus with effect for the expulsion of demons; but when the sons of Sceva, the Jew, undertook to exorcise in the same way, the demoniac fell upon them, and drove them naked and wounded from the house. They were quacks. Ezekiel prophesied in the valley of dry bones, and there was a noise and great shaking; but when a preacher, with nothing of Ezekiel's strength, lays himself out to excite noise and bodily action, as though *this* must certainly include the breath of life, the whole business sinks into a solemn farce. The Spirit of God, on the day of Pentecost, came like a mighty rushing wind on the disciples in Jerusalem, causing them to speak with tongues; but when a religious meeting is turned into a babel, to make it pentecostal, it deserves to be reprobated as savoring more of hell than heaven. Life is always beautiful in its place; but hideous and ghastly are the muscular actings of a galvanized corpse. An apostrophe from the lips of Whitefield might thrill, like an electric shock, through a whole congregation, and yet be no better than a vulgar mountebank trick, as imitated by an ordinary revivalist, affecting to walk in his steps. An Edwards might so preach the truth as to force his hearers from their seats, and yet be no pattern whatever for those who with design and calculation call in the device of "decision acts," as they are termed, to create a similar show of power. Whitefield and Edwards needed no new measures to make themselves felt.* They were genuine men of God, who had strength from heaven in themselves. They were no quacks.

The system of New Measures then is to be deprecated, as furnishing a refuge for weakness and sloth in the work of the ministry, and in this way holding out a temptation, which, so far as it prevails, leads ministers to undervalue and neglect the cultivation of that true inward strength without which no measures can be at last of much account. This is a great evil.

---

*Whitefield and Edwards! exclaim the champions of the Bench; they were both thorough going New Measure men, and it is a slander upon their names to speak of them as belonging to the opposite interest. Now it is not said here that they tolerated no new things in the worship of God; but only that they *needed* nothing of this sort to make themselves felt. What was new, in their case, was not sought; it came of itself, the free natural result of the power it represented. Whitefield had recourse to new methods himself to some extent, and Edwards carried his toleration of such things far in favor of others; but in neither instance could it be said that any value was attached to what was thus out of the common way, for its own sake, or as something to be aimed at with care and design beforehand. The judgment of Edwards in this case moreover, it should be remembered, as given in his *Thoughts on the Revival in New England*, had respect to the particular things it sanctions, not in a general way, but as related to an extraordinary work of God, of great extent and long continuance, most amply authenticated on *other* grounds. It is a widely different case when we are required to accept such things on their *own* credit as the evidence of a revival, or as the power of which it is to be secured.

It is a vastly more easy thing to carry forward the work of religion in this way than it is to be steadily and diligently true to the details of ministerial duty as prescribed by the apostle Paul. To be "vigilant, sober and of good behaviour"—not "self-willed, not soon angry"—"just, holy, temperate"—"one that ruleth well his own house, having his children in subjection with all gravity"—holding fast the faithful word in such sort "that he may be able by sound doctrine both to exhort and convince the gainsayers;" to "follow after righteousness, godliness, faith, love, patience, meekness," so as to be "an example of the believers in word, in conversation, in charity, in spirit, in faith, in purity;" to be "gentle unto all men, apt to teach, patient, in meekness instructing those that oppose themselves;" to meditate on divine things, and to be wholly given to them, so as to be continually profiting in the view of all; to "endure hardness as a good soldier of Jesus Christ;" to be a scribe well instructed in the law, a workman that need not to be ashamed, able to bring forth from the treasury of God's word things new and old, as they may be wanted; to preach week after week, so as to instruct and edify the souls of men; to be earnest, faithful, pungent in the lecture room and catechetical class; to be known in the family visitation, in the sick chamber, in the dwelling places of poverty and sorrow, as the faithful pastor, "watching for souls," whose very presence serves to remind men of holiness and heaven, not at certain seasons only, but from month to month, from one year always to another; all this is something great and difficult, and not to be compassed without a large amount of inward spiritual strength. But it calls for comparatively little power for a man to distinguish himself as a leader in periodical religious excitements, where zeal has room for outward display, and wholesale action is employed to discharge within a month the claims of a year. It is not asserted that a minister *must* be destitute of the qualifications that are required to make a regularly faithful and efficient pastor in order that he may be fitted to make himself conspicuous in this way; but most assuredly such *may* be the case. A man may be mighty in the use of new measures, preaching every day if need be for three weeks to crowded congregations, excited all the time; he may have the anxious bench filled at the close of each service and the whole house thrown into disorder; he may have groaning, shouting, clapping, screaming, a very bedlam of passion, all around the altar; and as the result of all, he may be able to report a hundred converts or more, translated by the process, according to his own account, from darkness into God's marvellous light. He may be able to act the same part in similar scenes, at different places, in the course of a winter; and, for the time being, his name may be familiar to the lips of men as a *revivalist*, whose citizenship might be supposed to hold in the third heavens. All this *may* be, where to an attentive observer it shall soon be painfully evident, at the same time, that the true and proper strength of a man of God is wholly wanting. A man may so distinguish himself and yet have no power to study, think or teach. He may be crude, chaotic, without cultivation or discipline. He may be too lazy to read or write. There may be no power whatever in his ordinary walk or conversation to enforce the claims of religion. Meet him in common secular connections, and you will find him in a great measure unfelt in the stream of worldliness with which he is surrounded. Often he is covetous, often vain; often without a particle of humility or meekness. His zeal, too, seems to exhaust itself in each spasmodic "awakening" through which it is called to pass. The man who appeared to be all on fire for the salvation of souls, and ready to storm even the common proprieties of life for the sake of the gospel, shows himself now marvellously apathetic towards the whole interest. He has no heart to seize *common* opportunities, in the house or by the way, to say a word in favor of religion. It is well indeed if he be not found relaxing altogether his ministerial activity, both in the pulpit and from house to house. The truth is, he has no capacity, no inward sufficiency, for the ordinary processes of evangelical labor. Much is required to be a faithful minister of the New Testament; whilst small resources in comparison are needed for that semblance of power to which a man may attain by the successful use of the system now in view.

Here, then, is a strong temptation presented to ministers. They are in danger of being seduced by the appeals which this system makes to their selfishness and sloth. It offers to their view a "short method of doing God's great work," and a sort of "royal road," at the same time, to ministerial reputation. How easy, in these circumstances, for even a good man to have his judgment warped and his practice disturbed. And how natural that weakness, under every form, should rejoice to take refuge in the shelter thus brought within its reach.

It should be considered a calamity in any community, or in any religious denomination, to have this system in fashionable and popular use. Let the idea prevail that those who employ new measures in the gospel work are the friends pre-eminently of serious heart religion, and of all evangelical interests; whilst such as frown upon them are to be regarded with suspicion, as at best but half awake in the service of Christ. Let it be counted enough to authenticate the power of a pastor's ministrations that he shall be able to furnish, from winter to winter, a flaming *report* of some three weeks' awakening in his charge, in the course of which scores of sinners have been drawn to the anxious bench, and immediately afterwards hurried to the Lord's table. Let some religious paper, known as the organ of the Church, herald these *reports*, from week to week, without inquiry or discrimination, as "revival intelligence," proclaiming them worthy of all confidence, and glorifying both the measures and the men concerned in the triumphs they record. Let those who are counted "pillars in the church" give their sanction to the same judgment, openly honoring the new system, or quietly conniving at what they may not entirely approve, so as by their very cautions and exceptions to forward the whole interest in fact. Let the sentiment be industriously cherished that with this interest is identified in truth the cause of revivals itself, and that lukewarmness, and dead orthodoxy, and indifference, if not absolute hostility, towards prayer-meetings, missionary efforts, and all good things, characterize as a matter of course all who refuse to do it homage. Let this state of things hold with respect to the subject, and it needs no great discernment to see that it is likely to work disastrously upon the character and fortunes of the Church so circumstanced. The attention of ministers will be turned away from more important, but less ostentatious methods of promoting religion. Preaching will become shallow. The catechism may be possibly still treated with professed respect, but practically it will be shorn of its honor and force. Education may be considered to some extent necessary for the work of the ministry, but in fact no great care will be felt to have it either thorough or complete. Ignorance, sciolism, and quackery will lift up the head on all sides and show themselves off as the "great power of God." Novices will abound, "puffed up with pride," each wiser in his own conceit than seven men that can render a reason. Young men, candidates for the sacred office, will be encouraged to try their hand at the new system before they have well commenced their studies, and finding that they have power to make themselves felt in this way, will yield their unfledged judgment captive to its charms, so as to make no account afterwards of any higher form of strength. Study and the retired cultivation of personal holiness will seem to their zeal an irksome restraint; and making their lazy, heartless course of preparation as short as possible, they will go out with the reputation of educated ministers, blind leaders of the blind, to bring the ministry into contempt, and fall themselves into the condemnation of the devil. Whatever arrangements may exist in favor of a sound and solid system of religion, their operation will be to a great extent frustrated and defeated by the predominant influence of a sentiment, practically adverse to the very object they are designed to reach.

Thus will the ministry be put, more or less, out of joint by the force of the wrong judgment involved in the system of New Measures, where it has come to be fashionable and popular. The Church must suffer corresponding harm, of course, in all her interests. The old landmarks grow dim. Latitudinarian views gain ground. Fanatical tendencies gather strength. The ecclesiastical body is swelled with heterogenous elements loosely brought together and actuated by no common life, except sectarian bigotry may be entitled to such name. False views of religion abound. Conversion is everything, sanctification nothing. Religion is not regarded as the life of God in the soul that must be cultivated in order that it may grow, but rather as a transient excitement to be renewed from time to time by suitable stimulants presented to the imagination. A taste for noise and rant supersedes all desire for solid knowledge. The susceptibility of the people for religious instruction is lost on the one side, along with the capacity of the ministry to impart religious instruction on the other. The details of Christian duty are but little understood or regarded. Apart from its seasons of excitement, no particular church is expected to have much power. Family piety and the religious training of the young are apt to be neglected.

    It is a calamity, then, in the general view of the case now taken, for a community to be drawn into the vortex of this system as a reigning fashion. The occasional use of it might be comparatively safe; in some hands, *perhaps*, without harm altogether. But let it be in credit and reputation for a short time on a given field, and its action will be found to be just as mischievous as has now been described. It will prove the refuge of weakness and the resort of quacks. It will be a "wide and effectual door" to let in fanaticism and error. It will be as a worm at the root of the ministry, silently consuming its strength; and as a mildew on the face of congregations and churches, beneath whose blighting presence no fruit can be brought to perfection.

CHAPTER IV.

Action of the Bench.—It creates a false issue for the conscience.—Unsettles true seriousness.—Usurps the place of the Cross.—Results in widespread, lasting spiritual mischief.

Let us now fix our attention on the action of the new system, directly and immediately considered. Without regard to its more remote connections and consequences, let us inquire what its merits may be in fact, as it respects the interest it proposes to promote, namely, the conversion of souls. Is it the wisdom of God and the power of God, as its friends would fain have us believe, for convincing careless sinners, and bringing them to the foot of the Cross? Let the Anxious Bench, in this case, be taken as the representative of the entire system. No part of it carries a more plausible aspect. If it be found wanting and unworthy of confidence here, we may safely pronounce it to be unworthy of confidence at every other point.

As usually applied in seasons of religious excitement, I hold the measure to be spiritually dangerous; requiring great skill and much caution to be used without harm in any case, and as managed by quacks and novices (who are most ready to be taken with it) more suited to ruin souls than to bring them to heaven. This view is established by the following positions.

1. *The Anxious Bench, in the case of an awakened sinner, creates a false issue for the conscience.* God has a controversy with the impenitent. He calls upon them to acknowledge their guilt and misery with true repentance, and to submit themselves by faith to the righteousness of the gospel. It is their condemnation that they refuse to do this. When any sinner begins to be sensible in any measure of his actual position in this view, he is so far awakened and under conviction. Now in these circumstances what does his case mainly require? Clearly, that he should be made to see more and more the true nature of the controversy in which he is involved, till he finds himself inwardly engaged to lay down the weapons of his rebellion and cast himself upon the mercy of God in Jesus Christ. He needs to have his eyes fastened and fixed on his own relations, spiritually considered, to the High and Holy One, with whom he is called to make his peace. The question is, will he repent and yield his heart to God or not? This is the true issue to be met and settled; and it is all-important that he should be so shut up to this in his thoughts that he may have no power to escape the force of the challenge which it involves. That

spiritual treatment must be considered best in his case which serves most fully to bring this issue into view, and holds him most effectually confronted with it in his conscience, beneath the clear light of the Bible. But let the sinner in this state be called to come forward to a particular seat in token of his anxiety. He finds himself at once under the force of a different challenge. The question is not, will he repent and yield his heart to God, but will he go to the anxious bench; which is something different altogether. Thus a new issue is raised, by which the other is obscured or thrust out of sight. It is a false issue too; because it seems to present the real point in controversy, when in fact it does not do so at all, but only distracts and bewilders the judgment so far as this is concerned. While the awakened person is balancing the question of going to the anxious bench, his mind is turned away from the contemplation of the immediate matter of quarrel between himself and God. The higher question is merged, for the time, in one that is lower. A new case is created for the conscience of artificial, arbitrary form and ambiguous authority. Can it be wise thus to shift the ground of debate, exchanging a strong position with regard to the sinner for one that is weak? Suppose it were made a point with awakened persons that they should rise up and confess before the congregation all their leading sins, in detail and by name, to break their pride, show their desire to be saved, excite prayer in their behalf, &c.; would not this requirement, interposed as a preliminary to the main point of conversion itself, and enforced by no proper sanction for the conscience, serve only to turn away the attention of such persons from the object with which it should be employed, thwarting the very interest it might affect to promote? And is there not room for objection to the Anxious Bench on the very same ground? It is certainly a little strange that the class of persons precisely who claim to be the most strenuous in insisting upon unconditional, immediate submission to God, scarcely tolerating that a sinner should be urged to pray or read the Bible, lest his attention should be diverted from that one point, are as a general thing nevertheless quite ready to interpose *this* measure in his way to the foot of the cross, as though it included in fact the very thing itself. And yet a pilgrimage to the Anxious Bench is in its own nature as much collateral to the duty of coming to Christ as a pilgrimage to Jerusalem. In either case a false issue is presented to the anxious soul by which for the time a true sight of circumstances is hindered rather than promoted.

It may be thought, indeed, that the movement of going to the Anxious Bench is so easily performed as not to be properly open to this exception. It may be considered a mere *circumstance* that can have no weight practically in the view now presented. But we shall see that this is not the case. However small the point involved may seem, it is not only of account, as producing for the moment a factitious case of conscience, open to "doubtful disputation," but it includes also actual difficulty that cannot fail to be felt. Whether the challenge be refused or accepted, it becomes in most cases more than a circumstance, and is of no small force in fact in the way of embarrassing the proper exercises of an awakened soul.

2. *The Anxious Bench, in the case of those who come to it, is adapted by its circumstances to disturb and distract the thoughts of the truly serious, and thus to obstruct the action of truth in their minds.* It is no doubt quite a common thing for persons to be carried into this movement who have little or no seriousness at the time, urged forward by sympathy, or superstition, or a mere taste for distinction. There is much reason in the remark of the Rev. Dr. Miller when he tells us that he should expect, in calling out the anxious, to find the persons rising and presenting themselves to be, for the most part, the "forward, the sanguine, the rash, the self-confident and the self-righteous," while many who keep their seats would prove to be the modest, the humble, the brokenhearted, the very depth of whose seriousness had restrained them from coming forward in this way.* And yet the measure may be expected to prevail of course with many persons also who are truly under conviction, and whom nothing but the fear of losing their souls could engage to thrust themselves thus into view. In any case, however, the genuine religious feeling that may exist is likely to be in a great measure overwhelmed by the excitement that must be involved in the very act of coming to such a resolution, and subsequently in carrying it into effect. The truth of this remark will be more clear when we remember that young persons, and females especially, form the main body commonly of those who are drawn to the anxious bench. Their susceptibility fits them to be wrought upon more readily than others to the extent that is necessary to secure this point. But the same susceptibility renders it certain that in circumstances so exciting it will be impossible for them to hold their thoughts or feelings in any such balance as the interest of religion requires. They of all others would *need* to be sheltered from stimulating impressions in this form at such a time instead of being forced to face them in their weakness.

Take a single case in illustration of the way in which the system may be expected to work. Here is a gentle girl, sixteen or seventeen years of age. She finds herself in the midst of a large congregation where at the close of the sermon the minister, encouraged by the general seriousness of the house, invites all who are concerned for the salvation of their souls to come forward and place themselves on the anxious seat. She has been perhaps a long time under some concern, or it may be that God's truth has been felt for the first time on this occasion; not with *great* force perhaps, but so at least as to bring her spirit to a solemn stand in the presence of

---

*Appendix to Sprague on Revivals, p. 38.

her Maker. She hears the invitation, but shrinks from the thought of doing what the minister demands. The call however is reiterated, and enforced by the most exciting appeals to the imagination. After a few moments there is a stir; one is going forward to the bench, and then another, and another. She is struck, moved, agitated. A struggle has commenced in her bosom, which she herself is not prepared to understand. May she not be fighting against God, she asks herself, in refusing to go forward with the rest? May it not be in her case, at this moment, now or never? All this is solemnly crowded on her alarmed conscience by the whole character of the occasion, in the way in which it is managed by the minister. Already her soul has passed from the element of conviction into the element of excitement. The "still small voice" of the Spirit is drowned amid the tumult of her own conflicting thoughts. But see, she yields. With a desperate struggle, she has thrown herself forth into the aisle. Trembling and agitated in every nerve, poor victim of quackery, she makes her way, consciously in the eye of that large watching assembly, from one end of the house to the other, and sinks, half fainting with the effort, into a corner of the magic seat. And now, where is she, in spiritual position? Are her tears the measure of her sorrow for sin? Alas, she is farther off from God than she was before this struggle commenced in her father's pew. Calm reflection is departed. Her hold upon the inward has been lost. Could any intelligent Christian parent, truly anxious for the salvation of his daughter, deliberately advise her in circumstances which have been supposed, to seek religion in this way? Can the pastor be wise, who is willing to subject the lambs of his flock to such a process, with the view of bringing the good seed of the word to take root and vegetate in their hearts?

3. *The Anxious Bench is adapted to create and foster the ruinous imagination that there is involved in the act of coming to it a real decision in favor of religion.* It is well known in the Church of Rome certain observances are held to carry with them a sort of inward merit in this way, as though by themselves they had power to secure a spiritual blessing. There is a constant tendency with men, indeed, to invest the outward under *some* form with the virtue that belongs only to the inward, so as if possible to "get religion," and hold it as property or means for some other end, instead of entering into it as the proper home of their own being. It is not strange then that the Anxious Bench should be liable to be so abused. It is only strange that sensible persons should make so little account of this danger, as is sometimes done. We are gravely told, it is true, that coming to the anxious bench is not considered to be the same thing as coming to Christ.* The measure is represented to be important on

---

*"Who ever pretended that going to the anxious bench is *conversion*?" *Luth. Observer, Dec.* 15, 1843. And yet, in the same article, it is said again of one who yields to the measure: "Does he not *resolve* no longer to resist the influences of divine grace, and

other grounds, and for other purposes. Certainly it is not imagined for a moment that any one in his senses will be found ready to *say* that coming to the bench is itself religion. But still that some such impression is liable to be created by the measure, and is extensively created by it in fact as it is commonly used, admits of no dispute. It is not uncommon indeed for those who make use of it to throw in occasionally something like a word of caution with regard to this point; and in some few instances, possibly, such prudence may be observed as fully to guard against the danger. But this is not common. As a general thing, even the cautions that are interposed are in such a form as to be almost immediately neutralized and absorbed by representations of an opposite character. The whole matter is so managed as practically to encourage the idea that a veritable step towards Christ at least, if not actually into His arms, is accomplished in the act of coming to the anxious seat. I have had an opportunity of witnessing the use of the measure in different hands and on different occasions; but in every case it has seemed to me that room was given for this censure.* Indeed I do not see well how the measure could be employed in any case with much effect without the help of some such representation. We find accordingly that the whole process, as it were in spite of itself, runs ordinarily into this form. Sinners are exhorted to come to the anxious bench as for their life by the same considerations precisely that should have force to bring them to Christ, and that could have no force at all in this case if it were not confounded more or less to their perception with the other idea. The burden of all is presented in the beautiful but much prostituted hymn usually sung on such occasions,

---

wage war against God, and the efforts of his faithful minister?" Such submission is commonly taken to be conversion.—In another place the editor finds the principle of the Bench in John vii., 37, *If any man thirst, let him come unto me and drink*, and in Matt. xi., 28, *Come unto me all ye that labor and are heavy laden*, &c. The parallel is monstrous, and has a rank smell of pelagianism. In like strain Mr. Davis, of Pittsburgh, calls the bench a "test," and compares it with the "*device* of the forbidden fruit" in the garden of Eden, and with the "anxious river" in which Naaman, the Syrian, was required to wash, 2 Kings v., 10–12, that he might be cured of his leprosy. "If no *test-questions* are presented, how can men ever *act*, or *determine* whether they will serve God or not?" "Viewed as a means of bringing sinners to an *immediate decision* on the subject of religion, no reasonable objection can be brought against it."—*Plea for New Measures*, p. 23–30. Right bravely spoken again; but, I repeat it, the very dialect of QUACKDOM!

*"He exhorted them to repent of their sins, and go to their forsaken God. To aid them in their return, an anxious seat was prepared on Sabbath evening, &c." *Corresp. Luth. Obs., Dec.* 16, 1842. "The anxious seat was introduced through some opposition—and at it the high and the low, the rich and the poor, the old and young, the male and female bowed. They were not ashamed of the despised seat, but presented themselves there with as much avidity as if they were certain of getting a fortune there. And so they did. There they received a title to mansions in the skies, &c." *Jan.* 6, 1843. "On Sunday night the anxious were invited to occupy the front seats, for the usual purposes, and O what a crowding was there to the foot of the cross!" *June* 8, 1843.

Come humble sinner. The whole of this is made to bear with all the weight the preacher can put into it on the question of coming to the anxious seat. Every effort is employed to shut up the conscience of the sinner to this issue; to make him feel that he *must* came or run the hazard of losing his soul. Advantage is taken of his hopes and fears in every form of awakening and stimulating appeal to draw him from his seat. The call is so represented as to make this the test of penitence. Those who come are welcomed as returning prodigals who have decided to come out from the world and be on the Lord's side; while all who refuse to come are treated as showing just the opposite temper; and it often happens that the preacher, in the warmth of his zeal, charges upon their refusal in this view the same guilt and madness and peril precisely that lie upon the deliberate rejection of Christ himself. Now it is an easy thing to say, in these circumstances, that after all the Anxious Bench is not substituted for Christ. So the Puseyite and Papist disclaim the idea of putting into His place the Baptismal Font. But in both cases it is perfectly plain that Christ is seriously wronged notwithstanding. In both cases the error is practically countenanced and encouraged that coming to Christ and the use of an outward form are in whole, or at least to some considerable extent, one and the same thing; with the difference only that the form in one case is of divine prescription, while in the other it is wholly of man's device.

It is true indeed that the "mourners," as they are sometimes termed, are still treated after coming to the bench or altar as persons yet unconverted. This should neutralize, it might seem, the idea of any such saving virtue in the measure as is here supposed to be encouraged in the usual style of calling out the anxious. But this is not the case. The coming is not accepted at once as conversion, though exhibited apparently as the same thing immediately before; but still it is taken practically for something closely bordering on conversion. The mourners are counted nearer to the kingdom of heaven than they were before. They are exhorted now to "go on," as having actually begun a divine life. The process of conversion is commenced. They have come to the birth; and all that is wanted to bring them fully into the new world of grace is the vigorous prosecution of the system of deliverance to which they have now happily committed their souls. The Anxious Bench is made still to be the laver of regeneration, the gate of paradise, the womb of the New Jerusalem. Conversion is represented to be far easier here than elsewhere. We find accordingly that this idea fairly carried out leads certain sects of the full New Measure stamp to profess a peculiar tact and power in carrying the process of spiritual delivery regularly out at once to its proper issue. It is only for want of proper treatment, they say, and because "there is not strength to bring forth," in other cases, that souls are brought thus far without being born at once into the kingdom. *Their* Anxious Bench, or the altar where their mourners kneel and roll, is commended to the world as a more perfect organ of conversion. Once fairly within its grasp, the soul as a general thing is quickly set free; often in the course of a few minutes, and very commonly before the close of the meeting. They know how to "get the anxious *through*." All this is sufficiently extravagant; but still it is only a gross expression of the feeling, commonly encouraged by the use of the Anxious Bench with regard to its virtue as a help to conversion. The whole measure is so ordered as to promote the delusion that the use of it serves *some* purpose in the regeneration of the soul.

4. *Harm and loss to the souls of men flow largely from the use of the Anxious Bench.* It is an injury in the case of an awakened sinner to have his attention diverted, in the first place, from the real issue before him to one that is false. It is an injury farther to have reflection arrested, and the working of true conviction in part or altogether overwhelmed, by the excitement of obeying a call to come out in this way. It is an injury again to be induced to lean upon such a movement; as though it could have any efficacy at all to bring the soul near to God. But the harm and loss occasioned by the system reach much farther than this.

The inward tumult resulting from the occasion is in a high degree unfavorable to genuine seriousness while it lasts, and is sure to be followed by a reaction still more hurtful to the spirit when the occasion is over."All means and measures," says the Rev. Dr. Alexander in his letter to Dr. Sprague, "which produce a high degree of excitement, or a great commotion of the passions, should be avoided; because religion does not consist in these violent emotions, nor is it promoted by them; and when they subside, a wretched state of deadness is sure to succeed."

A most unhappy influence is often exerted on those who are drawn to the anxious bench, and afterwards fall back again openly to their former careless state. They may have had but very little conviction, perhaps none at all. But their feelings have been excited, and without knowledge or reflection, they have gone forward among the professed mourners, vaguely expecting to gain religion in this way. Afterwards they find themselves completely stripped of all feeling. They have too much understanding to set any value on their experience, and too much conscience to be willing that it should pass for more than they know it to be worth in fact; or possibly they have swung clear over to the opposite quarter, and have no wish at all to be, or to be considered religious. And yet they have been on the anxious bench, and in great distress apparently for their sins. They have publicly committed themselves in the case in a way that is not likely soon to be forgotten. All this works injuriously on their minds now. Rash vows are always hurtful. The posture with regard to religion is altogether worse than it was before. Often disgust and irritation towards the whole subject are the unfortunate consequence.

But in a vast multitude of instances, the operation of the measure is worse still. The slightly convicted are full as likely to go forward in the way of profession as they are to go back. Powerful considerations are at hand besides the interest of their own salvation to hold them to the course on which they have entered. They are committed, and have no prospect of coming honorably or comfortably out of their present posture, except by *getting through* on the side towards the Church and not towards the world. There is room too for the workings of ambition and emulation; a desire to be noticed, and an impatience of being left behind by others in the career of spiritual experience. "It ought not to be forgotten," says Dr. Alexander, "that the heart is deceitful above all things, and that strong excitement does not prevent the risings of pride and vainglory. Many become hypocrites when they find themselves the objects of much attention, and affect feelings which are not real."* And if all such impure motives might be supposed to be out of the way, there is still enough to render the danger of spurious conversion in such circumstances alarmingly great. The mourner strives of course to *feel* faith. The spiritual helpers standing round are actively concerned to see him brought triumphantly through. Excitement rules the hour. No room is found either for instruction or reflection. A sea of feeling, blind, dark and tempestuous, rolls on all sides. Is it strange that souls thus conditioned and surrounded should become the victims of spiritual delusion? All high wrought excitement must, in its very nature, break when it reaches a certain point. How natural that this relaxation, carrying with it the sense of relief as compared with the tension that had place before, should be mistaken on such an occasion for the peace of religion, that mysterious something which it is the object of all this process to fetch into the mind. And how natural that the wearied subject of such experience should be hurried into a wild fit of joy by this imagination, and stand prepared, if need be, to clap his hands and shout hallelujah over his fancied deliverance. Or even without this mimic sensation, how natural that the mourner at a certain point should allow himself to be persuaded by his own wishes, or by the authority of the minister perhaps, and other friends telling him how easy it is to believe and urging him at last to consider the thing done; so as to take to himself the comfort of the new birth as it were in spite of his own experience, and be counted among the converted. Altogether the danger of delusion and mistake where this style of advancing the cause of religion prevails must be acknowledged to be very great. The measure of the danger will vary, of course, with the extent to which the characteristic spirit of the system is allowed to work. A Winebrennerian camp-meeting, surrendering itself to the full sway of this spirit, will carry with it a more disastrous operation than the simple Anxious Bench in a respectable and orderly church. But in any form the system is full of peril as opening the way to spurious

---

*Sprague on Revivals. Appendix, p. 7.

conversions and encouraging sinners to rest in hopes that are vain and false.

There need be no reserve in speaking or writing on this subject. Neither charity nor delicacy require us to be silent where the truth of religion is itself so seriously concerned. To countenance the supposition that the souls which are so plentifully "carried through" what is called the process of conversion under this system are generally converted in fact, would be to wrong the Gospel. "Let God be true, though every man should be a liar." Of all the hundreds that are reported, from year to year, as brought into the kingdom among the Methodists, United Brethren, Winebrennerians, and others who work in the same style, under the pressure of artificial excitement, how small a proportion give evidence subsequently that they have been truly regenerated. The Church at large does not feel bound at all to accept as genuine and worthy of confidence the many cases of conversion they are able to number, as wrought with noise and tumult at camp-meetings and on other occasions. It is taken for granted that a large part of them will not stand. And so it turns out, in fact. In many cases the fruits of a great revival are reduced almost to nothing before the end of a single year. So the system unfolds its own nakedness in a practical way. And this nakedness comes to view, in some measure, wherever much account is made of the Anxious Bench. There may be no methodistical extravagance, no falling down or rolling in the dust, no shouting, jumping or clapping; only the excitement and disorder necessarily belonging to the measure itself; still it is found that conversions made in this way do not as a general thing wear well. No one whose judgment has been taught by proper observation will allow himself to confide in the results of a revival, however loudly trumpeted, in which the Anxious Bench is known to have played a prominent part. He may trust charitably that out of the fifty or a hundred converts thus hurried into the Church some will be found "holding fast the beginning of their confidence firm unto the end;" but he will stand prepared to hear of a great falling away in the case of the accession as a whole in the course of no considerable time. Of some such revivals scarce a monument is to be found at the end of a few months, unless it be in the spiritual atrophy they have left behind. And it often happens that churches instead of growing and gathering strength by these triumphs of grace as they are called, seem actually to lose ground in proportion to their frequency and power. If any weight is to be attached to observations which are on all sides within the reach of those who choose to inquire, it must be evident that as this system is in all respects *suited* to produce spurious conversions, so it is continually producing them in fact, to a terrible extent. For the evil is not to be measured of course simply by the actual amount of open defection that may take place among those who are thus brought to "embrace religion." So many and so strong are the considerations that must operate upon a supposed convert to hold fast at least the form of godliness after it has been once assumed, though wholly ignorant of its power, that we may well be surprised to find the actual falling away in the case of such ingatherings so very considerable as now represented. As it is, it becomes certain in the very nature of the case that this apostacy forms only a *part* of the false profession from which it springs. While some fall back openly to the world, others remain in the Church with a name to live while they are dead. This presumption is abundantly confirmed by observation. Very many thus introduced into the Church show too plainly by their unhallowed tempers, and the general worldliness of their walk and conversation, that they have never known what religion means. They have had their "experience" centering in the Anxious Bench, on which they continue to build their profession and its hopes; but farther than this they give no signs of life. They have no part nor lot in the Christian salvation.

Notoriously, no conversions are more precarious and insecure than those of the Anxious Bench. They take place under such circumstances precisely as should make them the object of earnest jealousy and distrust. The most ample evidence of their vanity is presented on every side. And yet the patrons of the system are generally ready to endorse them, as though they carried the broad seal of heaven on their face. Of conversions in any other form, they can be sufficiently jealous. They think it well for the Church to use great caution in the case of those who have been led quietly under the ordinary means of grace to indulge the Christian hope. They shrink perhaps from the use of the Catechism altogether, lest they might seem to aim at a religion of merely human manufacture. But let the power of the Anxious Bench appear, and, strange to tell, their caution is at once given to the winds. *This* they proclaim to be the finger of God. Here the work of religion is presumed at once to authenticate itself. With very little instruction, and almost no examination, all who can persuade themselves that they are converted, are at once hailed as brethren and sisters in Christ Jesus, and with as little delay as possible gathered into the full communion of the Church. And this is held to be building on the true foundation gold, silver, and precious stones, while such as try to make Christians in a different way are regarded as working mainly, almost as a matter of course, with wood, hay, and stubble. Wonderful infatuation! Stupendous inconsistency!

CHAPTER V.

The Bench vindicated on insufficient grounds:—1. As bringing the sinner to a DECISION;—*2. As involving him in a* COMMITTAL;—*3. As giving* FORCE TO HIS PURPOSE;—*4. As a penitential* DISCIPLINE;—*5. As necessary for the purposes of* INSTRUCTION;—*6. As opening the way for* PRAYER.

In view of such disastrous action as we have now been called to contemplate, we ask on what grounds the use of the Anxious Bench is vindicated. These should be of great force to counterbalance the weight of mischief with which it is attended. No divine appointment is pleaded in its favor.* We could not suppose for a moment indeed that any appointment of God could be associated with such bad influences and tendencies as are found to hold in connection with this invention. But it is not pretended to make it of Scriptural authority. It is vindicated on other grounds with variable argument to suit the occasion. These, however, are by no means satisfactory.

1. It serves, we are told, to bring awakened sinners to a *decision*. They are disposed to avoid this. They halt between two opinions. They should not be allowed to leave the sanctuary in this state. The Gospel calls for a present determination. It is well, therefore, to shut them up to that point. This is done by the Anxious Bench.†

---

*A good deal has been said indeed of the *principle* of the Old and New Testaments. But Mr. Denig has just been as successful in vindicating woman-preaching, shouting, rolling, &c., in this way, as the editor of the *Lutheran Observer* has been in justifying the anxious bench. All fanatical sects are able to muster something from the Bible which seems to cover, in sound at least, the principle of their peculiarities. So every abuse in the Church of Rome came in, under the shadow of pretended Scriptural precedent. Her fasts, her vigils, her relics, her penances, &c., all found a show of support in the word of God. The angelic institute of *monkery* was abundantly commended by the same authority. Was not John the Baptist a monk, and Elijah the Tishbite; and Elisha the son of Shaphat; and the sons of the prophets of Jordan; and the Rechabites; were they not examples in point so far at least as the *principle* of the system was concerned? So argued the fathers of the fourth century; and it must be confessed with full as much reason on their side as the friends of New Measures have when they appeal to the Bible in like strain for the support of their favorite system.

†"It presents the conscience with the *true* issue, and invites the sinner, without delay, to manifest his choice of God by coming forward. The 'anxious bench' does not suffer the sinner to go away simply meditating upon what he has heard; to go away in a state of rebellion, &c. But it calls upon him at once to submit to God." "Coming to the 'anxious bench' is a token of submission, and is used as a means wholly to that end."—*Davis' Plea*, p. 56.

This sounds well. But what is it that the sinner decides when he rises and goes forward to the anxious seat? He is encouraged to come, singing,

> "I'll go to Jesus, though my sin
> Hath like a mountain rose;
> I know His courts, I'll enter in,
> Whatever may oppose."

Is *this* the decision which the movement really involves? Then it is the same thing with conversion; the resolution of the prodigal carried into effect when out of a deep sense of his poverty and misery he *arose and went to his father*. And so much as this the considerations by which he is urged to come forward would seem to imply. But when the point is pressed, we learn that no such extravagant supposition is entertained. Coming to the anxious bench is *not* coming to Christ. The sinner seated upon it is unconverted still; hangs still between Christ and the world; and may still go away halting between two opinions, as fully as if he had not come out in this way at all. What shall we say of such a *decision*? A decision that decides nothing? The apostles, we are told, insisted on men's coming to the point at once in the business of religion, and we should do the same thing. So certainly we should. But is this such a point as the apostles were accustomed to press? When Peter found the multitude awakened on the day of Pentecost, he called them to an immediate decision. But what was the form in which this was done? "Repent, and be baptized every one of you in the name of Jesus Christ, for the remission of sins," cried the preacher. "Come," roars the modern revival-monger, pleasing himself with the thought of being like Peter, on the day of Pentecost, "Come humble sinner, in whose heart a thousand thoughts revolve, come, come without delay this night, this moment, come—to the altar or to the anxious bench." Alas for the parallel!* If it *be* conversion to come out in this way, let the thing be openly affirmed at once; but if not, why mock us by calling it a decision, and pretending to find precedents for it in the Acts of the Apostles?

2. But the ground now is shifted; sinners are not brought exactly to a decision by the Anxious Bench, but they are brought at least to a *committal*; and this is considered to be of great account. Let them go away from the house of God without this, and there will be a reason to fear that their seriousness may evaporate before the next meeting. We should take

---

*"We do not disparage baptism by comparing it to the anxious bench. By no means; we regard it as a sacrament, and intended for high purposes; but it also involved the precise principle in that day that the anxious bench does not. It afforded an opportunity for a public manifestation on the part of those who submitted to it, of their determination to be Christians. So also does the anxious bench."—*Luth. Obs., Dec.* 1, 1843. Alas, one may well be pardoned for whispering, *"Why are you a* LUTHERAN?"

advantage of their feelings when they are excited, and engage them, if possible, to take a step by which they shall feel themselves committed to the world, as well as to their own consciences, in favor of religion. This is done when we get them out to the anxious bench. They bind themselves by this act to seek the Lord. The thing is known and talked about. They *feel* themselves bound, and their shame and pride come in to fortify the higher influences, by which they are urged to go forward and not "draw back unto perdition."

Low and jejune must be the conception of religion which can allow such a view as this to be entertained. It is well indeed that sinners should bind themselves by an inward resolution to seek the Lord, while He is to be found; and it is right that they should be urged to do this on all suitable occasions. But such a resolution, to be of any account, must proceed from intelligent reflection and inward self-possession; and it can have no salutary force, except as entertained in the consciousness of God's presence and God's authority, to the exclusion comparatively of all inferior references. Nothing can be more irrational than to think of making the sinner's feelings in this case a trap for his judgment, and then holding him fast by the force of an outward bond. The circumstances in which he is urged to put his soul thus under pledge are the very worst that could well be imagined for the purpose. Volney, in the storm at sea, was not more fully at the mercy of an element beyond himself. Death-bed resolutions, notoriously hollow as they are, embrace just as much rational freedom. The vows of a drunkard, in ordinary cases, are but little respected. But here, where excitement, sympathy and passion combine, to wrap all spirits in a moral tornado, till the brain is found to reel with the bewildering, intoxicating element that surrounds it, the greatest account is made of such engagements, and every art is employed to secure them, even from hysterical girls if need be,* that they may feel themselves bound subsequently to "follow on to know the Lord." A large proportion of such resolutions must necessarily be without inward force; and now the sense of the *committal* is indeed required to sustain the solemn step which has been taken. But what is this, in such circumstances, but the substitution of low worldly references, as far as it prevails, for that consciousness of the soul's relations to God, in which alone, as we have already seen, any resolution of this sort can truly stand. So far exactly as the anxious person may be swayed by the thought of consistency, credit, or any similar interest, in continuing to seek religion, the true posture of conviction is wanting altogether. "How *can* ye believe," said Christ, "which receive honor one of another, and seek not the honor that cometh

---

*"Have not *hysterical girls* souls to be saved?" *Luth. Obs.*, Dec. 15, 1843. After due reflection, it seems necessary to answer this searching interrogation in the *affirmative*.

from God only." A reigning respect to the authority of the world under any form disqualifies the soul for transacting honestly in the great interest of religion.

In a multitude of instances these committals are followed by a reaction, in the minds of those who are drawn into them, of the most unhappy kind. They fall back openly to the world, but not without a feeling of humiliation and spite, in the recollection of their own weakness; and their state subsequently is worse than it was before. In the case of many others, the committal has its force, no doubt, in carrying them forward till they get fully into the Church; and their profession possibly may have the same power to hold them to the forms of religion afterwards, even to the end of life. But it is for the most part a false hope to which they are thus conducted. The Church, in this way, is filled with hypocrites, and not with true converts.

3. But the ground may be slightly shifted again, so as to present the measure, not in the light exactly of a bond upon the sinner's soul, but as a *prop* and *support* rather to his weakness. A first step often costs more than a hundred that follow. A world of hesitation, in certain circumstances, is surmounted by a single effort to move. The sinner, when first awakened, shrinks from making his case known, and his concern, pent up in his own bosom, is not likely to be as strong and active as it would be if it could appear in an outward form. Let him come then to the altar or the anxious bench. The man who signs a temperance pledge finds his resolution to be sober supported by the act. Hundreds of drunkards have been enabled in this way to reform completely, who without this help would have had no power to rise.

This is plausible; but it will not bear examination. A first step is of great account in religion; but only where it springs freely from the will; which it cannot do without reflection and self-command. An outward engagement to seek the Lord can be of no use, without a certain measure of intelligent conviction at work within; and where this is present, it will not be difficult to secure whatever may be proper or desirable in the other form, without having recourse to an expedient so full of danger. It is a part of the spiritual policy of the Romish Church to entice those who are serious, by means of vows, into positions from which they cannot draw back, with the view of thus establishing them in the purpose of a religious life. But we all know how little is gained in the Romish Church by this policy. It is true, indeed, that a drunkard may sign the temperance pledge even when he is drunk and afterwards keep it. But there is a vast difference between the object of the temperance pledge and that which it is proposed to reach by means of the Anxious Bench. The one is fully within the compass of human will and human strength; the other is beyond it entirely.* The one may be mastered in the flesh; the other cannot be approached or understood except in the spirit. In any case, however, vows and pledges that spring from excitement rather than reflection are to be considered fanatical, and as such neither rational nor free; and though in certain cases men may seem to be strengthened and supported by them in the prosecution of good ends belonging to a lower sphere, they are ever to be deprecated in the sphere of religion as tending only to delusion and sin.

4. The measure is sometimes recommended on the ground that it is well suited to humble and break the sinner's pride. The carnal mind is not willing to stoop to the shame of the cross in the view of a sinful world. It is difficult at the same time to bring it to a clear sight of this fact in its own case. But the anxious bench reduces the question to a present point. If unwilling to stoop to the self-denial involved in coming to this, how can the awakened person be willing to do anything that religion requires. Thus the pride and wickedness of the heart, in relation to the gospel, are forced home upon the individual's consciousness; and when at length, under the pressure of this conviction, he goes forward and joins himself openly with the anxious, his pride is prostrated, and he is no longer ashamed to appear earnestly concerned for the salvation of his soul.

But it is easy to see that on the same principle any *test* which might be imagined, for the same purpose, could be justified with equal ease. The sinner might be required to sit at the church door, clothed in sackcloth and ashes, begging an interest in the prayers of all the entering worshippers; or to travel through all the aisles of the church on his knees, in token of his humiliation. If unwilling to bend to such a requirement, how should he be counted truly in earnest with respect to the main point? In this way the whole system of Romish penance might challenge our respect. In truth, however, no account is to be made of any such outward demonstration as a test or token of the sinner's feelings in the particular view now considered! Popish penances involve commonly no spiritual mortification, and have no tendency whatever to reconcile men to the reproach of Christ. The sinner may be brought to lick the dust, if need be, under the pressure of an alarmed conscience, without a particle of that inward humiliation before God, which the idea of religion demands. So it is possible, and no

---

*Mr. *Finney* holds the pledge in the one case, a fair exemplification of the advantage gained by bringing a sinner to the bench in the other. The idea is quoted also with approbation by the *Lutheran Observer,* Dec. 1, 1843. Mr. *Davis* finds gross heresy, antinomianism, fatalism, &c., in the statement of the tract just at this point, *Plea,* p. 50–54. He speaks forth boldly the error that lies wrapped up in the very heart and core of the system he represents. "Does the sinner submit to God," it is asked with an air of triumph, "or does the Holy Ghost?" The only proper answer to such a question is, The Holy Ghost *in the sinner,* or the sinner as born of the Spirit of Christ, submits to God. Any view that stops short of this is rotten as Pelagianism itself.

doubt exceedingly common, for persons to take their seat on the anxious bench with very little if any feeling at all of this sort. Where the idea prevails that there is religion to some extent in the very act itself of coming out in this way, hundreds may easily be engaged to do so, just as under parallel circumstances they might be engaged to flagellate themselves publicly through the streets, without the least benefit in the way of a conquest over their carnal pride. In some cases, the occupancy of the bench may indeed be attended with the wholesome discipline of humiliation in the way supposed, preparing the spirit to follow Jesus "without the camp, bearing his reproach;" but it is just as certain that the same result has been secured in *some* cases by the penitential castigations of the Church of Rome, or the wilful self-inflictions of fanaticism in its worst forms. Where the soul is already prepared for spiritual humiliation, either the scourge or the bench, if duly accredited to the mourner's conscience as the power of God for the purpose, may serve as an occasion to promote this end. This is no reason, however, why we should have recourse to one or the other in seeking to advance the interests of religion. There is no direct adaptation in either to produce evangelical humiliation. They are suited rather, as has been shown already in the case of the bench, to blind the soul to the true nature of such humiliation by fixing its attention unduly on outward references and outward acts, and challenging it to a *wilful* more than to a *willing* service. It is well to remember here what the apostle says most profoundly on the subject of all such "will-worship," with its "show of wisdom," at the close of the second chapter of his epistle to the Colossians.

5. But again the use of the Anxious Bench is vindicated, as affording an opportunity for meeting the case of awakened sinners with suitable *instruction*. When they are called out in this way, they become known. They can be addressed collectively, and conversed with individually. What they need is particular instruction suited to their particular states. It is not by dashing water in a large way over a congregation of empty bottles that a minister can expect to get even a few of them filled; if he would labor to any purpose he must come down and take each bottle separately by the neck, and pour the water in according to the capacity of its mouth.

But when we look a little into the matter, we shall find this object of instruction reduced to a perfect farce. There are two ways in which the occupants of an Anxious Bench may be addressed. What is said may be spoken to all at once, or they may be taken one by one in succession. If there are too many for the minister to manage himself in this way, he may engage others to take part with him in the work. This must be considered the method most congenial with the idea of the system. For the object, we are told, is to make instruction particular and specific; and how can this be accomplished so well as by taking each case separately? It is customary accordingly, when the anxious are fairly in their place, for the process of instruction to commence in this way. The minister comes to one, the first on the bench, and bending forward proceeds in a low voice to ask a question or two with regard to the person's spiritual condition. These are answered commonly in the most general and confused way. Then follows a short exhortation, for the most part, in the same general strain. The whole conference may not last more than some three or four minutes; for there are a number to be conversed with; and regard must be had, at the same time, to the patience of the congregation. So the ceremony passes forward to a second, and then to a third, and so on, till all have their turn. And this is called spiritual instruction! If a physician were seen handling a dozen of patients in the same style, the spectacle might well call for derision. But after all, it would be no such mummery as we have here. One of the most difficult and delicate functions a minister is called to perform, is that of giving counsel to awakened sinners. None calls for more caution and discrimination. It is hard to ascertain correctly the state of the spiritual patient, and hard to suit the prescription wisely to his particular wants. It is so where there may be the fullest opportunity for free, calm investigation, in the family visit or in a private interview. But here, where all surrounding influences conspire to complicate the difficulty to the greatest extent, in the midst of commotion without and commotion within, it is pretended to dispose of a dozen such cases perhaps in the course of half an hour. And to make the matter worse, if the number of the anxious be considerable, this, that, and the other helper is called in, some crude exhorter perhaps, some stripling student just starting on his way *towards* the ministry, or some forward novice, himself still in the swaddling clothes of the new birth, to take part in the solemn ghostly work, under the same form. And is it possible that sensible men, in the fair use of their senses, can fail to be struck with the absurdity of such a process? The only fair parallel to it in the medical sphere would be the mockery of three or four raw practitioners going the rounds of a hospital, and administering to fifty cases of diversified diseases, within the same time, as many doses of Thompson's mixture, *Number Six*. In the latter case the thing would be counted and called *quackery* of the first degree; and it is hard to see why it should go under any softer appellation in the former. The only difference might seem to be in the solemnity of the interests involved in the two different circles of action. The Thompsonian tampers only with the life of the body, while the spiritual practitioner plays blindly with the precious life of the soul.

If "profitable for instruction" at all then, the Anxious Bench mast be made subservient to this end in a different way. Considering the circumstances of the case, the only rational course with a company thus brought forward is to spend the few minutes that can be devoted to them in counsels and exhortations addressed to them collectively. Let it not be said that such instructions must needs lack point. The cases of the truly awakened are always sufficiently near alike to admit of a large amount of most pointed and pertinent direction in the same form for all; and one who is truly a well instructed scribe in the Gospel will be able to address an Anxious Bench to much more purpose in this way than if he were to pass round directing a few remarks to each one separately. But is it necessary to call them out from the congregation for this purpose? The same truths may just as well be presented to inquirers, as included in the general audience, and it might reasonably be expected, in the case of the truly serious, with much better effect. But is it not desirable, we are asked, to have inquirers together by themselves? No doubt, there may be an advantage in this. But let it be with fitting time and place; not under circumstances which can hardly fail to obstruct and defeat all the purposes that should be aimed at the case.*

The Anxious Bench is of no account, in any view, as a help to instruction; and it is not hard to perceive, that as a general thing, where it is used, this does not form in reality its main recommendation in the eyes of its friends. It may be convenient to advocate the use of the measure on this ground, and consistency will require always some show of improving it accordingly. The anxious, in one way or another, must be instructed and directed after they have come out. But just at this point, there is apt to appear a sort of giving way in the general pressure of the occasion as though the main object of it had been already reached in the coming out itself. It often happens that a very short exhortation is allowed to wind up the whole scene; or it becomes evident that the conversation with the anxious is protracted amid the flagging interest of the congregation, with mechanical rather than with living force. This, where order and sobriety still continue to assert their proper rights, in the feelings of the people. Where that is not the case it will be contrived to keep up the excitement still, in connection with the show of instruction, in such way that this shall come but little into view, while all stress is laid upon the first. The anxious then are encouraged to weep aloud, cry out and wring their hands. Now they are enveloped in the loud tones of some stimulating spiritual song. Then there is prayer which soon becomes as loud; commencing perhaps with a single voice, but flowing quickly into a sea of tumultuating

---

*"Let it not be said, that inviting to "anxious seats" is the only effectual method of ascertaining who are under serious impressions and who are not. Why is it not quite as effectual to give a public invitation to all who are in any degree seriously impressed, or anxious, to remain after the congregation is dismissed or to meet for the purpose of disclosing their feelings, and of being made the subjects of instruction and prayer? Nay, why is not the latter method very much preferable to the former? It surely gives quite as good an opportunity to ascertain numbers and to distinguish persons and cases. It affords a far better opportunity to give distinct and appropriate instruction to particular individuals."—*Dr. Miller. Letter to Dr. Sprague.*

sounds from which no sense can be extracted even by the keenest ear. The mourners besiege the "altar" pell-mell, kneeling, or it may be floundering flat upon the floor, and all joining in the general noise. Then may be heard perhaps the voice of the preacher shouting some commonplace word of exhortation which nobody hears or regards; while at different points vague, crude expostulations and directions are poured into the ears of the struggling suppliants by "brethren," now suddenly transformed into spiritual counsellors, who might be at a loss themselves to explain at any other time a single point in religion. In due time one and another are *brought through*; and thus new forms of disorder, shouting, clapping, &c., are brought into play. In this way the interest of the occasion, such as it is, may be kept up till a late hour. But who will pretend to say that *instruction* has been regarded or intended as a leading object in any part of the process?

6. Lastly it is said that the anxious should be called out in order that they may be made the subjects of *prayer*. They need the prayers of the Church; and the Church, it may be supposed, has a heart to plead with God in their behalf. But how shall this be if they are not known? By the Anxious Bench they are brought into view, piteously seeking an interest in the prayers of God's people; whose bowels of compassion cannot fail to be stirred by the spectacle.

This might seem to be the great object in the case of such methodistical displays as we have just had under observation. But scenes of this sort have no tendency to stimulate the spirit of prayer. They form an element, unfriendly, if not absolutely fatal to the true idea of devotion. This is evident generally from a certain character of irreverence, often grossly profane, that is sure to put itself forward in such circumstances, in proportion exactly to the strength of the reigning excitement. And in any case, there is reason to believe that more is lost than gained for the anxious, as it regards this interest, by the commotion necessarily connected with their movement to the anxious bench. It is a suspicious kind of prayer at best that can be engaged in such circumstances only by the *sight* of its objects, theatrically paraded to produce effect, without the power of a more general interest. But it is not necessary that the awakened should be unknown in the church to which they belong. They can be discovered without the aid of the Anxious Bench, and can be carried so upon the hearts of God's people, in the sanctuary and in the closet, with an interest far more deep and active than any that is produced in the other way.

I know of no other ground than those which have now been considered on which the use of the Anxious Bench can be vindicated with any plausible defence. And as these separately taken have no force, so neither can they be allowed to weigh any thing collectively against the condemnation in which the system is properly involved.

CHAPTER VI.

The system of the bench tends to disorder.—Connects itself readily with a vulgar and irreverent style in religion.—Women praying in public. —Influence unfavorable to deep, earnest piety.—Relation of the system to that of the CATECHISM.

The Anxious Bench tends naturally to disorder. Where any considerable excitement prevails, it is almost impossible for the measure to be applied without confusion and commotion. It is common indeed to have it said in the accounts given afterwards of such occasions that they were conducted in a quiet and orderly way. But the true idea of quiet and order is apt not to be understood; for it not unfrequently happens that these accounts themselves, in close connection with such a statement, present evidence sufficient to show it not strictly correct.* Some appear to think that there is no disorder at such times unless it comes to loud noise and gross confusion, in the style of the Methodists. But the proper order of the sanctuary may be seriously unsettled long before it has gone so far as this. The measure involves irregularity to some extent in its very nature, and opens the way for extravagance. It is always ready accordingly to run into

---

*"In giving accounts of similar visitations of mercy in other places our correspondents sometimes take especial care to let us know that all things were done 'decently and in order.' If by this is meant that all was quiet, and conducted with measured propriety and entire regard to the prejudice of those who are opposed to religious excitements; then we cannot say so much of the revival in —— church. For there was *noise* there not a little, *measured propriety* not much, &c."—*Luth. Obs.*, Nov. 11, 1842.—"We had no confusion, but considerable noise—and, dear brother, how could it be otherwise? Fifty and sixty souls crying to God for mercy, some finding peace and praising God, Christians conversing with, and praying for mourners, &c." *Corresp. Luth. Obs.*, *Apr.* 14, 1843.—The following would seem to be quite orderly. "On one occasion the whole church, that is the mass of professors of religion who were present, came forward in a body, including men and women, old and young, married and unmarried, and prostrating themselves around the altar and in the aisles, renewed their covenant with God and solemnly pledged themselves to increased efforts for the conversion of the impenitent." *Dec.* 2, 1842. Also the following as reported *Apr.* 7, 1843, by one who has written a book on revivals. Mr. S., a very moral and worthy man, "became awakened and converted in his own house, just the night before our meeting commenced." The next evening, when the call was given for the anxious to come forward, he passed up to the altar and asked leave to speak. This granted, he cried out, "O my old companions and friends, who of you will now come and take me by the hand, and go to heaven with me! Last night at midnight, God blessed my soul, and I must now tell you what He has done for me!" The effect was electric. "Where are you, my brethren, who have covenanted with God?" he asked again. "Instantly there was a general rush from all parts of the house, and I suppose every male member in the church came up to the altar to grasp our dear br. by the hand, and covenanted to go to heaven together. O what a scene! We all wept together. It happened the first night of our meeting, and a most glorious revival followed."

disorder. It leads naturally, if encouraged, to more striking deviations from the line of Christian sobriety. It forms the threshhold properly to the whole system of New Measures. We may pretend to draw a line between it and other more noisy and disorderly forms of action but the line will be an arbitrary one, separating things that after all are inwardly related. The general principle of the Anxious Bench and its proper soul are substantially the principle and soul of the entire system to which it belongs. Let it be considered orderly and edifying to call out the anxious in this way, and why should they not be encouraged as well to surround the altar on their knees, or to lay themselves down in token of their humiliation in the dust?* If one measure of irregularity and noise may be allowed on the principle that we should give room to the Spirit, why should not a larger amount of the same be tolerated on the same plea? "Should *man* enforce 'decent' silence"—asks the editor of the *Lutheran Observer*, in view of a scene where "crushed sinners," it is said, "prostrate upon their knees, lay scattered around the altar, the females in one group and the males in another what is grating discord to one ear, may be charming concord to another," and the united tones of all together reminded him of the noise of many waters—"Should *man* enforce 'decent' silence when *God's power* had produced 'strong crying and tears?' Should we prescribe limits to the workings of divine grace, and say to the swelling waves of overwhelming contrition, thus far shall ye come and no further?" The apology was intended to cover only a certain measure of noise and confusion. But it is of sufficient breadth plainly for any extent of extravagance we may be pleased to imagine. The most frantic disciple of Winebrenner could ask no more, to justify his greatest outrages on common decency and common sense. Screaming, shouting, jumping, tumbling, and in one word the whole wildfire of fanaticism, including the "holy laugh," and the "holy grin," might be vindicated in the same way. Only let persons persuade themselves that the "power of God" within them *must* reveal itself in this style, and all becomes at once rational and right. For there are *diversities of operations*; and it should be remembered that "rules of propriety are conventional and often very arbitrary things, and

---

*"If I were to place myself on what is called an *anxious seat*, or should kneel down before a whole congregation to be prayed for, I know that I should be strangely agitated, but I do not believe that it would be of permanent utility. But if it should produce some good effect, am I at liberty to resort to anything in the worship of God which I think will be useful? If such things are lawful and useful, why not add other circumstances to increase the effect? Why not require the penitent to appear in a white sheet or to be clothed in sackcloth with ashes on his head? and these, remember, are Scriptural signs of humiliation. And on these principles, who can reasonably object to holy water, to incense, and the use of pictures or images in the worship of God? All these things came into the Church upon the same principle, of devising *new measures* to do good." *Thoughts on Religious Experience*, by Dr. Alexander, page 72.

so is taste; what is thought decent in one community may be deemed very disorderly in another, what is grating discord to one ear, may be charming concord to another." Even Mr. Winebrenner himself, when interrogated on the subject of noise, only answers, "What is from heaven I approve of, but what is from men I disapprove of;" though he goes on immediately to sanction "loud groaning, crying, shouting, clapping of hands, jumping, falling down, &c." as forms in which a divine influence may be expected at times to work. Still he "has no inclination to justify all sorts of noise and bodily exercises." The truth is, as already said, that no satisfactory stopping place can be found in the system of New Measures. It has a life and spirit of its own, that begin to be developed in the simple Anxious Bench, and naturally flow onward from that point, to the very worst excesses. Good men may try to hold the stream in check, some at one point and some at another; but it will not consent to be held within the limits imposed upon it by *their* sense of propriety. It claims to have its origin in heaven, and who in such case shall presume to say to it, "Thus far shalt thou come, but no farther, and here shall thy proud waves be stayed?"

As the spirit of the Anxious Bench tends to disorder, so it connects itself also naturally and readily with a certain vulgarism of feeling in religion that is always injurious to the worship of God, and often shows itself absolutely irreverent and profane. True religious feeling is inward and deep; shrinks from show; forms the mind to a subdued humble habit. "The language of experience is," says one whose word should have weight, "that it is unsafe and unwise to bring persons, who are under religious impressions, too much into public view. The seed of the word, like the natural seed, does not vegetate well in the sun." We may say then that there is a measure of rudeness connected with this particular style of action in the Church from the very nature of the case. It is a wrong feeling in this respect that makes it seem desirable at all, that awakened persons should be dragged thus theatrically into public view; and the process is well suited to generate wrong feelings, under the same form, in those who are subjected to its rough operation. The circumstances of such an occasion are by no means favorable to true inward solemnity, such as causes the heart to exclaim, "How awful is this place!" High excitement always tends to destroy men's reverence for God and sacred things. And so this "high pressure" system, as it is sometimes called, in proportion as it prevails, is always found to work. It gives rise to a style of preaching which is often rude and coarse, as well as uncommonly vapid; and creates an appetite for such false aliment, with a corresponding want of taste for true and solid instruction. All is made to tell upon the one single object of *effect*. The pulpit is transformed, more or less, into a stage. Divine things are so *popularized* as to be at last shorn of their dignity as well as their mystery. Anecdotes and stories are plentifully retailed, often in low, familiar, flippant style. Roughness is substituted for strength, and paradox for point. The preacher feels *himself*, and is bent on making himself felt also by the congregation; but God is not felt in the same proportion. In many cases self-will and mere human passion, far more than faith or true zeal for the conversion of souls, preside over the whole occasion. Coarse personalities, and harsh denunciations, and changes rung rudely on terms the most sacred and things the most solemn, all betray the wrong spirit that prevails. But to see the character of the system in the aspect now considered fully disclosed, we must look at it again in its more advanced positions, where the genius that animates it is permitted to work with full scope. Here the so-called awakening, on the camp ground or at the quarterly meeting, is often presented under a form that is absolutely shocking to a truly serious mind. Noise and confusion unite to overwhelm every right sentiment in the soul. Decency and order are given to the winds. A dozen perhaps are heard praying at once, in all unseemly postures, and with the most violent gestures. And then the form and spirit of these prayers, as far as they can be heard! What rude familiarity with the High and Holy One; what low belittling and caricaturing of all that is grand in the Gospel; what gross profanity in the style of many of the petitions with which it is pretended to storm the citadel of God's favors! The atmosphere of such a meeting may be exciting, intoxicating, bewildering; but it has no power whatever to dispose the mind to devotion. There is nothing in the scene to impress those who are present, with the sense of God's awful, heart-searching presence. Very frequently while such a chaos of prayer is going forward in full strength at one end of the house, the lookers-on at the other show themselves as much at their ease, and betray as little emotion, as though they were sitting in a bar-room. They have grown obtuse to the stirring show, and feel themselves in no connection with what is going forward, except as they find an opportunity, from time to time, to fall in with the catch of some familiar revival-song, which they shout forth as boisterously as any body else. Fanaticism has no power to make God's presence felt. It is wild, presumptuous, and profane where it affects to partake more largely of the power of heaven. No wonder that the religion which is commenced and carried forward under such auspices should show itself to be characteristically coarse and gross. Wanting true reverence for God, it will be without true charity also towards men. It is likely to be narrow, intolerant, sinister, and rabidly sectarian. All that is high will become low, and all that is beautiful be turned into vulgarity, in its hands.*

---

*"Fanaticism often blazes with a glaring flame, and agitates assemblies as with a hurricane or earthquake; but God is not in the fire, or the wind, or the earthquake. His presence is more commonly with the still, small voice. There is no sounder characteristic of genuine devotion than reverence. Where this is banished, the fire may burn fiercely, but it is unhallowed fire. Fanaticism, however much it may assume the garb and language of

One striking illustration of the coarseness of this spirit is found in the disposition it has shown in all ages to set aside the rule, which forbids women to speak publicly in religious assemblies. Nature itself may be said to teach us that woman cannot quit her sphere of relative subordination with regard to man without dishonoring herself, and losing her proper strength. And it is no small argument for the divine origin or the gospel that while it teaches the absolute personal equality of the sexes as it had never been understood before, it still echoes, while it rightly interprets, the voice of nature with regard to this point. "I suffer not a woman to teach," says the apostle, "nor to usurp authority over the man, but to be in silence." And again, "Let your women keep silence in the churches; for it is not permitted unto them to speak.—It is a shame for a woman to speak in the church." True religion this judgment. No female with the Gospel in her heart can wish to have it reversed. She would feel her nature wronged rather in being required to appear in the way here forbidden before the public. But of *such* delicacy, no account is made, by the fanatical temper now under consideration. It is coarse and vulgar, and would fain show itself wiser at this point than Paul himself. It encourages women to pray in public, and to address promiscuous meetings, and by the spirit it infuses makes them willing to unsex themselves in this way. There can be no surer sign of grossness and coarseness in religion than a disposition to tolerate this monstrous perversion under any form.

The general system to which the Anxious Bench belongs, it may be remarked again, is unfavorable to deep, thorough, and intelligent piety. This must be the case, of course, if there be any truth in the observations already made with regard to its character. A system that leads to such a multitude of spurious conversions, and that makes room so largely for that low, gross, fanatical habit which has just been described, cannot possibly be associated to any extent with the power of godliness in its deeper and more earnest forms. The religion which it may produce so far as it can be counted genuine, will be for the most part of a dwarfish size and sickly complexion. The "experience" of the Anxious Bench is commonly shallow. The friends of the new method often please themselves, it is true, with the idea that *their* awakenings include a vast amount of power in this way; and they are not backward to insinuate that those who oppose their measures are ignorant of what pertains to the "depths" of experimental piety. Were such persons themselves experimentally acquainted with the pangs of the new birth, it is intimated, they would not be so easily offended with the noise and disorder of poor souls *agonizing* at the altar; and if they had ever themselves tasted the joys of pardoned sins they

---

piety, is its opposite; for while the latter is mild, and sweet, and disinterested, and respectful, and affectionate, the former is proud, arrogant, censorious, selfish, carnal, and when opposed, malignant."—*Dr. Alexander's Letter to Dr. Sprague.*

might be expected to have other ears than they now have for the shouts and hallelujahs of the redeemed, suddenly translated in these circumstances from the power of Satan into the glorious liberty of the family of God. But in fact no "experiences" are more superficial commonly than those which belong to this whirlwind process. The foundations of the inward life are not reached and moved by it at all. All that would be wanted often to hush an "altar-full" of chaotic cries to solemn stillness, would be that the hearts of the "agonizing" mourners should be suddenly touched with some real sense of the presence of God and their own sins. "I have heard of Thee," says Job, "with the hearing of the ear; but *now mine eye seeth Thee*: wherefore I abhor myself, and repent in dust and ashes." Alas, it is not the *depth* of these anxious bench and camp-meeting conversions, but their utter want of depth that exposes them to complaint. They involve little or nothing of what the old divines call *heart work*. They bring with them no self-knowledge. They fill the Church with lean professors, who show subsequently but little concern to *grow* in grace, little capacity indeed to understand at all the free, deep, full life of the "new man" in Christ Jesus. Such converts, if they do not altogether "fall from grace," are apt to continue at least babes in the Gospel, as long as they live. The natural fruit of the system is a sickly Christianity that is sure to be defective or one-sided, both in doctrine and practice. It proceeds upon a wrong conception of religion from the start, and error and heresy in the nature of the case are wrought plentifully into the very texture of all that is reached by its operations. There is involved in it a spirit of delusion which cannot fail to show its power disastrously after a short time in any community in which it is suffered to prevail.

Here is another most serious charge, demanding our special attention. I have denominated the system a *heresy*, not inconsiderately or for rhetorical effect simply, but with sober calculation and design. In religion, as in life universally, theory and practice are always inseparably intertwined in the ground of the soul. Every error is felt practically; and wherever obliquity in conduct comes into view, it must be referred to some corresponding obliquity in principle. It is not by accident then that the system of New Measures if found producing so largely the evil consequences which have been thus far described. Error and heresy, I repeat it, are involved in the system itself, and cannot fail sooner or later, where it is encouraged, to evolve themselves in the most mischievous results. Finneyism is only Taylorism reduced to practice, the speculative heresy of New-Haven actualized in common life. A low, shallow, pelagianizing theory of religion runs through it from beginning to end. The fact of sin is acknowledged, but not in its true extent. The idea of a new spiritual creation is admitted, but not in its proper radical and comprehensive form. The ground of the sinner's salvation is made to lie at last in his own separate person. The deep import of the declaration,

That which is born of the flesh is flesh, is not fully apprehended; and it is vainly imagined accordingly that the flesh as such may be so stimulated and exalted notwithstanding as to prove the mother of that spiritual nature, which we are solemnly assured can be born only of the Spirit. Hence all stress is laid upon the energy of the individual will (the self-will of the flesh) for the accomplishment of the great change in which regeneration is supposed to consist. The case is not remedied at all by the consideration that due account is made at the same time *professedly* of the aids of God's Spirit as indispensable in the work of conversion. The heresy lies involved in the system. This is so constructed as naturally, and in time inevitably, to engender false views of religion. Sometimes the mere purpose to serve God in the same form with a resolution to sign a temperance pledge, is considered to be the ground of regeneration. At other times, it is made to stand in a certain state of feeling, supposed to be of supernatural origin, but apprehended notwithstanding mechanically as the result of a spiritual process which begins and ends with the sinner himself. The experience of the supposed supernatural in this case stands in the same relation to the actual power of the new birth that magic bears to the true idea of a miracle. The higher force does not strictly and properly take possession of the lower, but is presumed rather to have been reduced to the possession and service of this last, to be used by it for its own convenience. Religion does not get the sinner, but it is the sinner who "gets religion." Justification is taken to be in fact by *feeling*, not by faith; and in this way falls back as fully into the sphere of self-righteousness as though it were expected from works under any other form. In both the views which have been mentioned, as grounded either in a change of purpose or a change of feeling, religion is found to be in the end the product properly of the sinner himself. It is wholly subjective, and therefore visionary and false. The life of the soul must stand in something beyond itself. Religion involves the will; but not as self-will, affecting to be its own ground and centre. Religion involves feeling; but it is not comprehended in this as its principle. Religion is subjective also, fills and rules the individual in whom it appears; but it is not created in any sense by its subject or from its subject. The life of the branch is in the trunk. The theory we have been contemplating then, as included practically in the system of New Measures, is a great and terrible heresy; which it is to be feared is operating, in this connection, to deceive and destroy a vast multitude of souls.

The proper fruits of Pelagianism follow the system invariably, in proportion exactly to the extent in which it may be suffered in any case to prevail. A most ample field for instruction with regard to this point, for all who care to receive instruction, is presented in the history of the great religious movement over which Mr. Finney presided some years ago in certain parts of this country. Years of faithful pastoral service, on the part of a different order of ministers, working in a wholly different style, have hardly yet sufficed in the northern section of the state of New York to restore to something like spiritual fruitfulness and beauty the field over which this system then passed, as a wasting fire in the fulness of its strength. The perfectionism of Oberlin, with its low conceptions of the law of God, is but a natural development of the false life with which it is animated. The wide West abounds in every direction with illustrations of its mischievous action, under all imaginable forms. In many places, a morbid thirst for excitement may be said to exhaust the whole interest that is felt in religion. The worst errors stand in close juxtaposition with the most bold pretensions to the highest order of Christian experience. All might seem to begin in the Spirit, and yet all is perpetually ending in the flesh. It were an easy thing, too, to gather exemplifications supporting the same lesson from the past history of the Church. For the system, properly speaking, is not new. The same theory of religion has led, in all ages, to substantially the same style of action, and this has been followed by substantially the same bad fruits.

The question of "New Measures" then, as it claims at this time particularly the attention of the German Churches, is one of much greater importance than some might be disposed to imagine. The truth is, this system, as we have said, has a life and spirit of its own. It may be associated to some extent, in certain hands, with the power of a more vigorous life derived from a different quarter, so as to seem comparatively sound and safe. But it ought not to be thought, on this account, that it may be incorporated practically with one order of thinking on the subject of religion as easily as with another. It is not by accident only that it is found connecting itself with the faults and defects that have now been mentioned. A false theory of religion is involved in it, which cannot fail to work itself out and make itself felt, in many hurtful results wherever it gains footing in the Church. No religious community can grow and prosper, in a solid way, where it is allowed to have any considerable authority; because it will always stand in the way of those deeper and more silent forms of action, by which alone it is possible for this end to be accomplished. It is a different system altogether that is required to build up the interests of Christianity in a firm and sure way. A ministry apt to teach; sermons full of unction and light; faithful, systematic instruction; zeal for the interests of holiness; pastoral visitation; catechetical training; due attention to order and discipline; patient perseverance in the details of the ministerial work; these are the agencies by which alone the kingdom of God may be expected to go steadily forward, among any people. Where these are fully employed, there will be revivals; but they will be only as it were the natural fruit of the general culture going before, without that spasmodic, meteoric character which too often distinguishes excitements under this name; while the life of religion will show itself abidingly at work, in the reigning temper of the Church, at all other times. Happy the congregation that may be placed under such spiritual auspices! Happy for our German Zion, if such might be the system that should prevail, to the exclusion of every other within her borders! We may style it, for distinction sake, the system of the *Catechism*. It is another system wholly from that which we have been contemplating in this tract. We find the attempt made in some cases, it is true, to incorporate the power of the Catechism with the use of new measures. But the union is unnatural, and can never be inward and complete. The two systems involve at the bottom two different theories of religion. The spirit of the Anxious Bench is at war with the spirit of the Catechism. Where it comes decidedly to prevail, catechetical instruction and the religious training of the young generally are not likely to be maintained with much effect; and it will not be strange if they should be openly slighted even, and thrust out of the way as an incumbrance to the Gospel, rather than a help.* What is wrought in the way of the Catechism is considered to be of man, what is wrought by the Bench is taken readily for the work of God. And the reason of this is near at hand. The Catechism is indeed weak in the hands of those who have this judgment. They have no inward power to make themselves felt in this way. But they *seem* to have power in the use of the Bench; and it is no wonder they should magnify it accordingly. The systems are antagonistic. Particular men standing under one standard may be to some extent entangled in views and practices properly belonging to the other; but so far they must be inconsistent with themselves. Each system, as such, has its own life and soul, in virtue of which it cannot truly coalesce with the other. They cannot flourish and be in vigorous force together. The Bench is against the Catechism, and the Catechism against the Bench. I mean of course not the Catechism as a mere dead form, in the way in which the original order of the Church, has been too often abused; and it is silly, if not something worse, to insist upon *this* view of it, when the two systems are drawn into contrast, as though there could be no other alternative to the Bench than the Catechism without life. It is the living Catechism, the Catechism awakened and active, that is intended in this opposition. As

---

*A graphic illustration of this point was furnished lately, it is said, by a minister of the New Measure school in this neighborhood. On the morning of a sacramental Sabbath, his catechetical class was admitted by profession of faith to the Lord's table and the full communion of the Church. On the very same evening, they were drawn forward to the anxious bench for the purpose of conversion! Towards the close of the year 1842, we find in the *Lutheran Observer* a glowing report from this same workman of splendid results effected by his ministry, on a different field, which he was obliged soon after to leave. In a single protracted meeting in one case he was able to muster "about one hundred and fifty" converts. Since that time, he has reported another revival, which came and went so rapidly that the community generally had no knowledge of it till it was all over. No wonder such a man should put honor on the Bench and scorn on the Catechism, and rail out from the pulpit against the present tract, as though it were the "abomination of desolation" itself.

such it stands as the representative and symbol of a system, embracing its own theory of religion, and including a wide circle of agencies, peculiar to itself, for carrying this theory into effect. These agencies, in the pulpit and out of it, will be understood, and honored, and actively applied in proportion exactly as the spirit of the system may prevail; and in the same proportion the Christianity of the Church may be expected to show itself large, deep, full, vigorous, and free. Between such a Christianity and that which is the product of the Bench, there can be no comparison; and it must be counted an immense misfortune in the case of any religious denomination when the views, feelings, and forms of action that are represented by this, through the force of a perverse judgment, gain such ground as to push the other system aside. It must be ever a wretched choice, when the *Bench* is perferred to the *Catechism*.

CHAPTER VII.

System of the Catechism.—Its theological ground and constitution.—Its general methods and forms of action.—Historical exemplification.

It seems to be due to the whole subject that the system of the CATECHISM, as here opposed to the system of the *Bench*, should be a little more fully described. This might well form the theme of a separate tract. As a closing chapter to the present publication, it can claim our attention only in a very general way.

The Anxious Bench has stood before us as the representative and type of a certain religious system, having its own theory and its own practice, both replete with dangerous error. In the same way, we exhibit the Catechism as the representative and type of another system, including in like manner both theory and practice of an opposite character. It is not meant, of course, that the whole system originated in the Catechism, or that it must stand or fall in every instance with the use of the Catechism; but simply that this belongs to it in principle and constitution, and is well fitted at the same time to stand as a specimen of its general meaning and force.

The theory of religion in which the system of the Catechism stands, is vastly more deep and comprehensive, and of course vastly more earnest also, than that which lies at the foundation of the other system. This last we have seen to be characteristically pelagian, with narrow views of the nature of sin, and confused apprehensions of the difference between flesh and spirit; involving in the end the gross and radical error, that conversion is to be considered, in one shape or another, the product of the sinner's own will, and not truly and strictly a new creation in Christ Jesus by the power of God. This is an old heresy of which notice is taken by the apostle Paul in the second chapter of his epistle to the Church at Colosse, and which has been actively at work in the Christian world, under various forms and disguises, from that time to the present. It has often put on the fairest appearances, seeming even to go beyond the general life of the Church, in the measure of its zeal and spirituality. It can easily affect also, deceiving itself as much as others, to honor the grace of God, and to derive all its life from a source beyond itself. But still the imagination remains, that this life is something that stands in the individual separately taken, the property of a particular *self*, rather than a more general power in which every such particular self is required to lose itself, that "old things may pass away and all things become new." The man *gets* religion, and so stands over it and above it, in his own fancy, as the owner of property in any other case. From such monstrous perversion, the worst consequences may be expected to flow. The system may generate action; but it will be morbid action, one-sided, spasmodic, ever leaning towards fanaticism. In opposition to this, the true theory of religion carries us continually beyond the individual, to the view of a far deeper and more general form of existence in which his particular life is represented to stand. Thus sin is not simply the offspring of a particular will, putting itself forth in the form of actual transgressions, but a wrong habit of humanity itself, a general and universal force, which includes and rules the entire existence of the individual man from the very start.* The disease is organic, rooted in the race, and not to be overcome in any case by a force less deep and general than itself. As well might we look for the acorn to forsake in growing the type of its proper species, and put forth the form of a mountain ash or stately elm. "That which is born of the flesh is flesh." So deep and broad is the ruin from which man is to be delivered by the Gospel. And here again, the same depth and breadth are presented to us also in the Christian salvation itself. Man is the subject of it, but not the author of it in any sense. His nature is restorable, but it can never restore itself. The restoration to be real, must begin *beyond* the individual. In this case as in the other the general must go before the particular, and support it as its proper ground. Thus humanity, fallen in Adam, is made to undergo a resurrection in Christ, and so restored, flows over organically, as in the other case, to all in whom its life appears. The sinner is saved then by an inward living union with Christ as real as the bond by which he has been joined in the first instance to Adam. This union is reached and maintained, through the medium of the Church, by the power of the Holy Ghost. It constitutes a new life, the ground of which is not in the particular subject of it at all, but in Christ, the organic root of the Church. The particular subject lives, not properly speaking in the acts of his own will separately considered, but in the power of a vast generic life that lies wholly beyond his will, and has now begun to manifest itself through him as the law and type of his will itself, as well as of his whole being. As born of the Spirit in contradistinction from the flesh, he is himself spiritual, and

---

*This point is well maintained in a Defence of the Second Article of the Augsburg Confession, ("gegen alte und neue Gegener,") by Dr. *Sartorius*, one of the most distinguished Lutheran divines of the present age. Had the treatise been written expressly against the theory of sin brought forward some time since, in this country, by Dr. Taylor of New Haven, of whom probably the German theologian had never heard, it could hardly have furnished a refutation of it more thorough and complete. It is directed against the Rationalism of modern Germany which only reiterates here the Pelagianism of the Romish Church as we find it withstood in the ever memorable Confession of Augsburg. This shallow theory, as exhibited by Dr. Taylor, constitutes as we have seen the very soul of Finneyism, which is simply another name for the system of the Anxious Bench.

capable of true righteousness. Thus his salvation begins, and thus it is carried forward till it becomes complete in the resurrection of the great day. From first to last it is a power which he does not so much apprehend as he is apprehended by it, and comprehended in it, and carried along with it as something infinitely more deep and vast than himself.

Now as one or the other of the two opposite theories of religion, thus briefly described, may be found to reign, not in the written or oral creed of those who take an interest in the subject, but in the inmost core of their life, the result will appear, with characteristic difference, in the whole tenor and bearing of their religion, practically considered. And this difference will be substantially that of the two systems now compared, the religion of the Catechism and the religion of the Bench.

It might seem indeed, at first view, that the theory which sets the particular before the general in this case would be found more favorable than its opposite to earnest and vigorous religious action, in every direction. And so it is often taken to be, in fact. The other scheme, involving as it seems to do a helpless dependence of the individual upon a generality deeper and more comprehensive than himself, first as it regards sin, and then again as it regards righteousness, is held up to reproach, as a view that cuts the sinews of moral action, and may be expected, where it prevails, to lie like a paralysing incubus on all the energies of the Church. But this idea is contradicted by universal experience, as well as by the true philosophy of life. To be moved deeply and strongly in any case, man *must* be wrought upon by a force, deeper and more comprehensive than his separate self. Great purposes and great efforts appear only when the sense of the general overpowers the sense of the particular, and the last is constrained to become tributary to the tendencies and purposes of the first. There may be a great show of strength, where the man acts simply from and for himself; noise, agitation, passion, reaching even to violence; but it will be only a display of imbecility when all is done. The will acting in this way is very weakness itself; and all the blustering and violence it may put on serves but to expose the deficiency of strength that prevails within. To acquire, in any case, true force, it must fall back on a power more general than itself. And so it is found that in the sphere of religion particularly, the pelagian theory is always vastly more impotent for practical purposes, than that to which it stands opposed. The action which it produces may be noisy, fitful, violent; but it can never carry with it the depth, the force, the fullness that are found to characterize the life of the soul when set in motion by the other view.

Conviction of sin is never deep and thorough, till it comes to a clear consciousness, with the sinner, that his sinful life is rooted in a sinful nature, older and broader than himself, which he has no power to renovate or control. Nor is the Christian salvation rightly understood, till it is felt that it must be something more deep and comprehensive than the will of the individual subject himself, in whom it is to appear. Such experience carrying the man beyond himself, and merging the consciousness of the particular in the consciousness of the general, may be much less ostentatious and much more quiet than the experience generated by the other view; but it will be so only because it is far less superficial, and far more full of truth. Religion in this form becomes strictly a life, the life of God in the soul. So far as this life prevails it is tranquil, profound, and free. It overcomes the world; "not by might and by power," the unequal, restless, fitful, and spasmodic efforts of the flesh, "but by the Spirit of the Lord." The believer can do all things, standing in Christ.

And as this theory of religion is the ground of all deep experience in the case of the individual Christian, so it gives rise to the more vigorous and comprehensive action, on the part of the Church, for carrying into effect the provisions of the gospel for the salvation of men. In proportion exactly as it is understood and felt, will such action display itself in all its proper forms; and under no other circumstances can any agency be employed for the same end that will be entitled at all to take its place.

From first to last, the action now mentioned will go forward, under a due practical recognition of the truth, that both the ruin of man and his recovery rest in a ground, which is beyond himself as an individual. If saved at all, he is to be saved by the force of a spiritual constitution, established by God for the purpose, the provisions of which go far beyond the resources of his own will, and are expected to reach him, not so much through the measure of his own particular life, as by the medium of a more general life with which he has to be filled and animated from without. This spiritual constitution is brought to bear upon him in the *Church*, by means of institutions and agencies which God has appointed, and clothed with power, expressly for this end. Hence where the system of the Catechism prevails, great account is made of the Church, and all reliance placed upon the means of grace comprehended in its constitution as all-sufficient under God for the accomplishment of its own purposes. The means are felt to be something more than mere devices of human ingenuity, and are honored and diligently used accordingly as the "wisdom of God and the power of God" unto salvation. Due regard is had to the idea of the Church as something more than a bare abstraction, the conception of an aggregate of parts mechanically brought together. It is apprehended rather as an organic life, springing perpetually from the same ground, and identical with itself at every point. In this view, the Church is truly the *mother* of all her children. They do not impart life to her, but she imparts life to them. Here again the general is left to go before the particular, and to condition all its manifestations. The Church is in no sense the product of individual Christianity, as though a number of persons should first receive the heavenly fire in separate streams, and then come into such a spiritual connection comprising the whole; but individual Christianity is the product, always and entirely, of the Church as existing previously, and only revealing its life in this way. Christ lives in the Church, and *through* the Church in its particular members; just as Adam lives in the human race generically considered, and through the race in every individual man. This view of the relation of the Church to the salvation of the individual exerts an important influence in the case before us, on the whole system of action, by which it is sought to reach this object.

Where it prevails, a serious interest will be taken in the case of children as proper subjects for the Christian salvation, from the earliest age. Infants born in the Church are regarded and treated as members of it from the beginning, and this privilege is felt to be something more than an empty shadow. The idea of infant conversion is held in practical honor; and it is counted not only possible, but altogether natural, that children growing up in the bosom of the Church under the faithful application of the means of grace should be quickened into spiritual life in a comparatively quiet way, and spring up numerously "as willows by the watercourses," to adorn the Christian profession, without being able at all to trace the process by which the glorious change has been effected.* Where the Church has lost all faith in this method of conversion, either not looking for it at all or looking for it only in rare and extraordinary instances, it is an evidence that she is under the force of a wrong religious theory, and practically subjected, at least in some measure, to the false system whose symbol is the Bench. If conversion is not expected nor sought in this way among infants and children, it is not likely often to occur. All is made to hang methodistically on sudden and violent experiences belonging to the individual separately taken, and holding little or no connection with his relations to the Church previously. Then as a matter

---

*To cut off occasion from such as *seek* occasion for misrepresentation, it may be well enough to remark here (though in ordinary circumstances the remark might seem to be wholly superfluous) that the idea of such a comparatively silent process of conversion, as something to be desired and sought in the case of infants and children, does not imply at all that regeneration in any case is a *gradual* change. Nor is it intended to throw discredit by any means on all sudden conversions in later life, attended with experience more or less violent and marked in the case of those who have grown up to some age in an impenitent state. Conversions of this sort under proper circumstances are entitled to entire confidence, and may be expected to occur frequently under faithful ministrations on the part of the Church. But the error is in making this the exclusive conception of the process. It is of immense account to hold fast with Luther and the other Reformers to the other conception at the same time. Regeneration is instantaneous, but as such not to be perceived directly in any case by the subject. It can be perceived only in its effects. But these belong to *conversion*, the change that flows from regeneration. Regeneration may take place in the womb, or in infancy, or in early childhood, or in adult age. In every case its symbol is the *wind*; "thou hearest the sound thereof, but canst not tell whence it cometh, nor whither it goeth."

of course, baptism becomes a barren sign, and the children of the Church are left to grow up like the children of the world, under general most heartless, most disastrous neglect. The exemplifications of such a connection between wrong theory and wrong practice, in this case, are within the reach of the most common observation. Only where the system of the Catechism is in honor and vigorous force, do we ever find a properly earnest and comprehensive regard exhibited for the salvation of the young; a regard, that operates, not partially and occasionally only, but follows its subjects with all-compassing interest, like the air and light of heaven, from the first breath of infancy onwards; a regard, that cannot be satisfied, in their behalf, with the spasmodic experience of the anxious bench, but travails in birth for them continually till Christ be formed in their hearts the hope of glory.

Thus due regard is had to the *family*, the domestic constitution, as a vital and fundamental force in the general organization of the Church; and all proper pains are taken to promote religion in families as the indispensable condition of its prosperity under all other forms. Parents are engaged to pray for their children, and to watch over them with true spiritual solicitude, continually endeavoring to draw them to Christ. With such feelings they will have of course a family altar, and daily sacrifices of praise and prayer, in the midst of their house. They will be careful, too, to instill into the minds of their children the great truths of religion "in the house and by the way." Catechetical instruction in particular, will be faithfully employed from the beginning. And to crown all, the power of a pious and holy example will be sought as necessary to impart life to all other forms of influence. All this belongs properly to the system of the Catechism.

In close connection with this domestic training, the ministrations of the Church come in, under a more public form, to carry forward the same work. The Church feels herself bound to watch over the children born in her bosom, and to follow them with counsel and instruction and prayer, from one year always on to another. They are required to attend upon the services of the sanctuary. Especially, the process of Catechetical instruction is employed with constancy and patience, to cast if possible both the understanding and the heart into the mould of evangelical doctrine.

The regular administration of the word and sacraments, forms of course an essential part of the same system. The ordinances of the sanctuary, being of divine institution, are regarded as channels of a power higher than themselves; and are administered accordingly with such earnestness and diligence as bespeak a proper confidence in their virtue, under this view.

Then again, the system includes the wide range of the proper pastoral work, as distinguished from that of the pulpit. The faithful minister is found preaching the gospel from house to house as well as in a more public way; visiting the families that are under his care, expressly for this purpose; conversing with old and young on the great subject of personal religion; mingling with the poor, in their humble dwellings, as well as with those in better circumstances; ministering the instructions of religion, or its consolations, at the bed-side of the sick or dying; and in one word laying himself out in continual labors of love towards all as the servant of all for Jesus' sake. The holiness of his own life particularly becomes, in these circumstances, an agency powerful beyond all others to recommend and enforce the gospel he is called to preach. To all who know him, his very presence carries with it the weight of an impressive testimony in favor of the truth.

The object in all these efforts, is not simply to bring sinners in the first instance to repentance and faith, but to build them up through the knowledge of the truth, in all righteousness, unto everlasting life. The ministry with all the resources of the sanctuary is made to look to "the perfecting of the saints," and "the edifying of the body of Christ," as its main end. Individual Christians, and each congregation of believers as a whole, are to be established, strengthened, and carried forward with regular and symmetrical growth to the "measure of the stature of the fulness of Christ." It is characteristic of the opposite system, that it makes conversion, in its own sense, to be the all in all of the gospel economy, and the development of the Christian life subsequently a mere secondary interest; as though by bending all efforts immediately towards the accomplishment of the first object, separately taken, the last might be safely left, in a great measure, to take care of itself. All this on the false principle again that the Church is to be enlarged by additions mechanically brought into connection with it from without, rather than by the extension of its own organic life from within. But in the gospel, all is made to hang on the growth of the Church itself, in grace and living power. This is the great object to be reached after in the ministerial and pastoral work; and it is only as this is in some good measure secured, that this work can be brought to bear with proper efficiency on the world beyond. Where the Church is in a living and growing state, "fitly joined together and compacted by that which every joint supplieth, and according to the effectual working in the measure of every part, making increase of the body unto the edifying of herself, in love," she becomes by this very process of growth itself the fountain of spiritual life to the dead mass with which she is surrounded; taking up the element of humanity as "flesh," and by the assimilating force of her own vitality, changing it into humanity as "spirit and life." In such circumstances, all the functions of the mystical body, and that of the ministry of course among the rest, will be carried forward through their proper organs with full power and effect. Where this order is not maintained, there may be exhibited often in the work of the gospel, vast excitement and great show of strength, and what for the moment shall seem to be immense effect; but it will be a manifestation of comparative weakness in fact, by which only the surface of life's broad stream has been tossed into waves, while its interior depths roll quietly forward as before. "Not by might, nor by power, but by my Spirit, saith the Lord." It is in the kingdom of grace, as in the kingdom of nature; the greatest, deepest, most comprehensive and lasting changes, are effected constantly, not by special, sudden, vast explosions of power, but by processes that are gentle, and silent, and so minute and common as hardly to attract the notice of the world, which is so deeply affected by their action. God is not with so much effect in the whirlwind, earthquake, and tempest as in the "still small voice" of the falling dew or growing grass. And so in the Church, the common and the constant are of vastly more account than the special and transient; the noiseless and the unseen of immensely greater force than that "which cometh with observation," and fills the world with the sound of its presence.

Such, in a general view, is the action generated by the system of the Catechism for the great purposes of the gospel, as compared with that which flows legitimately from the system of the Bench.

This system then gives no encouragement to religious torpor or sloth. That some take shelter under its name who are opposed to all that is serious or earnest in religion, while they affect to magnify the Catechism, and the common ministrations of the sanctuary, only shows that they have no communion in fact with the system in its true life. They resemble the Jews of old, who trusted in the outward temple, while they showed themselves false to all that made the temple sacred. Dead churches and dead ministers that turn catechetical instruction into an empty form, and make no account of inward living piety, as a necessary qualification for membership in the Church of Jesus Christ, have no right most assuredly to identify themselves with the system of the Catechism; and it is a gross wrong inflicted upon it by such as seek to bring it into discredit, when such instances of orthodox formality and deadness are taken to be proper exemplifications of its character and power, as though it had a natural tendency to beget death in this way rather than life. It produces action and calls for strength to a far greater extent than the system of the Bench. It is the greatest and most difficult work in the world to be a faithful minister of Jesus Christ in the spirit of this system; which might well constrain even an apostle to exclaim, *Who is sufficient for these things?* God forbid that we should countenance for a moment the dreadful supposition that the work of the ministry calls for no special zeal, no missionary devotion, no full and entire consecration to Christ, no earnest concern for the salvation of immortal souls; or that a church may be considered in a right state, where the voice of prayer is silent, the tear of penitence unknown, the hand of benevolence palsied, the language of Canaan despised, and the power of godliness treated as an idle dream. A church without life is an abomination in the sight of God. The ministry is horribly profaned, when it is made a retreat for worldlings, drones, hirelings that care not for the flock, but only for the fleece. "*Instant, in season and out of season,*" is its proper watchword, the motto that floats on its heaven-descended banner; and it is under the system of the Catechism precisely that the power of this is fully understood and felt, and may be expected to come, in a practical way, broadly into view.

In this system, room is found naturally and easily, of course, for all evangelical interests. It is a prodigious abuse of terms when some of the most vital and prominent of these are crowded out of their proper place, and made to stand in another connection entirely; when social prayer-meetings, for instance, and the various missionary and benevolent operations of the Church, are divorced in imagination from the regular life of Christianity, and ranked in the same bad category with such tricks of human device as the anxious bench. Family prayer, and social prayer, belong as much as private prayer itself, to the very nature of the Church. The spirit of missions is identical with the spirit of Christianity. For a church or a minister to oppose prayer-meetings, or efforts to send the gospel to the heathen, or efforts to raise up faithful ministers, or to circulate Bibles and tracts, for the promotion of genuine godliness at home, is to oppose Christ. We hear, it is true, of churches and ministers that look upon all these things as fanaticism, while they pretend to honor the good old way of the Catechism; but such ministers and churches, in the emphatic language of the apostle, "lie and do not the truth." They honor neither the Catechism, nor the Bible, or Christ. And the evidence of this appears invariably in the fact, that the same ministers and churches hate all serious, earnest godliness, are perfectly worldly in their temper, make no account of the new birth, and show no sense of religion whatever any farther than as it may be supposed to consist in a decent morality, and an outward use, to some extent, of its standing ordinances.

It is a most unfair view again of the system of the Catechism to think of it or speak of it as unfriendly to all special and extraordinary forms of action in the work of the gospel. The system, it is true, makes more account of the regular, the ordinary, and the general than it does of the occasional and the special; more account of rills and the perpetually flowing breezes of heaven than of mountain torrents, water-spouts, and storms. But it does not by any means preclude the presence of what is out of the usual way, or refuse to suit itself to its requirements when it comes. The extraordinary in this case however is found to stand *in* the ordinary, and grows forth from it without violence, so as to bear the same character of natural and free power. It is not the water-spout, but the fruitful, plentiful shower, causing the fields to sing, and the trees of the wood to clap their hands for joy. Such is the true conception of a *Revival*. For such special showers of grace, it is the privilege of the Church to hope, and her duty to pray, at all times. To call in question either the reality or the desirableness of them, is a monstrous scepticism, that may be said to border on the sin of open infidelity itself. They are the natural product of the proper life of the Church. Wherever the system of the Catechism is rightly understood, and faithfully applied, it may be expected to generate revivals in this form; though in proportion to the measure of this faithful use, it may be said, the ordinary and the extraordinary as here distinguished will be found continually coming closer and closer together, till in the end they may appear almost identical, and the church shall seem to bask, as on the "Delectable Mountains," in the perpetual sunlight of heaven itself. This may be denominated of a truth, her "best state," and we may add her most true, proper, and natural state. Churches that hate revivals, may be said emphatically to "love death." Every faithful pastor will be concerned to see his ministrations crowned with such special effusions of God's Spirit; and will stand prepared at the same time to hail with joy the first indications of their approach, and to put forth special efforts for the purpose of turning them to the largest account. These efforts, however, will be in the general form of his ordinary ministrations and services. If need be, however, they may be allowed to involve, to some extent, modes of action entirely *new*; it is not the mere circumstances of novelty of course, that forms the true ground of objection to "New Measures," technically so called, but the spirit, life, principle, of a certain system rather, as old as Christianity itself, which the measures thus designated are found to embody and represent. A revival, in the very nature of the case, so far as it may be a special visitation, transcending the ordinary life of a particular church, must call forth special action on the part of both minister and people. Meetings for prayer will naturally be multiplied. The call for preaching will be increased. Protracted meetings, as they are styled, may be required. Visiting from house to house, and direct personal conversation with sinners on the state of their souls, are carried forward of course with more diligence and vigor than before. Sermons and exhortations may be expected to become more earnest and pungent. A greater amount of feeling will prevail in meetings. It will become necessary to have special conferences with the awakened. All this is a simple extension of the processes by which the ordinary life of the Church is to be maintained, made necessary by the special outpouring of God's Spirit, and fairly comprehended from first to last in the system of the Catechism as distinguished from the system of the Bench.

It is true indeed that the spirit of the Bench may take possession of these measures, and infuse into them its own life and complexion. It is not by merely mechanical and formal distinctions that we can hold ourselves always to the territory of one of these systems as distinguished from the other. What we are most concerned to understand, is the spirit or soul by which each is animated. Thus it often happens that all the processes by which a revival is carried forward show themselves to be in fact pervaded with the false spirit of the Bench, at every point. But so far as this is the case, the revival itself ceases to be such, in the true sense of the term. It becomes a mere mock revival, a bastard imitation of the truth, the mushroom product of feeling and fancy wrought into a compost of fanaticism from which it shoots forth as it were in the course of a single night, without substance or strength. In such case, the various forms of action which have been mentioned, may be so exhibited as to breathe throughout the spirit of the system represented by the Bench; and there may be good reason for condemning the whole as quackery and wildfire. And no doubt it is owing to the frequent caricaturing to which revival measures have been thus subjected, more than to any other cause, that so strong a prejudice is found to prevail sometimes against everything of the sort. But still such measures as have been mentioned are not, in their own nature, of the same complexion with the Anxious Bench. They spring from the very conception of a revival; and no abuse to which they may happen to be subjected in the hands of revival-manufacturers, should be suffered to bring them into discredit, under their legitimate form. They belong constitutionally to the system of the Catechism.

It was on this system emphatically the Reformers of the 16th century relied in carrying forward the great work, for which they were raised up by the Spirit of God. It might be denominated indeed with great propriety, the system of the Reformation. Luther, Zuingli, Calvin, were all, in the fullest sense, men of the Catechism; and it was in this character pre-eminently, they showed themselves so mighty and so successful, in laying foundations, and rearing the superstructure, of that vast spiritual work which has since been associated with their names. They had ample opportunity, if they had seen proper to use it, for going to work by the other method. The age was ripe for agitation and commotion, in the name of religion, to any extent. Luther could have created a revival in this form that would have made all Europe rock with whirlwind excitement. But he left such work to the Anabaptists; or rather his giant strength was successfully opposed to it, in their hands. The Anabaptists were the men of the Bench in that day. Luther belonged wholly to another school.

I cannot perhaps close the subject better, than by exhibiting a most interesting and instructive exemplification of the true character and force of the system now explained and recommended, as furnished from the history of the century following the Reformation in England, by the celebrated *Richard Baxter* and his parish of *Kidderminster*. Switzerland, Germany, Holland, and most of all, Scotland, present in their history innumerable attestations to the same point. But it is well to fix our attention for a moment on a single case peculiarly striking in its character, and more than commonly prominent through the world-wide reputation of the pastor.

Baxter, it is well known, lived in the most stormy period of English history, during which for more than half a century, both Church and State might be said to rock perpetually, as with the earthquake throes of revolution. He was intimately connected, at the same time, with public affairs and public men, and deeply concerned in the political changes which were going forward. He was moreover a scholar and a writer, with such attachment to his books, and such a zeal in the use of his pen, as have characterised but few ministers in any age. Add to all this, he labored under such a complication of bodily infirmities and ailments, that one can hardly help wondering how he was able to do anything at all. It is distressing only to think over the catalogue of his disagreeable maladies, as they are presented in his life.

Kidderminster, when he began to preach there, was a most neglected, unpromising charge, like many others in England at that time. His predecessor had been a common tippler and drunkard, without any fitness whatever for his work. The congregation was large, but composed for the most part of ignorant, careless, rough-mannered people. At the end of two years, the excitement produced by the civil wars compelled him to withdraw. After the lapse of some time however, he was permitted to resume his labors in the same place, and continued in them about fourteen years, till separated from his charge by the new order of things, brought in with the restoration of the Second Charles. His ministry at the first was by no means generally palatable. It seemed to be altogether too serious and strict, for the views that reigned commonly among the people, and called forth in fact no small amount of opposition. But he was not a man to be discouraged with difficulties of this sort. He went forward patiently and faithfully with his work, and in the end saw it crowned with complete success.

The parish of Kidderminster would seem to have been one precisely of that sort, which those who glorify "New Measures" in our day are accustomed to consider specially in need of being wrought upon in this way. Were one of this school planted down in the midst of such a congregation, rude, ignorant, immoral, and having no sense whatever of the power of godliness as distinguished from its forms, his very first thought would be probably that nothing could be done to purpose, till the whole community should be roused and stimulated into violent action, in some sudden wholesale way. So perhaps he would appoint a protracted meeting, call in the aid of some professional revivalist, bear down with the whole apparatus of his favorite system upon the people, drive excitement to the uttermost; and then when the field should seem to be carried in this style, it might be trumpeted, with due flourish, in some religious paper, that the parish had become morally regenerated. A most summary and convenient method of turning a dry, barren Kidderminster into a fruitful field, and causing it to put forth blossoms as the rose. But after, all it did not suit the views of Richard Baxter. Mere excitement was of little account in his eyes, except as it might spring from the truth; and he had no conception or expectation of any general good to be accomplished by his ministry, except in the way of a patient, constant attendance upon the work itself, in its most minute details, kept up with prayer and faith from one end of the year to the other. Besides his Sabbath work and occasional sermons at other times, he preached once every Thursday. On Thursday evening he held a religious conference at his own house, calling sometimes on one, and sometimes on another, to lead in prayer. The young people held besides a weekly prayer-meeting. On Saturday evenings the people were encouraged to meet together at some of their houses to repeat the sermon of the preceding Sabbath, and to prepare themselves by prayer for the following day. "Two days every week," he tells us, "my assistant and myself took fourteen families between us for private catechising and conference; he going through the parish and the town coming to me. I first heard them recite the words of the Catechism, and then examined them about the sense; and lastly urged them with all possible engaging reason and vehemency, to answerable affection and practice. I spent about an hour with each family, and admitted no others to be present; lest bashfulness should make it burthensome, or any should talk of the weakness of others. All the afternoons on Mondays and Tuesdays, I spent in this way."

Such was the general method of Baxter's ministry. It was constant, regular, earnest; not marked with noise and parade; but like the common processes of nature, silent rather, deep, and full of invisible power. He was a man of prayer, and his whole soul was in his work. Thus his ministrations were clothed with uncommon interest and force. Prejudice and opposition gradually gave way. The pastor became the centre of all hearts. In the end the change was complete. We hear of no sudden general excitement, no pains taken to secure anything of that sort; no *revival*, in the ordinary acceptation of the term, as denoting an occasional and transient awakening in the history of a church. But the life of religion in the place was constantly progressive, and the power of a quiet revival might be said to reign at Kidderminster all the time. The result was wonderful. "The congregation," he says, "was usually full, so that we were fain to build about five galleries after my coming thither; the church itself being very capacious, and the most commodious and convenient that ever I was in. Our private meetings, also, were full. On the Lord's days there was no disorder to be seen in the streets; but you might hear a hundred families singing psalms and repeating sermons, as you passed through them. In a word, when I came thither first there was about one family in a street that worshipped God and called on His name; and when I came away, there were some streets where there was not one poor family in the side that did not so; and that did not by professing serious godliness, give us hopes of their sincerity. And in those families which were the worst, being inns and ale-houses, usually some persons in each house did seem to be religious." The church numbered six hundred communicants; "of whom there were not twelve," says Baxter, "that I had not good hopes of as to their sincerity."

Most happy would it be for our Reformed German Church, if all her pastors could be engaged to lay to heart the weight of this great example. Let no one think within himself that his circumstances make it impossible for him to work and prevail, in the same style. It would be hard to find among all our charges a field so rough and unpromising as was the parish of Kidderminster, when first subjected to the labors of Baxter. And it is only the zeal and faithfulness of Baxter that are needed, to transform the worst among them, in the course of a few years, into the image, at least in part, of what Kidderminster was when his ministry in the place was brought to a close. He has himself drawn a most stirring picture of what the pastor should be in his small work entitled, "GILDAS SALVIANUS: *The Reformed Pastor; showing the nature of the pastoral work, especially in private instruction and catechising.*" I consider it a privilege to close the present work, with a pointed reference to this most excellent publication. If any wish to see the SYSTEM OF THE CATECHISM explained and enforced, as with a pencil dipped in heavenly light, let them read Baxter's "Gildas Salvianus." One sentence of his own with regard to it should never be forgotten. "If God would but reform the ministry, and set them on their duties zealously and faithfully, the people would certainly be reformed: all churches either rise or fall, as the ministry doth rise or fall; not in riches and worldly grandeur, but in knowledge, zeal, and ability for the work."

"The *Reformed Pastor*," says the distinguished Dr. Doddridge, "is a most extraordinary performance, and should be read by every young minister before he takes a people under his stated care; and, I think, the practical part of it reviewed every three or four years. For nothing would have a greater tendency to awaken the spirit of a minister to that zeal in his work, for want of which many good men are but shadows of what, by the blessing of God, they might be, if the maxims and measures laid down in this incomparable treatise were strenuously pursued."

ANTICHRIST;

OR THE

SPIRIT OF SECT AND SCHISM.

BY

JOHN W. NEVIN,

PRESIDENT OF MARSHALL COLLEGE.

NEW-YORK:
JOHN S. TAYLOR, 151 NASSAU-STREET.
1848.

Entered according to Act of Congress, in the year 1848,

BY JOHN S. TAYLOR,

in the Clerk's Office of the District Court of the United States
for the Southern District of New-York.

PREFACE.

THE subject of the following tract has been partially presented, in three different places, during the course of the past year, from the pulpit; and in each case a call was made for its publication. It is now issued accordingly, with new and more complete preparation, in its present form.

A review of my work on the "Mystical Presence," which has appeared in the last number of the "Princeton Biblical Repertory," attributed to the pen of Dr. Hodge, makes it proper for me to say a word here of my relation to Schleiermacher; with whose whole system that article has found it convenient to invest me, in the way of borrowed drapery, for the purpose of bringing my theology into discredit.

I have read Schleiermacher some, and consider him certainly a genius of the very highest order in the modern theological world. But I am not aware at all of having taken him, in any sense slavishly, for my master and guide. I am not so foolish, indeed, as to set up for an *original* in Christian science; the most I lay claim to is the exercise of some proper independence in thinking after others; and I am ready to acknowledge always my obligations, in this way, to the great organs of theological knowledge, wherever they may come in my way. I am debtor thus, with lasting gratitude, both to the English and the Germans, both to Princeton and Berlin. So, no doubt, I owe much to Schleiermacher. But it is simply in the way, in which all the evangelical thinking of Germany, at this time, is, more or less, impregnated with the deep suggestive power of his thoughts. Schleiermacher, it is well known, left no school behind him, in the strict sense of the word. But he left behind him a vast number of prolific ideas, which have taken root in other minds, and shot up in different spiritual creations, that own no farther common bond among themselves, and no fixed dependence whatever on his system as a whole. Such men as Neander, Nitzsch, Julius Müller, Dorner, Richard Rothe, Ullmann, Umbreit, &c., all feel and own his genial influence, though in very different ways; just as the influence of Coleridge is felt, in England and this country, by hundreds perhaps, who have no other connection whatever as members of a common school. It is not possible to come under the influence of German theology at all, without some participation at the same time, indirectly at least, in the workings of Schleiermacher's mind.

But Schleiermacher was not orthodox; his system, as it is called, ran out, in his own hand, into gross and dangerous errors. Granted. It is allowed, on all hands, by those who most honor his memory. Does it follow still, however, that all his thinking was for this reason false, or that no part of it can be turned to account in such a way as to leave his errors behind? Princeton, I would say respectfully, has been too apt to deal in this sort of logic. At one time, all sympathy with the mind of Coleridge is denounced, because Coleridge himself was an admirer of Schelling, and an eater of opium; at another, the pantheism of Hegel is made the burden of the sweeping question, Can any good thing come out of Germany? I mean no apology for Schelling, Coleridge or Hegel; but such indiscriminate judgments serve not, in the end, the cause, either of religion or science. They are moreover particularly inappropriate to the case immediately in hand. Schleiermacher's ideas have already entered, as we have just seen, into various theological tendencies and systems, quite different at many points from his own. What could well be more unreasonable, in this case, than to charge all these with the errors of Schleiermacher himself, as necessarily involved in such correspondence? The "Repertory" might just as well denounce the whole system of Origen, on account of its acknowledged faults, and charge these as necessary consequences on all the great and good church fathers, who walked more or less in the light of his powerful mind, during the fourth and fifth centuries.

Let us be just to the memory of Schleiermacher. He stood in the bosom of a generation, which he found wholly destitute of faith in Christianity. Penetrated himself with the persuasion of its divine character, he sought to enforce its claims to rational respect, in the face of the learned and polite infidelity with which he was surrounded. In this mission his life was not passed without effect. It stands intimately associated with the process of theological regeneration, which is now going forward in the German church. Is it much to be wondered at, however, that he himself, in the circumstances mentioned, should not have been able to clear himself fully of the rationalistic connections in which be stood; or that his own ideas, in many cases, should be found leaving him behind, when brought to vegetate and expand, under more favorable relations, in other minds? Few of his disciples occupy now his own ground.*

This charge of holding Schleiermacher's system, brought against me by Dr. Hodge, has reference mainly, it seems, to two ideas, which run through the present tract as well as the "Mystical Presence." First, the *person* of Christ is made to be the ultimate fact of Christianity, rather than his doctrine merely, or work; secondly, the supernatural life which this included, is represented as coming through him into *organic* union with the life of nature, for the redemption of the world. But surely it is not necessary that either of these ideas should remain bound to the Rationalism and Sabellianism, which are charged by Dr. Hodge on the theory of Schleiermacher himself. To my mind at least, they fall in much more easily with the full doctrine of the Athanasian creed; and it is in this form generally, if not universally, that they come into view, in what may now be called the reigning evangelical theology of Germany. This may be seen in the admirable article from Ullmann, which I have prefixed as a preliminary essay to my work on the "Mystical Presence;" where the posture of Schleiermacher in regard to Christianity is properly appreciated, while at the same time it is *condemned* as inadequate and unsatisfactory, on the score of its not doing justice to the ideas of sin and atonement; in consequence of which the whole theory is carried forward to higher and more orthodox ground. Still Ullmann is full throughout of the two great thoughts already mentioned, not dreaming, as it would seem, of any difficulty in the way of holding them in such form. In the January number of the *Studien und Kritiken*, for the present year, he has a fine article on the theological position of this widely influential journal, with which he

---

*The great feature of Schleiermacher's thinking, is commonly considered to be his tendency to resolve religion into a system of subjectivity. In this view, he stands opposed to Hegel, whose philosophy makes all rather of the objective. Dr. Hodge then is rather wide of the mark, when he holds him up as the author of what he calls, in his review of "Bushnell on Christian Nurture," the German philosophical form of ritual or church Christianity. No doubt some of his ideas have had a wholesome influence, in this direction. But Schleiermacher is one of the last men to be charged with a disposition to trust in rites and forms. As to Neander, his style of thinking is unchurchly, almost to the extreme of Quakerism itself—a sore fault in that great master of church history.

has been connected for so many years, bearing directly and strongly on this very point. The theology, in whose service he and his colleagues stand, and in which he sees more and more the central movement of the age, he defines as resting in a new way, on the "ground-fact of Christianity, that God was *in Christ* reconciling the world to himself." All is made to hang on the mystery of the incarnation. "Christianity, more than before, is apprehended as *life*; as the life in which God and humanity are first fully united in an organic way, and thus a new principle is furnished for the restoration and completion of man's nature; and for this very reason, also, more than was the case ever before, the *person* of the Redeemer is recognized in its *central*, all conditioning, and all pervading *significance*, so that from this as its great spiritual heart, the Christian system is made to flow, in the living union of its parts."

Besides fortifying myself here with the preliminary essay, borrowed from Ullmann, I had taken all proper pains, as I thought, in the body of my work itself, to show that I stood in no fellowship, either with the errors of Schleiermacher on the one hand, or with those of Hegel on the other. I have been somewhat surprised, I confess, that in spite of all these precautions, I am set down by Dr. Hodge as a simple borrower of some "cast-off clothes" of the first, with a rag here and there perhaps from the second, just as though no such care whatever had been taken to prevent this very wrong. The only natural construction to be put on this is, that Dr. Hodge holds me incapable of seeing clearly to what issue my system necessarily runs, and feels himself authorized accordingly to load it with all these as he has them clearly in his own mind. Even in that case, however, he should have given me the full benefit of my ignorance, by noticing at least the honest endeavors it has made to keep clear of these errors. And how does it stand then with Ullmann? Is he too mistaken, in supposing that the theology of which he makes so much account, can by any possibility be sundered from the rationalistic Sabellianism of Schleiermacher, or the pantheistic Mysticism of the middle ages? And must we believe the same thing of all his colleagues and associates, as represented in the *Studien und Kritiken*? Such would seem to be the opinion of Dr. Hodge.

But let us now, for a moment, look a little more closely at the two theological ideas which have been named, that we may see for ourselves how far this judgment is entitled to our respect. The case is such, it seems to me, that all may very easily bring it, in their own minds, to a satisfactory solution.

Take first the view, by which Christ's *person* is made the central fact of Christianity. Can any one see, how this should remain necessarily wedded to Schleiermacher's defective doctrine of the Trinity; and not rather acquire its highest force, when associated, as it is in the hands of Dorner, Ullmann, and Rothe, with the ancient faith of the church? For my own part, I know no more overwhelming argument against all Socinianism and Unitarianism, than the "History of the Doctrine of Christ's Person" as handled by Dorner. So also I can easily understand Rothe, that great master of Christian speculation, and sympathize with him too as speaking in good faith, when he says: "The foundation of all my thinking, I can honestly say, is the simple Christian faith, as it has ruled the world for eighteen hundred years. This is for me the last certainty, for which I am ready to sacrifice, unhesitatingly and cheerfully, every other show of knowledge that may stand in its way. I know no firm ground besides, on which to cast the anchor, as of my whole human existence in general, so also of my thinking in particular, save the historical manifestation which bears the holy name of Jesus Christ. This is for me the inviolable all-holiest of humanity, the highest that has ever entered the consciousness of man, and a glorious sunrise in history from which alone all other objects derive light."* In proportion precisely as the person of Christ is felt, in this way, to be the all in all of the gospel, we must be urged, it seems to me, to make the highest account of the history of the incarnation, as the only proper support of such world-momentous weight. It is just what is needed, to give to every article of the old Apostles' Creed its full significance and proper majestic intonation. Nor is it easy to see certainly, how it should wrong in the least a single function or act of Christ, as concerned in our salvation. It disturbs not necessarily the orthodox ideas of atonement, imputation, justification, the agency of the Spirit, &c.; but only provides for them a suitable basis in the deep christological reality which lies beyond. It rejects neither the doctrine of Christ nor his work,

---

*Theologische Ethik. Preface.

but simply resolves their *value* into the constitution of his life. Can it impair at all the dignity of his prophetical, priestly, or kingly offices, to say that all these serve merely to unfold the full import of the "grace and truth," previously comprehended in his mediatorial person? Is it any more difficult in the end to combine the two views into one system, than it is to unite the doctrinal scheme of St. Paul with the more contemplative theology of St. John?

And then, as to the other idea, immediately flowing from the first. Will it be pretended, that the conception of an *organic* union between the natural and the supernatural, through the person of Christ, is not capable of being joined with full faith in the doctrine of his separate divinity and the reality of the incarnation? It is only in connection with such faith, it appears to me, that it can be steadily and satisfactorily held at all. Or must we be told, that God can come into no real union of this sort with the world, and that every imagination of the kind runs out ultimately to Naturalism or Pantheism? So Dr. Hodge appears to think and affirm. He objects to all such expressions, as that the divine has become human or the supernatural natural; and says that the view of a historical incorporation of the power of Christ's life, by the Spirit, with the actual constitution of the world, tends to destroy the doctrine of the Trinity, and leaves no room especially for the objective personal existence of the Holy Ghost. But now, is not this virtually to deny the fact of the incarnation itself? Either the supernatural entered into organic, that is, real and historical union, with the natural, in the person of Christ, or we must say of the whole mystery, that it was an optical illusion simply, or at most a passing theophany in the style of the Old Testament. The difference between such a theophany and a real incarnation, does not depend certainly on the measure of mere duration in the two cases. It rests altogether in this, that the last involves a true organic entrance into the stream of the world's life, which the other does not. And so it follows, that Christianity too is the perpetual presence of the same new creation, historically at work in the Church, and gradually assimilating the world into its own nature. This involves no such resolution of the Christian life into the force of a more natural law, as Dr. Hodge presumes to charge upon the whole theory. The difference between Adam and Christ, the old creation and the new, is still very wide, as I have endeavored at least always to show, in the "Mystical

Presence." Adam was a "living soul," says the apostle; Christ "a quickening spirit." It is the *personality* of Christ precisely, as an active, conscious, all-present fountain of life, and not his mere nature as in the case of Adam, that carries forward supernaturally, from age to age, the life of his people under the same free personal form.

The ancient church fathers abound with this view, of the organic union of the divine life with the human in Christ; and through him in the Church, as lying at the foundation of all Christianity. Particularly is this the case with those, who occupy that most brilliant period in the history of theology, which immediately followed the Sabellian and Arian heresies. Such men as Athanasius, the Gregories, and Basil, plant themselves continually on this high ground, as the only secure platform of the Christian faith and salvation. They insist clearly on the distinction between the show and the reality of an incarnation. To make Christ a mere theophany or avater, involved, to their apprehension, the overthrow of the gospel. They felt too, and say over and over again, that the incarnation was of force, for the race, and not simply for the single person of Christ himself. They speak of him always, not as the cause merely, but as the *principle* of the new creation, which is represented accordingly as flowing organically from his person, onward to the last resurrection. Dr. Hodge indeed declares the theory to be a departure from the faith of the universal Church; but without going to the original sources themselves, any one may easily see the contrary, who will take the trouble of reading what is exhibited on the subject by Dorner, in his Christology. "Not only one or two, but *all* the most distinguished church fathers," he tells us, "show one mind in regard to the real, living person of the incarnate Word. With one voice they agree, that the personality of Christ has not simply a limited force, such as any other historical personality may claim, but that it holds rather an *essential* relation to the *whole race*; for which reason only, this person, though single in itself, is made th*e object of an article of faith*, as of abiding and everlasting significance for all. Whether it be expressed, that he is the archetype, after whose image as existing in God, Adam was formed, and so our entire humanity; or that he is the principle, ἀρχή, for the whole new creation, in which first the old is made complete; or that he is the ἀπαρχή of the entire human mass, united to its substance, with all-pervading power; or that he is the everlasting head of humanity, himself a member of it indeed, but by the complete union of the divine and human in his person, at the same time, the plastic, organizing principle also, the universal soul, of its general organism; and on the other hand such a *head*, conveying life to all, only by being also in truth a *member*, essentially incorporated into this organism—of such universal significance, only in virtue of his individual personality, as comprehending the presence of the divine itself in a real way: however the general view, we say, might be expressed, one thing is certain, that the Church *in all this continued simply in the track of the apostolic faith.*"*

If Christ and Christianity come not into organic union with the previous constitution of the world, in such a way as to complete its whole sense, by linking the supernatural with its life in an abiding and real new creation, is not the mystery of the incarnation shorn of all its significance and credibility at the same time?

Dr. Hodge charges me with Eutychianism, because I affirm the divine and human natures to have become so united in Christ, as to constitute one undivided life. The proof, as he gives it, is short; one life, he tells us, is only another word for one nature or φύσις, under which term Eutyches taught such a union of the two sides of our Savior's person as in fact reduced his humanity to a mere show; whence I am made to teach the same thing, or at least something no better. Words here, as we all know, are of most precarious force. I can only say that for me, *life* is not the same thing with nature, in the hypostatical mystery. I use the term rather to express, what I conceive to be involved in the idea of personality. But now, without pressing terms at all, is it not but too plain from the whole form and tenor of his thinking, that Dr. Hodge himself (I would speak it respectfully) stands fully in the system of Nestorius, by which the life of

---

*Entwicklungsgeschichte der Lehre von der Person Christi. p. 78, 79. First edition.—In the second greatly enlarged edition, the authorities are given in full, p. 837–840. 940–962. Ὁ λόγος ἐνηνθρώπησεν, says Athanasius, ἵνα ἡμεῖς θεοποιηθῶμεν. Through the body of Christ, a divine life is conveyed into our bodies, making them immortal. They describe him as τὸν ὁλικὸν, and not merely τόν τινα ἄνθρωπον, homo *universalis*, and not simply *singularis*. For one who has come to take any inward interest in the subject, it is indeed refreshing to commune with the deep christological ideas of this old patristic divinity. Better *such* mysticism, a thousand times, than the barren abstractions, which have taken the place of it, in much at least of what is called popular theology at the present day.

Christ was so divided as to fall asunder really into two persons? The constitution of his being was such as to involve, in his view, two lives; by which he must mean, of course, two forms of consciousness, that is, two subjects of thought and will, mechanically joined together in what he denominates the single person. But what is personality, if it be capable of this broad dualism? Is it not a unity, by its very conception, representing in the form of consciousness the inmost life of its subject? In what sense can the union of the two natures in Christ be *hypostatical*, if both are not brought to meet and rest in a strictly common centre? Would Dr. Hodge admit a strict ἕνωσις in the case, at all, instead of the mere συνάφεια of Nestorius?

His general theology, as presented in this article, if I understand it rightly, implies the contrary. It carries a decidedly Nestorianizing aspect throughout. This is shown particularly in what may be termed the bald abstraction, in which all doctrinal ideas are made to stand. The Trinity is taken as a logical formula, rather than a living revelation of God through Jesus Christ. The relation of God to the world, is that of an artificer over against the mechanism of his own work. The last principle of things, is an outward decree, which it is his business to execute in a like outward way. Man is no organic whole, evolving itself as a single process from first to last, but a vast multitude of living units placed on the same theatre, by successive generations, for moral trial. God imputes the sin of Adam to his posterity, not on the ground of any real unity of life between the parties, but purely of his own sovereign pleasure, just as he might have imputed the sin of the fallen angels to men, if he had thought proper. It is in virtue of his own arbitrary covenant simply, that it is said, metaphorically, "All mankind descending from Adam by ordinary generation, *sinned* IN HIM, and *fell with him*, in his first transgression." They fell not so in the actual reality of life, but only in God's purpose and plan. Parallel with this mechanism of the curse, runs the mechanism also of redemption. The incarnation is an expedient, *contrived* to solve the problem of the atonement, and must be carefully held aloof from the whole process of the world's history under any other view, lest it should lose this "ex machina" character. Why it should have been delayed four thousand years, or why its action since should have been suspended on the common laws of our life in such a way as to move at so slow a rate over the face of the globe, is not clear; such however has been the divine will. After all, no absolutely new order of life has been introduced into the world by the occasion. The Old Testament saints stood substantially on the same ground, as to consciousness or and inward relation to God, with the saints of the New Testament; though the least of these last *is* said to be more than the greatest of the first. The person of Christ itself, as such, forms not the specific revelation of the gospel, but simply his word and work as instrumentally disclosed through its agency. Divinity and humanity were indeed united in his life, but not in such a way as to be conjointly concerned at all in the same process of birth, growth, affection, work, suffering, and death. The humanity moreover, in this case, stood in no organic relation to our human life generally; it was simply the theophanic form, in which it was thought good that the Word should at this time appear. The second Adam, thus constituted, was made our representative again, like the first, by pure covenant and decree, and not on the ground at all of any real inward qualification he had, by the constitution of his person, to become a new organic root for the race. He was in truth no such root whatever, but the outward author simply of a redemption, which is to be made over to his people in a foreign way. Inspiration here, as before, rests on no life-relation established between the parties; to suppose any thing of this sort, is to fall, we are gravely told, into the error of mediate justification, as taught by Placaeus! The virtue of the sacrifice on Calvary is made over to us by sheer divine thought, just as we might have had the benefit of some similar sacrifice, for aught we can see to the contrary, had God been pleased to order it in some other nature, and on some other planet altogether. Christ, now in heaven, is bound immovably, so far as his human nature is concerned, to the right hand of God, under the same general limitations that attach to our present existence in time and space; and communicates with the world, only as he did before his incarnation, in his divine nature or by the Spirit as his substitute and proxy. To conceive of him as present personally in the Church, ἐν πνεύματι, under a peculiar mystical subsistence, of which the Holy Ghost is the medium, is said to involve virtually a denial of the objective personal existence of the Holy Ghost. Believers are indeed mystically united with Christ, as the Church has always believed; but only by the indwelling influence of the Spirit, as a wholly distinct agent; which moreover dwelt in good men, before Christ came, precisely in the same way, and is not to be regarded at all as coming into any new form of revelation for men in consequence of the Mediatorial mystery. Our mystical union with Christ in this view, is just like our mystical union at last with Moses, Abraham, and Isaiah, the animating life simply of one and the same Spirit which has dwelt in all. Dr. Hodge finds no particular mystery in the marriage relation, as noticed in Eph. v. 22–33, and just as little of course in Christ's relation to the Church, of which it is there made the type; the very judgment, which Calvin solemnly pronounced, in this case, preposterous and irreverently rash.

Such appears to me to be the general character of this theological scheme, as presented in the Repertory. I have tried to make the picture, not a caricature, but a bold outline simply of the system, as it shows itself to my mind. In view of the whole, I can only say: If *this* be Calvinistic orthodoxy, my soul, come not thou into its secret, and unto its assembly, mine honor, be not thou united.*

This is not the place, of course, to notice the argument of the article on the sacramental question, as it stands connected in the original proper faith of the Reformed or Calvinistic Church. Let it suffice to say, that so far as it may seem to have force, against the statements of the "Mystical Presence," it is by confounding two different things, which are there kept carefully distinct; the *substance* of Calvin's doctrine namely, and the scientific *form* into which I have tried to cast it, for the very purpose of escaping difficulties and contradictions that are acknowledged to accompany it as usually stated. What does it prove against the first and most

---

*The Rev. Albert Barnes, in his "Defence," representing New School Presbyterianism, as it is called, and the general divinity I suppose of New England, mentions three general theories of our relation to Adam (p. 196–218). First, the doctrine of "the abler Calvinistic writers," such as Edwards, Boston, Stapfer, Calvin himself, &c., that the human race is involved in Adam's condemnation, on the ground of a *real union* between them as the root and branches of a common life. Secondly, the doctrine of Princeton and the Biblical Repertory, that this is by mere arbitrary sovereign imputation. Thirdly, the view that simply admits the fact of our general human sinfulness, without any attempt to explain it. Mr. Barnes rejects both the two first views, and holds to the last. But speaking of the second, he says: "Whatever may be the defects of the old system, it has manifestly many advantages over this. It has the merit of consistency. It retains the Scripture use of language. It uses words as they are employed in common life. So the profound mind of Edwards saw; and greatly as *I* dislike that system, it has so many *consistencies* over that now under notice, that I should greatly prefer it to that which in our time has supplanted it."

material part of the work, to show that the second is not in full keeping with Calvin's position as a whole? That is assumed and confessed, in the book itself. The scientific statement there given, is a mere essay towards a satisfactory vindication of the sense contained in the old doctrine. If it should be found unsuccessful, let it perish. This can never change however the nature of the old doctrine itself. There it stands still, a matter of pure history, in all its force. Dr. Hodge has not shown at all, that Calvin and the Calvinistic symbols do not teach a real participation of believers in the life of Christ, by the Lord's Supper. The evidence of the contrary, as presented in the "Mystical Presence," is not disturbed or unsettled in the least, as it seems to me, by all he has said. It is agreed, by the most competent judges, that Calvin held in substance the same mystery that was taught by Luther, differing from him only as to the mode of its occurrence. This clearly too was his own judgment. He signed the Augsburg Confession, as this was accepted also in the beginning by the entire *German* Reformed Church.*

J. W. N.

Mercersburg, May, 1848.

---

*Dr. Hodge regrets that I should have surrendered myself so far to German modes of thinking. But am I not a teacher in the German church, and as such bound, in common honesty, to cultivate a proper connection with the theological life of Germany, as well as with that of Scotland and New England? Or is it meant seriously, that the *whole* evangelical theology of that land is false, so far as it may vary from our common English tradition? And yet at this very time a scheme is in progress in Scotland itself, and under the auspices as it would seem of all sections of the Scotch church, for a wholesale transfer of this same evangelical German divinity, into English form, and for English use! Surely it is high time for the Princeton Repertory to adopt a less summary tone, in disposing of its merits.

ANTICHRIST.

Beloved, believe not every spirit, but try the spirits whether they are of God; because many false prophets are gone out into the world. Hereby know ye the Spirit of God: Every spirit that confesseth that Jesus Christ is come in the flesh, is of God; and every spirit that confesseth not that Jesus Christ is come in the flesh, is not of God. And this is that spirit of Antichrist whereof ye have heard that it should come; and even now already is it in the world.—1 JOHN IV. 1–3.

INTRODUCTION.

CHRISTIANITY has been called to struggle, from the beginning, with two forms of opposition. It has been assailed from without by broad and open infidelity; and from within also, by the false spirit of error, under the disguise of its own name. It is only the outward aspect and posture of the war however that are changed in this case; the foe remains always and substantially the same. The first shock was of course with open infidelity, in the shape partly of Judaism and partly of Paganism, which continue also to constitute the proper reigning forms of such unbelief, onward to the end of the world. Very soon, however, as the power of the gospel became too great to be effectually withstood in this way, these same hostile forces, representing indeed the whole life of the world in its natural character, began to reveal themselves also under the other mode of opposition. The spirit of infidelity became a spirit of HERESY and SCHISM, in the bosom of the Christian Church itself, answerable in this new form again to its original distinction, as a Jewish tendency in one direction and a Gentile or Pagan tendency in another.

Heresy and schism are not indeed precisely the same thing. They are however most intimately related, as different aspects or sides only of one and the same bad life. Heresy is theoretical schism; and schism is practical heresy. They flow into each other continually, and serve to make one another spiritually complete. Their connection is like that of the understanding and the will, which with all their difference embrace and fill each other, with mutual interpenetration, at every point. All heresy is in principle schismatic; all schism is in its inmost constitution heretical.

In one view, it may be said of heresies that their name is legion. The history of the Church has been a struggle with endless forms of error and falsehood in her own bosom, from the beginning. On nearer examination, however, all these are found to gather themselves up into a single fountain or head.* In this way, to the eagle gaze of St. John, all heresies and schisms, in long prophetic prospect, fall back perpetually to one and the same grand starting point. With bold, graphic hand, he brings into view, as by a single stroke of the pencil, what may be called the universal generic character of this false power in the Church; and thus lays down, at the same time, a simple universal criterion, of easy application, by which to distinguish it in every age from the Christian life in its true form. "HEREBY know ye the Spirit of God: every spirit that confesseth that *Jesus Christ is come in the flesh*, is of God; and every spirit that confesseth *not* that Jesus Christ is *come in the flesh*, is not of God." All true Christianity owns the mystery of "God manifest in the flesh," not in word only but in deed; springs from the apprehension of it by faith; lives, moves and has its being here, from first to last. Every spirit, then, pretending to be Christian, which excludes from itself the force of this confession, whether this be done in a direct or merely indirect way, stands self-convicted of falsehood. It is not of God, but bears upon itself the universal stamp or mark of heresy; for this precisely is the fundamental and primary idea of all heresy in the church, that it "confesseth not that Jesus Christ is come in the flesh." This, in one word, is that *spirit of Antichrist*, whereof ye have heard, says the apostle, that it should come, and which is even now in the world.

Our subject then is ANTICHRIST, or the spirit of heresy and schism, under the aspect in which it is here presented to our view, by the glowing

---

*Schleiermacher (*Der chr. Glaube*, § 22), with his peculiar talent for distinction and classification, reduces all Christian heresies to four cardinal ground-forms, determined by the nature of Christianity itself. Christianity springs from the apprehension of a new life, on the part of men, in Christ; a relation that implies the need and capability of redemption on the one side, as well as the full presence of it on the other. It may be heretically wronged then in two ways; either by such a view of Christ's person, or by such a view of our common human nature, as serves to subvert, directly or indirectly, the idea of such redemption. In either case, there is room again for such wrong, in two ways. The human nature may be regarded as having no need, in fact, of redemption from beyond itself; or its need, on the other side, may be held to lie so deep as to preclude all possibility of a real redemption from the ground of its own life. Thus we have the *Pelagian* and *Manichean* heresies, both resulting in an unreal salvation. So again, Christ may be placed on such a level with our common humanity, as to have no power whatever to become the centre of a higher consciousness for the world; or so much may be made of his higher nature, as to leave no room for any real communication between him and other men in the way of life. Thus we have the *Nazaraean* (or Ebionitic) and *Docetic* heresies. Altogether four; capable of endless modification; ever playing into each other; but through all ages substantially the same, including every possible defection from the simplicity of the doctrine of Christ. It is easy, again, to see that the Pelagian heresy agrees at bottom with the Nazaraean or Ebionitic, and the Manichean with the Docetic. Thus all turns, at last, on the view of the Savior's person; and so all heresies resolve themselves into a denial, virtual or explicit, of the fact that Jesus Christ has truly and really appeared in the flesh.

pen of St. John the Divine. We will consider first its *Nature*; glance in the second place at its general *History*; and then endeavor to set forth some of the distinguishing *Marks* or features, by which it may be identified and recognized under all the Protean shapes it is found to assume from age to age, with reference more particularly to its great Protestant manifestation, at the present day, in the form of Rationalistic Sectarianism. The way will thus be open to represent, in conclusion, the moral *Misery* of our reigning sect plague, and its proper *Remedy*.

I. THE NATURE OF ANTICHRIST.

This can be properly understood, only by means of a correct apprehension, in the first place, of Christianity and the Church. It is its relation to Christ as revealed in the Church, which gives it at once both its constitution and its name. It is Antichrist only in virtue of its relation to Christ.

Christianity is not simply a divine *doctrine*. It does not consist in this, that a certain system of truths, made known by extraordinary revelation, has come to be embraced and professed openly by a body of people styling themselves the Church, who are at the same time more or less influenced by such faith in their character and life. The religion of Christ does indeed include doctrines, vast and momentous as eternity itself, such as the world has had no knowledge of under any other form of revelation; but these, after all, do not constitute its primary distinctive character. It is deeper than all doctrine.

Christianity again is not simply a divine *law*. It does not consist in this, that by means of the gospel, a body of people styling themselves the Church, have come to a clearer apprehension than the world ever had before, of the moral relation in which men stand to one another and to God, and of the duties that grow properly out of these relations. The religion of Christ is indeed a perfect system of ethics in this view; but this is not in the end its fundamental distinction. It is broader and deeper than any conception of this kind.

Christianity is not mere doctrine for the understanding, or mere law for the will, but a power which is formed to lay hold of the inmost consciousness of the world as the principle of a new creation. In this view, it comes to us in the character, not of a theory or rule, but primarily of a divine FACT. It is something which has taken place in the actual constitution of the world.

But we are not thus at once at the ground of the subject. We must carry our distinctions still farther.

Christianity, as a Fact, is not to be confounded with the idea of a mere *Event*. In this case, it must be considered the produce simply of such natural and spiritual forces as were at work in the world before its appearance. It would be a mere historical occurrence, of the same nature with the building of Rome or the destruction of Jerusalem; grand and stupendous, of course, and worthy to constitute the grandest epoch in the onward flow of time, but still one only, at last, among ten thousand other events that have taken place and continue to be followed still with important consequences, in the general movement of our human life. The rise of Mohammedanism may be fully resolved, in this way, into the action of resources and powers which were previously at hand in the process of history. But to conceive of the rise of Christianity, as a parallel product of the world's earlier life, a mere reformation, say of Judaism, or a simple evolution of what was comprised in causes previously at work, is to overthrow its true nature altogether. It challenges our faith as a strictly *supernatural* fact.

On the other hand, however, Christianity must not be confounded, in this view, with the idea of a mere passing *Miracle*. It is not the supernatural, as brought to reveal itself in the way of outward, startling phenomenon simply, the presence of the invisible forced abruptly, for a short season, on the sense of the visible world, and then withdrawn again into its own awful retirement. The miraculous, in such form, cannot be said to add any thing to the real contents of history. It falls over, at last, to the character of a naked occurrence, and can be felt at best only as an outward occasion, in its influence on the course of life. But Christianity, as already said, is the principle of a new creation in the life of the world. It is the supernatural, then, brought into real, organic, abiding union with the natural, raising it into its own sphere, and filling it permanently thus with powers it never possessed before. It forms no contradiction, in this way, to the constitution of the world, as it stood previously, but accomplishes rather its inmost meaning, by revealing itself, in the "fullness of time," as the great mystery of humanity, which had been the desire of nations through all preceding ages; while it becomes, from the period of its revelation onward, the central force of history itself, which may be said to comprehend and rule as such all other forces embraced in the process. It challenges our faith as a strictly *historical* fact.

As distinguished thus from a mere event, on the one hand, and a transient miracle on the other, Christianity must be regarded as a WORLD-FACT, in the broadest sense of the term. Thus to transcend the constitution of nature, and at the same time to fall in with it harmoniously and complete its sense, is necessarily to be more deep and comprehensive than this from the beginning. Christianity is not part of the world as it stood before, but, for this very reason, more than the whole of it, as now exalted, through Christ, into a new and higher order of existence. The New Testament rests not upon the Old as its basis, but on the contrary, the Old Testament could never come to any true and solid reality till it was made to rest finally upon the New. We have a right to say, accordingly, that the second creation is more universal or catholic than the first. It must be so, in the very nature of the case, to unite with this organically, without being the continuation simply of the same life. To suppose it less comprehensive, less world-embracing in its own inward meaning and power, is either to rob it of its supernatural character altogether, or else to thrust it out from the course of actual history, as the magical action simply of forces that come to no real union with our general life whatever. Christianity is the broadest and deepest form of humanity. As a world-fact, it is parallel with the creation of man in the beginning, only going beyond it in the depth, and compass, and far-reaching significance of its contents.

Christianity in the sense now described, is, of course, a *single* Fact. Innumerable particulars are indeed comprehended in its evolution, reaching as this does from the first to the second advent of the divine Savior; but all make up, in the end, the power of one and the same glorious life, the process and completion of the new creation in Christ Jesus.

All begins in the mystery of the incarnation. The whole Gospel is enunciated in that overwhelming declaration, *The Word became flesh.* The declaration is not, itself, however, the Gospel. This meets us primarily in the living person of our Lord and Savior Jesus Christ, in which is comprehended, for all time, the actual reality of the great mystery now named. He stood among men not as the proclaimer simply of truth and life, but as the very principle of both in his own person. He was not the prophetical organ only of the evangelical revelation, but the sum and substance of this revelation itself. As the constitution of the world, in its first form, served not merely to herald the name of God, but was itself an act of self-revelation, by which he came, to a certain extent, into actual view, so also the mystery of the incarnation is to be regarded, not as the medium simply of divine grace in its highest character, but as the very form under which this grace was brought to light. The person of Christ forms the last and most perfect act of self-revelation on the part of God, by which the process of all previous revelation became complete, and the deepest idea of the universe passed over from shadow to reality, in the actual inward and full union of the divine nature with the human, as one and the same life. The life of God, in the person of the incarnate Word, incorporated itself with the life of the human race, and became, in this way, the principle and fountain of a new creation for the world at large. This act itself brought righteousness and salvation, life and immortality, into the sphere of our fallen humanity; for it was not possible that the divine element, thus "made flesh," should not in the end triumph over sin and hell, and thus accomplish all the grand and glorious results that are comprehended in the idea of the Gospel. Christianity, the whole vast mystery of the Church, the new heavens and the new earth replete with righteousness, all rest originally included as a single fact in the mystery of the incarnation. Christ is himself the light and life of the world. The last ground of its salvation is his person, not his work. All resolves itself into what he is, and not simply what he does. The great truths of the Gospel hold only in the new order of life, which is constituted and unfolded by the fact of the incarnation itself, and beyond this they have no reality whatever. The resurrection and immortality which Christ proclaims spring forth directly from the power of his own life. The atonement finds all its value in the theanthropic mystery with which it is supported from behind. The ultimate, specific distinction of Christianity, as compared with all other systems of religion, is neither the doctrine nor the work of Christ, but the economy of his person, as the indispensable basis of both. It is constituted here, once forever, by the perfect, everlasting union of the human nature with the divine. This *fact*, apprehended and appropriated in the way of faith, (which in such case is the consciousness of a true life-union with the Savior himself,) carries along with it, to the end of time, the whole force and value of the Christian redemption.

The nature of Christianity, starting in such form, and passing over into the world's life in the way now stated, is happily illustrated by what may be considered the germ of the Apostles' Creed, as presented to us in the memorable confession of Peter, of which we have so full an account in the sixteenth chapter of the Gospel according to St. Matthew.

"Whom do men say that I, the Son of Man, am?" To this question, addressed, we are told, by our Lord himself, on a certain occasion, to his twelve disciples, the reply was, "Some say that thou art John the Baptist, some Elias, and others, Jeremias or one of the prophets." Here were various judgments, formed in the way of mere outward reflection and opinion, on the appearance of Jesus Christ in the world, without any sense of the divine reality which was actually at hand in his person. "But whom say ye that I am?" was the searching interrogation that followed. Simon Peter, in the name of all his brethren, promptly replied, "Thou art the Christ, the Son of the living God." Here was faith, in communication, however, not with any given doctrine concerning Christ, received from without, or fruit of his own reflection, but with the living person of the Savior himself, as be stood there before him, in the plenitude of his own glorious life. Peter's knowledge, at this time, was very imperfect. The plan of the Christian salvation remained for him still a profound, unfathomable mystery. He had probably no distinct theory whatever in his mind, with regard to Christ's nature. *How* he came to the inward conviction expressed by his confession, or *what* precisely this conviction might be found to include in the end, for the understanding, he was not prepared at all to tell. But he had been apprehended, in the inmost depths of his spirit, by the overpowering force of the Savior's personality, and felt himself irresistibly drawn towards it, as the true ground and centre of his own spiritual being. His faith was the act of his inmost life itself, going forth towards the divine reality which was before him in Christ, and resting upon it as the comprehension of all truth and all good; an act, not of thought or volition, or feeling merely, as such, but of the entire soul, as the yet undistinguished totality of all these, like the communication that holds between the infant and its mother, as it hangs upon her bosom, and gazes upwards into her face, and long before it has come to the use of speech or thought, or knowledge of any kind, *lives* itself into her very life, and rests in the overflowing fullness of her love as though it were identical with its own being. "To whom shall we go but unto Thee?" is the language of such faith. Christ has become for it a necessary fact, the *most* necessary, indeed, of all facts, in the consciousness of life itself. Peter had no theory of redemption whatever, no orthodox scheme of salvation, by which to square his hope of heaven. But he could say, with the unwavering assurance which he had of his own existence, "Thou hast the words of eternal life; and we believe and are sure that thou art that Christ, the Son of the Living God." (John VI. 68, 69.) In this personal apprehension of Christ's person precisely, stood the high value of his faith, as contrasted with the mere opinions of the surrounding world.

Hence that marvelous congratulation, "Blessed art thou, Simon Barjona, for flesh and blood hath not revealed it unto thee, but my Father which is in heaven!" What was it, that mere nature in this case could not reveal? The substance simply of what Christ was the deep, world-wide significance of the fact that stood revealed in his person. Transcending, as it did, the whole constitution of nature, this fact could be apprehended, only in a supernatural way, and by such a process as must carry the soul of the subject over into the same sphere of life. Only as it might be brought to reach over, in the reality of its own living nature, to the personal consciousness of those who embraced it, was it possible for it to come to any true and full revelation. So the case stood with Peter. He was in Christ by faith, one with him for the time in the inmost consciousness of his soul. And so it follows with thrilling, almost startling emphasis, "Thou art Peter, and upon this rock I will build my church, and the gates of hell shall not prevail against it." Not on Peter's person, apart from his confession, of course, was the church to be built; but not on Peter's confession either, be it remembered, apart from his person. *Peter in Christ*, as the representative especially of the whole apostolic college; the personality of Peter, as centered and poised now on the supernatural fact, which had entered into his consciousness, and become part of himself, by Christ's person; Peter's confession, not as an abstract doctrine, lying beyond himself, but as constituting here the inmost fact of Peter's own life;—this was the *rock* on which, from this time onward to the end of the world, the church should continue to rise as a holy temple unto the Lord, in defiance of all the powers of earth and hell; built, as it is said in another place, upon the foundation of the apostles and prophets, Jesus Christ himself being the chief corner-stone. (Eph. II. 20.)

Thus central and fundamental to the whole idea of Christianity and the church, do we find the mystery of the incarnation to be, not as a doctrine simply, but as a supernatural world-embracing fact, revealed in the person of Jesus Christ. The confession of Peter represents the universal Christian consciousness, as it was made to embrace this living revelation, from the beginning, in the form of life. That consciousness expressed itself in the Creed, which became thus the inward form as well as the outward bond of the Christian communion. The Creed was no product of reflection, no result of consultation, no work of abstraction or calculation in any way, but the free, spontaneous outbirth of the general life of Christianity itself. Its contents were not doctrines, but facts, the very process of the new creation itself, as a present reality apprehended by faith in Christ Jesus, who was felt to be the alpha and omega of the whole. All hung upon the mystery of the incarnation, as a divine, ever-during fact, unfolding at once the inmost nature of the adorable Trinity, and the boundless grace which is secured to man by the holy catholic Church.

But it is just this mystery in the church, which, above all, the natural sense of the world is unable to receive. "Flesh and blood," we are told, cannot reveal it. The spirit of the world, then, is necessarily here a spirit of infidelity, from first to last. "Whosoever believeth that Jesus is the Christ, is born of God," we are told by the holy apostle John; such inward apprehension of his true character, can come only from an actual transplantation. to some extent, into the new life sphere, which is constituted by his person. To be wholly out of this, involves of necessity an inward denial of its existence; and every judgment of its nature must be false, in proportion precisely as it springs from any such wrong position. Our human consciousness becomes complete only in Christ, who is literally the life of the world under its deepest and most comprehensive form; on which account it must ever be in vain to think of measuring or fathoming its true sense, as here revealed, by the force of any consciousness we can have of a different order. Every other consciousness, from the very nature of the case, is something not universal, but partial only, and as such inadequate altogether to serve as a rule for the right apprehension of the Christian mystery. On the contrary, by assuming to itself at all any such character as this, it can never fail to come into hostile relation to the truth as it is in Christ Jesus. Thus Judaism on the one side, in the beginning, as well as paganism on the other, showed themselves alike incapable of understanding Christianity, and set themselves in array against it with an open declaration of war. It was to the Greek foolishness, and a stumbling-block to the Jew; though in its own sphere, the wisdom of God and the power of God unto salvation. Foiled in its attempt to overthrow the church from without, we soon find the same spirit, in substance, introducing itself under the garb of friendship into the bosom of the church itself, ostensibly reconciled to Christ, and it might be to some extent led captive in fact by the overwhelming authority of his person. But in this simply outward transformation, it is still as much opposed to the actual sense of the christological mystery as before; and we have consequently only the spirit of infidelity converted into heresy and schism. The great distinctive character of all false Christianity is this accordingly, that it refuses to admit what we have seen already to be the grand distinction of that which is true. It will not confess that "Jesus Christ is come in the flesh." It may disguise itself beneath the Christian name, and pretend to honor Christ as a divine teacher and Savior; but it is radically opposed to him in fact. It will not allow his person to stand; but substitutes for it some spurious figment of its own brain, which it then dignifies with his glorious name, and seeks to pass off thus, to the view of the world, as the true and proper Christ of the Gospel. It is the great anti-christian lie, (the necessary life of the world out of Christ,) affecting to usurp the throne which belongs to the Divine Redeemer himself, and in this way warring against the Truth of truths in his person. "This is that spirit of Antichrist," says the apostle, "whereof ye have heard that it would come; and even now already is it in the world."

As the mystery of the incarnation is constituted, by the perfect union of humanity and divinity, in the single person of Jesus Christ, it is plain that it may be heretically assailed in two ways. The divinity may be sacrificed on the one side, in favor of the humanity; or the humanity, on the other side, may be sacrificed in favor of the divinity. Christ may be viewed as a mere man, invested with the show only of a divine life; or as a wholly supernatural being, invested with the show only of a common human life. In the first case, Christianity is shorn of its dignity as a strictly new creation, and simply carries on the process of history as it stood before; in the other case, it is such a creation as comes to no organic union whatever with the world's previous life, and runs out accordingly into the form of magic. Either view, of course, subverts fundamentally the great fact of the Gospel, which is at once, as we have seen, supernatural *and* historical—the power of a *new* creation, in which, at the same time, the *old* is comprehended and made complete. The two errors come in this way to the same thing at last; and, as the true idea of Christ is divided between them, and thus made false and unreal on both sides, each has ever shown a tendency to fall over dialectically to the form of the other, as being more or less consciously incomplete and unsteady in its own position; just as unbelieving Judaism and Paganism (the twofold principle of this twofold Antichrist), with all their opposition, are found also unable to maintain their separate independence, and come never to any true and solid rest, till both are made one in Christ. (Eph. II. 14.)*

The two phases of heresy now mentioned may be styled in a general way, the *Ebionitic* or Humanitarian, and the *Gnostic* or Docetic. The first is the product of Jewish infidelity, translated into the Christian sphere; the last represents, in the same circumstances, the infidelity of the Gentile.

Both are comprehended in the general idea of Antichrist, as exhibited by St. John; since both alike refuse to confess that "Jesus Christ is come in the flesh," and in this way turn the foundation fact of Christianity into a lie. It is however plainly the Gnostic error, which the apostle has here primarily in his mind. The Ebionitic theory was too poor, to be made the object of his special attention. It was only in the other form, that the antichristian spirit, transforming itself into an angel of light, could be said to come to its proper revelation in the Church. It was in this form besides, that it was already displaying its presence, particularly in the Church of Asia Minor, the region where John wrote. Gnosticism, as a system, had not yet, it is true, made its appearance. But the elements out of which it grew were all at hand, and the secret principle of its life was actively at work. The language of the apostle, accordingly, carries in itself a distinct reference to this particular system. The Ebionite, like the modern Unitarian, could hardly be said to allow that Christ had come at all; for he made him to be, when all was done, the simple continuation merely of what had been before. His christology was no new order of life whatever, but the

---

*Paganism, as well as Judaism, looks towards Christianity as its proper, necessary end. Both systems may be said to struggle from the start, towards the mystery of the incarnation, as the last sense of the world's life, though of themselves they fall short of it throughout. On the Gentile side, the human mind was never able to come to any true sense of the distinction between the divine and human; they appear always more or less confounded, and are always incapable thus, of course, of any true reconciliation. Judaism, as a divine revelation, unfolds a higher sphere of thought. Here the distinction between God and the world comes into view, and is made to rest upon its proper moral basis, securing the idea of a true personality on the side of God, and also on the side of men. But the distinction comes again to no real union; God remains perpetually *beyond* the world, sundered from it in the way of abstract opposition. Judaism was not complete in itself, save as the shadow only of things to come, but *required* the revelation of Christianity to fulfill its own sense. Refusing to accept it for this end and affecting to stand by itself, it became necessarily as false as Paganism on the opposite side. In these circumstances, moreover, the opposition between the two systems, that of the Gentile and that of the Jew, could not fail to become itself uncertain and fluctuating. As neither system was complete in itself, it followed that each, in seeking to stand for itself, must fall over perpetually to the standpoint of the other; for that is the necessary law of all such dialectic contradictions; so long as their opposite poles come not to a true reconciliation in the higher position which both seek, neither can sustain its own independence, but each is doomed to play continually into the sphere of the other. This we find exemplified in Judaism and Gentilism, as openly opposed in the first place to Christianity; and then, very strikingly again, in the two great heretical tendencies under which they have taken shelter in the Church, through all their varying history, from the beginning down to the present time.

old anthropology only of the world, as it had stood from the beginning. The Gnostic, on the other hand, *seemed* to admit the advent of a higher life into the world; but his Christ came in the end to no proper reality. The old dualism of heaven and earth, remained for him all that it had been before this pretended union took place. His Christ was no actual incarnation; came not at all *in the flesh*; carried in himself the show only, and not the substance, of our common human life. And such precisely is the heresy here delineated by St. John. This emphatically is that spirit of Antichrist, against whose continual coming the Church is warned so solemnly to stand through all ages on her continual guard.

Here then we reach the special idea of Antichrist, in the sense of St. John: a spirit, nominally Christian, and so not beyond the Church but in it, which seeks to overthrow the person of Christ, by resolving it into the mere show of an incarnation, that has never had place in fact.

The title designates thus, not a person, but a *spirit*. This is confined to no single age, but lives through all time. It is bound besides to no standing settled form; but is ever coming into view, from some new quarter, and under some new aspect; with such fair and plausible show, as might deceive, were it possible, nay, to a certain extent, at times, does deceive, the very elect. It had begun to reveal itself, when this warning was first uttered, in manifold cases of false doctrine. "Even *now*," says the apostle, "are there *many* Antichrists." (1 John II. 18.) It has been in the world ever since, sometimes under one form and sometimes under another; and it will continue to be in it still, with varying phase, till the whole thinking of the Church, as well as its entire life in other forms, shall have come to be fully transfused with the power of the new creation, the mystery of which is primarily comprehended in the divine-human person of Christ.

In this view, moreover, the bad power in question is not necessarily confined to cases, in which it may be said to reign with open opposition to the truth; but is capable of being associated also with forms of Christian character, that are prevailingly sound and good. In its own nature, or spirit or principle, first of infidelity, and then of heresy, it may notwithstanding insinuate itself at times, to a certain extent, into the thinking also of the truly pious and faithful; and thus appear as a false theory or scheme of religion, where yet the inward force of religion is perhaps deeply felt. The conflict between light and darkness in the church, is not simply that of system against system, outwardly opposed, but enters into the process of the Christian life itself; which is carried forward, only in the way of a constant struggle with the false tendencies of human nature, in those who are the subjects thus of its transforming power. The antichristian spirit accordingly, may reveal itself, in some cases, for a time at least, in close conjunction with the most active spirit of religion; though always of course, in such case, as a secret leaven, that tends directly to corrupt and destroy the good life with which it is thus unhappily combined.

It is the general character of Antichrist, to deny "that Jesus Christ is come in the flesh." It is not necessary, however, as must appear from what has been already said, that the denial should go always at once to this point, in a direct and open way. It may take place also indirectly, and by mere implication or consequence. In proportion indeed as the falsehood becomes incorporated with the life of the gospel itself, it must show always a more and more refined action, under this latter form. To deny the incarnation broadly and plainly, belongs to the heresy only in its primitive undisguised character. It lies in the very conception of an historical process, that its subsequent developments should be of a more inward, deep, and spiritually insidious character, corresponding continually with the development of the Christian principle itself, whose action must enter always more and more deeply into the life of the world, creating all things new. But whether as expressed or merely implied, in the form of an open heresy or as a leaven of falsehood secretly infecting the Christian consciousness itself, it remains in its own nature ever the same fearfully bad power, "whose coming is after the working of Satan," and which aims throughout at nothing less than the subversion of the whole gospel. No connections into which it may happen to come, can change its own true and proper intrinsic nature. It is still always the horrible enemy of Christ; usurping his name, and playing itself off as an angel of light, only to make war more successfully upon the truth which is comprehended in his person.

From its very nature, the antichristian spirit, as now described, must always be a spirit of *schism* as well as heresy. The true catholicity of the gospel rests ultimately in Christ's person; not in any doctrine or precept simply which he spoke, but in the new order of life brought to light, in the way of historical enduring fact, by the mystery of the incarnation. It could answer no purpose to preach the idea of a universal brotherhood in God, to the sense of the world as it stood before Christ came. The consciousness of the Jew on the one hand, no less than the consciousness of the Gentile on the other, was by its very constitution partial only and not universal. The genius of Paganism might seem indeed, to a superficial observer, to have been more catholic than Christianity itself. Heathen Rome stood ready, we are told, not simply to tolerate, but even to honor and worship, to a certain extent, the gods of all her conquered provinces. This, however, was only itself an evidence of what we now affirm; it showed that her sense of religion fell entirely short of the proper universal character, which belongs to it as the deepest idea of man's life. Her catholicity at best sought nothing more than a friendly alliance of different religions; as something parallel with a confederacy of different political states. Judaism had no such toleration for foreign systems of worship; but it had also no power, on the other hand, to embrace the world as a whole on the basis even of its own life. To become truly universal, it was absolutely necessary that it should descend far below its own depth, and so pass away in another form of consciousness altogether. Neither Judaism nor Paganism reached to the last ground of man's life; and how then was it possible, that they should represent its proper *wholeness* in the form of religion? This last ground of humanity, as something deeper than the whole previous constitution of the world, is revealed only in Christ; who is for this very reason the principle and fountain of all true catholicity and wholeness, as the only proper inward and enduring form of the Church, and the end thus at the same time of all contradiction and schism. (Eph. II. 14–22.) "In Christ Jesus, neither circumcision availeth any thing, nor uncircumcision, but a new creature." To be baptized into Christ is to put on Christ; and then "there is neither Jew nor Greek, there is neither bond nor free, there is neither male nor female;" but a consciousness more profound and universal than the sense of all these distinctions, "ye are all *one*, as the children of God, in Christ Jesus." (Gal. III. 26–28. VI. 15.) All this, let it be well considered, only *in Christ*, and in virtue of the concrete revelation of life which is comprehended in his person. It is the mystery of the incarnation itself, the christological fact in which it stands, brought home to the inmost sense of the soul through faith, that serves to break down all walls of partition in the sphere of religion, and to make its scope as broad and free as the idea of our universal life. To deny this fact, to be shut out from the sense of it in a living way, is to be thrown back necessarily upon a less comprehensive consciousness; which as such can never be truly catholic, but must include always at best a part only of the truth, with inward antagonism to the truth as a whole. In its own necessary constitution then, the antichristian spirit is ever more or less sectarian and schismatic. It involves a rent, or rupture, with the Christian life, in its last ground. To deny that Christ is come in the flesh, is to substitute the simply Jewish or simply Gentile consciousness, for the far deeper consciousness that should swallow up both in the form of Christianity; which is to overthrow of course, to the same extent, the entire idea of one holy catholic Church. Antichrist is thus the spirit at once both of heresy and schism.

II. GENERAL HISTORY OF ANTICHRIST.

No thought is had here, of course, of any thing like a regular methodical account of the manifold forms and phases, under which the evil power before us has been waging war with Christ and his Church, from the beginning down to the present time. This would require whole volumes for its execution, and resources of learning and science besides of the very highest order. Our historical survey at present is intended to be nothing more than the most cursory and rapid glance at some of the more striking manifestations of the spirit in question, at different periods; for the purpose of illustrating and identifying still farther its true distinctive character, as already described; and to open the way for a proper estimate of its presence, in the form under which it is found revealing itself, more particularly, in our own time.*

As already intimated, the heresy appeared at first without reserve or disguise, in what may be called its proper native character. The spirit of the world, which was at the time a spirit in general of wild tumultuating fermentation, while it took the attitude for the most part of open infidel opposition to the revelation of Christ, came still to some extent under its divine power from the very start. We find it accordingly, even in the days

---

*It is assumed here, of course, and throughout, that Christianity is itself *historical*, in the inmost sense of this term. Heresy becomes a process, developing itself through various phases, simply because the life of the Church is never stationary, but always passing forward from one stadium of perfection to another, all to become complete at last in the splendors of Christ's second coming. Some will have it indeed, that Christianity is not thus historical. They allow, to be sure, what they call a history of the Church; but by this, they mean only that the Christian religion has been in the world for eighteen centuries, passing through various hands and subject to various fortunes, till at length it has come to be the property of the generation now living. The idea of an organic process by which the thinking and working of the Church, in our age, is to be regarded as the growth continually of its life as it has gone before, they obstinately reject. Especially do they refuse to hear of a history of Christian doctrines, in any such sense as implies a real genesis of truth for the understanding of the Church. The principle of development they count dangerous, and cling, whether as Romanists or Protestants, to the principle of stability. But shall we put out our own eyes, to please this unreasonable school? The Church has *not* been stationary in her form, but always in a process of change, from the beginning. It is the height of ecclesiastical pedantry, for any section of the Christian world, as it now stands, to pretend to pass itself off as an accurate image of what the Church was in the second century or the first. Such affectation can lead only to hypocrisy at last, and blind traditional bigotry. All theology is historical; not a single doctrine do we hold, that is worthy of trust, which has not been wrought into form and shape for us, through the medium of the actual life of the Church, as it has stood in other ages. Take, for instance, the doctrine of Christ's person. Has it been held under the same form from the beginning? One of the greatest works of this age is Dr. Dorner's *Entwicklungsgeschichte* of this very doctrine; in which, what *seems* at least to be a history of its development is very learnedly, and at the same time very clearly, traced from the beginning down to the present time. Those who so boldly reject the idea of historical development, would do well to make themselves acquainted with this great theological performance, not to speak of others, that might be mentioned, on the same general field. Is this work of Dorner a mere dream? Are his facts false; or does he put them together like a fool, mistaking altogether their true sense? If our stability theologians would only read such a work, and pretend, at least, to *answer* it, one might have some patience with their dogmatic confidence. But it is really asking too much in such a case, to require that those who *have* thus read, should be content to take such dogmatic confidence as of itself conclusive on the other side. Stubborn assumption here, confronted with the power of facts which it will not condescend to notice, or of which, perhaps, it has never heard, is not entitled to much respect.

of the apostles themselves, entering into pretended friendship with Christianity, and in this way seeking to corrupt it into its own image. Captivated and excited in fact, to a certain degree, by the grandeur of Christ, it affected now to make common cause with his infant Church, and to yield him its homage as the true Savior of the human race. But in all this, it came to no apprehension of the "mystery of godliness" as embodied in his person; and instead of surrendering itself to him by faith, as the deepest fact in life and the last principle of all truth, it required rather that Christ should surrender himself to *its* authority, and be content to take such form and meaning as its own order of life might allow. It could not go out of itself, in order that it might be in Christ. It was willing to be modified, stimulated, etherealized after a fashion, by Christ; but it could not brook the idea of a new creation in Christ. On the contrary, Christ must be forced to come into its own false sphere, with whatever of violence and cost, to make it appear as though *this* were the truth which he came to reveal. In other words, the fact of the incarnation must be turned into an empty dream. Only so was it possible to escape in full the authority of an objective Christ, and set up a purely subjective idol in his room. A divine life was acknowledged in the person of the Savior; but only in such a form as necessarily overthrew the conception of his true and proper human life. The idea of a real living union between the divine nature and the human, lay quite beyond the whole philosophy of religion as here brought into exercise. The human, accordingly, was made to lose itself entirely in the divine or superhuman. The man Jesus became only the shadowy form, or outward sign at best, under which the true invisible and supernatural Christ discovered himself to the senses of other men. It could not be said, that this divine Christ had himself literally *come in the flesh*. He seemed indeed to come in this way, teaching and working wonders in Judea and in Galilee; but all this was in the end a phantasm only, and not a part of the world's real history. For how was the thought to be endured, that spirit should link itself thus in lasting inward marriage with gross matter? How could the infinite enter into living union with the finite, and not suffer fatal circumscription in the process?

Such Docetic views of the person of Christ, as we learn from various references in the New Testament, began to show themselves in the Church before the death of the Apostles. They are clearly identified as the arch error of the age, in particular by St. John. "This is that spirit of Antichrist, whereof ye have heard that it should come, and even now already is it in the world." So again, "Little children, it is the last time; and as ye have heard that Antichrist shall come, even now are there many Antichrists, whereby we know that it is the last time. Who is a liar but he that denieth that Jesus is the Christ? He is Antichrist, that denieth the Father and the Son. Many deceivers are entered into the world, who confess not Jesus Christ is come in the flesh. This is a deceiver and an Antichrist." (1 John

II. 18, 22. 2 John 7.)* In what forms precisely the heresy may have manifested itself during this period, remains for us to a great extent unknown. Most probably there was but little regularity in its character. It was more a spirit or tendency, than a system. Its general form was chaotic and confused; of Gentile aspect at one time, and then again of Jewish; most frequently, however, we have reason to believe, a contradictory amalgamation of features borrowed from both sides. The Ebionitic view of Christ had a tendency from the start to pass over, at least in part, into the Docetic; as the Docetic also, on the other hand, had a constant tendency to lose itself again in the Ebionitic.†

In the second century, the false spirit which had been thus chaotically at work from the beginning, assumed order and system, to some extent, in the vast creations of *Gnosticism*. Wonderfully diversified as these were in their particular forms and aspects, the christological theory on which they rested was always substantially the same. It denied that Christ had come in the flesh, and resolved the fact of the incarnation into a mere theophany, by which the divine life only *seemed* to unite itself organically with the life of the world in man, without doing so in fact. Either the humanity of the Savior was altogether rejected, his whole bodily appearance treated as a vision simply, or optical illusion; or else it was stripped of all proper reality, by being made to sink into the character of an external organ, or instrument only, through which the true spiritual Christ was pleased to manifest his presence among men. The human, even when thus accepted as something real by itself, had still no actual reality in the constitution of the Savior's person; it came into no living union with this

---

*The somewhat enigmatical exhortation, which closes the first epistle: "Little children, keep yourselves from idols," has reference probably to the same general subject; as if he had said: Be on your guard against spectral shadows (εἴδωλα, simulacra) that seek to pass themselves off for the true mystery of Christ. So Ignatius pronounces such as turned Christ into a phantasm, to be themselves no better than ghosts (ἀσώματοι καὶ δαιμονικόι).

†*Cerinthus* stands a prominent representative of such heresy, about the close of the first century, on the same field that was then honored by the presence of the apostle John. Jesus, in his view, was a mere man at first, born in a natural way; who, however, by his extraordinary virtues showed himself worthy to become the Son of God; and was accordingly raised to this distinction at his baptism, when Christ, a superangelic æon, descended upon him and entered into his person. He now knew the Father, and proclaimed him to the world, having power also to work miracles. At his death, the æon Christ withdrew from him again, and so took no part, of course, in his sufferings. Christ will return again, however, hereafter, and then the man Jesus will rise from the dead, and so enter upon his millennial reign. In all this, we have, it is clear, no *personal* union of the divine and human in the Messiah, but at best only a mechanical, magical connection. It serves to show, at the same time, how easily Ebionism and Gnosticism pass over into each other. The Savior is all man at the start; but his humanity is overpowered in the end by the higher life that descends upon it, as all outward foreign force; and thus all evaporates into sheer spirit. So the proper Gnosticism, on the other hand, starting with a Savior all superhuman, has a constant tendency to lose itself ultimately in the opposite extreme.

whatever, but stood out of it, and beyond it, as a mere transitory accident or appendage. The person was, in fact, divided into two Christs; a higher and a lower, a heavenly and an earthly Christ, bound together in an outward temporary way; the second being but an occasion or medium for the sensible revelation of the first. It was not thus a union that might be considered original and necessary at all in the Redeemer's life, but a mere economical device adopted to serve a particular purpose; which was referred accordingly, not to the origin of the human subject as born of the Virgin, but to his baptism in the river Jordan. Previous to this, Jesus had been, according to the theory, a mere man; born naturally, or it might be, as some were willing to allow, supernaturally; who, by a course of exalted virtue, became a suitable organ for the use of the heavenly Christ, now ready in the fullness of time to descend from the divine pleroma into the world. This descent had place at his baptism, the true *epiphany* of the Logos, which here took possession of his person, and continued to use it subsequently as an instrument of revelation, till the mission of mercy became complete. In some of the Gnostic systems more was made of the humanity of Christ than in others; but in all of them it remained at last an accidental appendage to his higher nature, rather than an essential element in his true and proper life. It was at best but the sign or symbol of the divine reality it represented; a sort of earthly copy or counterpart it might be of what belonged properly to heaven; but in no sense the actual presence of the divine heavenly fact itself. *This*, it was allowed on all hands, could not so *come in the flesh*.

There is nothing more grand and magnificent in the whole history of the Church, than its long, deep struggle with the gigantic strength of this Gnostic speculation. Had it not been founded upon the rock of Peter's life-confession, the *fact* of Christ's theanthropic person perpetually present to the inmost consciousness of the Church, through the power of faith, these gates of hell must assuredly have prevailed against it in the way of full and final overthrow. But it could not thus perish. The Gnostic heresies only served themselves to bring the Church, in the end, to a clearer understanding of what was contained in her own living creed. Christianity authenticated itself, as a divine reality and not a mere scheme of thought, by throwing off the huge weight of foreign element that sought on all sides to overwhelm it, and asserting successfully its own rightful supremacy, as the fountain of a new order of life for the world. The true nature of the fact comprehended in Christ's person, so far as the reality of both sides of his life was concerned, came gradually to a clear, steady enunciation. A long process was still needed, to settle the form in which the doctrine should be ultimately held; but so much at least was triumphantly established, that Christianity rested on a true union of the divine life with the human in the person of Jesus Christ; and in this way the contest with Gnosticism, in its open and undisguised character, was brought forever to an end. With all their magnificence, the Gnostic sects accordingly had no power to stand. They passed away, in due time, like the streams of the desert, or the coruscations of an aurora borealis.

But the *principle* of Gnosticism was not thus extirpated from the Church. It only betook itself to new forms of error, more plausible and refined, in which to continue its antichristian war against the person of Christ as before, under cover still of the Christian profession and name.

Its next most notable manifestation is in the character of the *Manichæan* heresy; which may be said to bring up the rear of the Gnostic period, in a certain sense, in the third and fourth centuries. It seems, on first view indeed, to base itself on quite different ground; having respect to the constitution of our common human nature, more than to the person of Christ. But the view we take of our common human nature and the view we take of Christ, in our theory of religion, always condition each other, and give us at last but different sides only of one and the same theological scheme. A false christology involves ever a false anthropology; and a false anthropology, on the other hand, can never be sundered from a christology equally unsound. The same system of thought precisely, which refused to admit the idea of a true reconciliation between Nature and Spirit in the person of Jesus Christ, made it necessary to assert a like abrupt and hopelessly hostile relation between the life of nature and the higher life of grace, in those who are the subjects of his redemption. We see an exemplification of this, to some extent, in all the Gnostic sects. But in the Manichæan heresy, it forms the grand characteristic distinction by which it is known. Humanity is here exhibited under the form of an absolutely helpless dualism; playing over continually into the sphere of an equally helpless pantheism; two principles, two kingdoms, that shut out all possibility of a real inward reconciliation, and thus allow no room whatever for the idea of a natural historical salvation, such as it is the object of Christianity to accomplish. The world as such, and the nature of man too so far as it partakes of its constitution, are regarded as intrinsically and incurably bad. Only the higher life which has become imprisoned in this dark sphere, but which forms at last no constituent part at all of its existence, is capable of being redeemed and saved; and the salvation which it requires resolves itself, when all is done, into a process that is full as much physical as moral, and which in the nature of the case, overthrows the whole conception of a real mediation in the work of redemption. The entire process assumes the form of magic. Natural and supernatural come to no true union. All ends in dark fanatical gloom, on the one hand, and fantastic, unreal cloud creations, on the other.

The natural counterpart of this heresy, standing in the same relation to it that the Ebionitic view of Christ's person sustains to the Docetic, is presented to us in the form of *Pelagianism*. Here, the human nature is regarded as capable of salvation, without the help of any higher principle in the form of life. Manichæism carries its view of the corruption of the world so far as to subvert its capability of redemption; Pelagianism makes the corruption so light, that no redemption is needed. The case is admitted to call for help; but the help is thought of only in the character of outward occasion or salutary inward influence; it resolves itself into the notion of doctrine, example, providential facilities, and gracious aids. Christianity, of course, is not accepted as a new creation in Christ Jesus; it is only the old creation, roused into the full exercise of the resources it included before. Thus the full sense of what is comprehended in the fact of the incarnation, is necessarily contradicted and wronged. Pelagianism inclines naturally to look upon Christ as a mere man, and thus finds its proper end in Unitarianism. The Manichæan and Pelagian heresies, with all their apparent contradiction, exhibit only opposite poles of the same antichristian falsehood; which, as such, have a constant tendency, like Ebionism and Gnosticism, to fall over each into the sphere of the other. Fatalism and licentiousness are strangely mixed together, in the history of error. Nothing is more common than the union of Pelagian and Manichæan principles to some extent, or rather perhaps an alternation of one system with the other, in the same sect. Augustine especially was the great organ of the Church, in the hand of God, for conducting the Christian consciousness safely through both extremes, into that form of faith which has since been acknowledged as Catholic orthodoxy on the subject of sin and grace. The Manichæan and Pelagian heresies however were not annihilated, by the formal condemnation to which they were thus brought, in their original form. They have entered largely into the history of Christianity, through all subsequent ages; sometimes in one form, and sometimes in another; more or less blended together; producing oftentimes the most contrary results, theoretical and practical, in strange combination; but involving always, at bottom, a dualistic apprehension of Christ's person, by which the great fact of the incarnation may be said to have been shorn continually of its true and proper force.

Our attention is next challenged by the momentous christological controversies of the fifth and sixth centuries through which the true doctrine of Christ's person was still further defined and affirmed, in opposition to the error of *Nestorius*, on the one side, and the *Eutychian* or *Monophysite* heresy, on the other. The question here respected not the constituent parts of the Mediatorial person, in themselves considered; he was allowed on all hands, in the Church, to be very God and very man; the point was now to determine, if it might be done, the relation in which the two natures must be supposed to stand to each other, in this mysterious union. The question lay in this case, of course, entirely within the sphere of the Christian faith itself; and yet the same false tendencies substantially, which had been encountered in a more open way before, were now to be met and conquered again; the field of controversy was changed, but the conflicting forces, so far as inward principle was concerned, were what they had been from the first. As brought nearer, however, to the central fact of Christianity, the two contrary phases of the antichristian error, which as we have already seen have a tendency from the start to play into each other, show themselves here less capable than ever of any clear and independent distinction. We have two extremes as before; but the falsehood which belongs to both, is found to be more clearly than before a common falsehood, from the fact that each is felt to include so largely in its own constitution, the very contradiction that seems to sunder it from the other; so that it is not always easy, by any means, to follow out in the action of either, the development of what might seem to be its own primary principle. Eutychianism appears to be on the whole a continuation of the old Docetic or Gnostic tendency; whilst Nestorianism, as its opposite, must be regarded as a sort of highly refined Ebionism. The first recognizes indeed the proper humanity of Christ, as the last recognizes also his proper divinity; but in the one case, the humanity is made to lose itself again in the divine life with which it is united; while on the other, this union is reduced to the form of a mere mechanical conjunction, that brings the divine personality into no proper oneness of life with the manhood of Christ whatever. In both cases, the historical fact of the incarnation is subverted; in favor of Christ's true humanity, it might seem, on one side, and to save his title to full divinity on the other; but with palpable confusion of these purposes, at the same time, in each direction.

Thus Nestorianism in particular, which appears to lay so much emphasis, in one view, on the human side of Christ's life, asserting as it did at the same time his proper full divinity, comes necessarily to be almost as much Gnostic as Ebionitic in its constitution. For Gnosticism was willing also, as we have already seen, to allow the real manhood of the Savior, if only it were left to stand in a simply outward and mechanical relation to the higher principle which it served to reveal. The Nestorian Christ, like the Gnostic, was in fact a divided Christ, two distinct subsistences, joined together in the show, but not in the reality, of a common life. The divinity must be so sundered from the humanity, as to have it in fact always beyond itself, and never in its own sphere; it cannot be born of the Virgin, it cannot enter into the process of human growth, it cannot participate in the sufferings of the garden and the cross. It is a separate consciousness, that merely broods or floats over the proper life, first of the child, and then of the man Jesus, without coming ever to any actual incorporation with it, in the way of inward personal unity. The hypostatical union is not organic and real, but the conjunction simply of two distinct forms of existence, which it is made to embrace in a visionary, magical way. Both sides of the antichristian principle are found here, dialectically wrought into the constitution of the same most plausible heresy; and under this form particularly, Jewish in one aspect and Gentile in another, Ebionism and Gnosticism smelted together, it has continued to show itself very extensively active in the Church ever since, with various modifications, down to the present time.

During the middle ages, we are met with the presence of St. John's cardinal heresy, under multitudinous and most complex manifestations. In the Roman Church, we have on the one hand a gross system of Pelagianism, sinking the Christian life into the sphere of mere nature; while on the other the natural is fantastically overwhelmed by the idea of the supernatural, and the whole system of grace converted into a system of magic. A conjunction of seeming opposites, which it need give us now, of course, no difficulty to comprehend or admit. Among the sects again, by which the reigning Church was opposed, it is easy to trace, from the Paulicians downward, a Gnostic and Manichæan taint, which must be allowed seriously to detract from their general merit as "witnesses of the truth." Their great defect is the want of a firm, full sense of the realness of Christianity, as an abiding objective revelation of the life of God in the flesh.

It was not to be expected, of course, that the Reformation should bring to an end the activity of the bad power, at whose history we are now glancing. On the contrary, if Protestantism be itself a higher stadium of the Christian life than all that went before, it might naturally be presumed that the antichristian heresy, whose very nature it is to keep pace always with the development of this life itself, would come here also to a corresponding revelation, and be something worse thus than all it had previously been. It is no compliment to Protestantism, to say that there is no Antichrist, save that which has been left behind in the Church of Rome; for this must imply, as the world now stands, that Protestant Christianity is comparatively impotent, as a true revelation of the presence and glory of Christ. Where the life of Christ is mainly active, in the way of historical force, we have reason to expect a corresponding activity of Antichrist, as the spirit of delusion and error. If then Protestantism be the truth of Christ in a higher form than Romanism, we ought not to be surprised certainly to find this false spirit here also, under its most subtle and dangerous character. In the nature of the case, moreover, the Protestant Antichrist must be sought, not beyond the pale of Protestantism, and in the posture of open opposition to its cause; but in the bosom of this cause itself, regarded as the most perfect style of the Church. He will be found, sitting in the temple of Protestantism, affecting to be no less than Christ, the Protestant Christ himself, whose right it is to exercise supreme control in the Church, and to be worshiped and served by the whole world.

Such a revelation we have presented to us, on a broad scale, in the *Rationalism* and *Sectarianism* which have become so widely characteristic of our Protestant Christianity, in its modern form. Antichrist is both rational and schismatic, as has been already shown, in his very nature; and his manifestations have exhibited always more or less of this twofold character, from the beginning. But never before was it made to stand forth so broadly to view, as the open and avowed form of the revelation itself. In the name of Protestantism, a large part of the Christian world has come to be rationalistic and schismatic now, on principle; holding this to be the true and proper form of Christianity; making no question of its power and right to shape theology and fashion the structure of the Church, as in its own eyes the case may seem to require. Nor is it difficult at all to identify the two forms of thinking here mentioned, as different sides only of one and the same false life. Their relation to each other is the same essentially which we have already found to hold between heresy and schism; the one is for the understanding what the other is for the will. Both, in their last ground, come together, as the power of a single error, and each accordingly including always the principle of the other in its own constitution, is secretly impelled towards it also, throughout, as the end in which alone it becomes naturally complete.

Rationalism, belonging as it does primarily to the sphere of theory and reflection, is naturally disposed to fall in with the Ebionitic tendency, and to reject thus at last the whole idea of any thing more than a common human life in Christ's person. It is not, however, necessarily restricted to this view; the very same theoretic principle may enter into a scheme of thinking, in which the supernatural side of Christianity is fully admitted. It deserves to be well understood and considered, that there is a supernaturalism which comes at last to the same thing precisely with rationalism in its lowest form; a rationalistic supernaturalism, we may term it, which acknowledges the presence of a divine life in Christ, but will not allow it, at the same time, to come into any organic union with his human life; so that the two forms of existence, thus held asunder, remain in truth, when all is done, two different spheres of consciousness altogether, and the proper divinity of the man Jesus is as much subverted as though it had been openly denied from the start. The supernatural, held in this way, becomes magic, and cannot be said to have truly "come in the flesh." This Nestorian theology, accordingly, if it be pushed out by thinking to its proper consequences, is found incapable in the end of maintaining its ground against the view that excludes the supernatural altogether. Rationalism indeed is in its very nature, a perpetual oscillation between these two extremes; it is constitutionally dualistic, and in this view comes to its most profound character finally, in the form of Pantheism. Such is the course through which it has run particularly in Germany, the land it has so long claimed openly as its own.

The spirit of Sect, on the other hand, would seem to carry in itself an original natural affinity with the Docetic or Gnostic way of looking at

Christ. More practical than theoretic at the start, it is disposed to lay peculiar stress on the spiritual side of Christianity, as the revelation of a higher life in the world. But this higher life is not apprehended, as the true universal sense of the world itself; comes to no full human revelation, in the person of Christ, as the principle and ground of all religion. Sectarianism is ever inclined to place Christ wholly in the clouds, or to turn him into an ideal phantom, that it may be left the more free in the exercise of its own subjectivity. In this way, however, it is carried over, by a sort of inward necessity, to the sphere of theoretic Rationalism. The divine which it affects to grasp and hold in such fantastic style, becomes identical at last with the simply human. That which has begun in the spirit finds its tame, flat conclusion, ultimately in the flesh.

It is by no accidental connection, then, that Sectarianism is found to be rationalistic. It belongs to its very constitution to have this character. The spirit of sect, wherever it may prevail, involves necessarily a false view of the person of Christ, and is utterly incompatible thus with sound Christian orthodoxy. As a spirit at once of heresy and schism, in this way, we pronounce it to be emphatically the Antichrist of the Church in our own time. So far as its power goes, it is at war with the whole fact of the incarnation.

III. MARKS OF ANTICHRIST:

With reference particularly to the Sect System.

To test the truth of the affirmation thus made, let us now pass in review some of the more striking marks or notes of the antichristian spirit, as they are found to accompany it through all its various phases and transmutations, applying them, at the same time, in the way of special trial, to the system here brought into view. For this we are prepared, in some measure, by the analysis and history which have gone before. It is the *spirit* of Antichrist, as something which is capable of diverse manifestations, that we are concerned especially to understand; and the only way of identifying the presence of the spiritual Proteus, in any particular manifestion, is to study well the features that belong to it in its universal character.

In this whole process, of course, we have to do, not with any particular sect or sects, as such, but only with the sect mind, as lying at the ground of all such divisions, and revealing itself through their general life. This is something which it is vastly important to understand, apart from all denominational distinctions and controversies with which it may be joined.

The ultimate, universal criterion of the Antichristian spirit is before us already, in the rule of St. John. It will not yield, in full, that Christ is *come in the flesh.* All other marks then, of course, by which it may be distinguished, must resolve themselves at last into this fundamental character. They will be the necessary consequences simply that flow from the want of faith in the incarnation as a real and abiding fact, and they will be found accordingly to fall back always to this point, as their principle and source.

First Mark.

Antichrist owns no *real mediation* between God and man to be necessary, in order to Christian salvation. It may affect, indeed, to feel the need of redemption, and to honor and trust in Christ at the same time as a Redeemer. But the only redemption it requires comes at last merely to this, that the parties which have been separated by sin should be brought together in form and fancy, without being reconciled in fact. The relation in which Christ stands to the whole object may be considered highly important and necessary, but it is altogether outward and mechanical, and no good reason appears why he should be a human Christ at all. He is the occasion by which men are brought near to God, not the real medium of this approach itself; the cause of the atonement in the divine mind, not the very fact in which it consists, as the actual self-revelation of God, *at one* with the world, and making the world to be *at one* with himself. (Rom. V. 11; 2 Cor. V. 18, 19.) To such an *at-one-ment,* accordingly, the salvation never comes in fact. The old dualism of nature remains without help, save in the way of pantheistic oscillations, that serve to mock in the end the weakness out of which they spring. All runs out into the form of an abstract, interminable disjunction and contradiction, between nature and spirit, earth and heaven, man and God. Salvation is something wholly subjective; made to rest in some measure, it may be, upon the *thought* of something which is supposed to have taken place also in the divine mind; but still, even in this form, a process which is such as to leave the subject always hopelessly in himself.

The Gnostic had no apprehension of Christ, as the objective medium of salvation; saw no need of any such medium in his own case; was strong rather in the imagination that he was called to rise above the world, in the way of direct personal transaction with God; for which only certain facilities had been provided by the gospel. His Christ became accordingly a mere phantasm.

So universally the antichristian spirit shows itself insensible to the necessity of a real mediation between God and man, and in this way thrusts the Savior aside, by clothing him with a false character. The Christ of the Quaker is the light of God in his own soul; which becomes again, in due time, the light of common reason. The Hegelian Christ is an idea. The history of sectarianism shows it to have a constant constitutional tendency to thrust the fact of real mediation aside in the same way. It is characteristic of the sect spirit, that it makes Christ auxiliary only to its own religious life, and not properly the medium in which it moves. A Docetic tinge, a character of fantastic unreality, is thus made to surround his person, which only too often pays the natural penalty of its own wrong again, by settling at last into the form of a cold rationalistic abstraction.

Second Mark.

Antichrist undervalues the mystery of Christ's *person*. Not, of course, professedly, and in a direct way, but indirectly and in fact, by sinking it into comparative insignificance in the work of redemption. It might seem, indeed, in one view, as if the heresy were inclined to make too much of Christ's person; carrying it wholly into the clouds, and counting it too high to come into any real connection with the world whatever. The Gnostic Christ is altogether supernatural and transcendental, and owns no fellowship at all with our natural humanity, in its common mortal form. But for this very reason, he stands shorn of all personal importance for the actual human world. His person, as such, is not the medium of salvation, not the main thing, therefore, in Christianity. Not by what he is, according to this system, but by what he speaks and does, are we redeemed and brought near to God. The proper contents of the Savior's personality are not discerned; their unutterably momentous import is not felt; the fact is not apprehended as real, but in place of it the fantastic figment of a Christ is made to swim in the mind, having no more reality or power finally than a mere idea or thought; so that all hangs, not upon the constitution of the real historical Christ at all, but only upon the truth and power revealed through his ministry.

The Sect life in the church is always infected, more or less clearly, with this way of thinking; bears upon itself always, more or less plainly legible, this mark of Antichrist. All sectarian, schismatic Christianity has a tendency to make Christ's actual person of small account, as compared with his doctrine and work. It affects to magnify, it may be, the mediatorial functions of the Redeemer; but sees not the proper and necessary root of all these in the *mediatorial life*; as that which goes before all, and includes all, in the form of a divine, historical, and perpetual fact. Its christology is, after all, the outward apparatus of its theory of redemption, the divine machinery of salvation, rather than the very substance and process of this salvation itself. It fails always to bring the fact of the incarnation to its full right and weight. The fact itself is admitted; but the necessity of it is by no means clear. One cannot see plainly, after all, as the case stands, why precisely the redemption of the gospel must be just in this form, and not in another; why it was absolutely needful for the Word to become flesh at all; why the ends of redemption might not have been about as well reached, if the whole gospel history had been a mere theophany, or a revelation of God's truth and love by some other medium altogether. For even where the evangelical salvation is made to go beyond the idea of doctrine merely or authority, so as to include the potion of a direct divine influence upon the soul, secured through the Savior Christ, it is still only the work of Christ externally considered, that opens the way for such grace, so that, for aught that appears in the theory itself, the same end might have been fairly reached, if the same work had been accomplished in some other form entirely; by an atonement, for instance, in the spiritual world, had it so pleased God, or under some other mode of existence than our common humanity, instead of that earthly sacrifice which actually took place for this purpose, when Christ died upon Calvary. The incarnation is viewed at best as the erection of the outward altar simply, on which this holocaust for the sins of the world might be made to ascend in sacred fire towards God; the platform of the work of salvation; the artificial theatre, wonderfully *contrived* by Heaven, on which should be enacted the vast scene of man's redemption. All is felt to be, at last, more or less shadowy, visionary, and fantastic; all tends to swim into the form of distant, dim, ideal abstraction. Invariably it will be found, the sectarian Christ lacks the character of true realness for the mind, and wears, on the contrary, a more or less magical, æon-like aspect, in which the gospel seems to look down upon us always only from the clouds.

Third Mark.

With this dim sense of what is properly comprehended in the person of Christ, is always associated necessarily a corresponding want of faith in the Church, as a *real supernatural constitution* always present in the world. Antichrist acknowledges of course the existence of the Church; owns also its divine origin, and pretends to find in it the presence of a divine life. But the Church thus allowed, comes to no true, organically historical revelation in the world's life, as an independent, abiding form of human existence, continuously distinct from all that the world has been, or still continues to be, under any other form. If Christ be the principle of a new creation, the point in which the earth and heavens have been brought into permanent living conjunction as never before, it follows at once plainly that the Church in which is comprehended the power of this fact, and which for this very reason is declared to be his BODY, the fullness of Him that filleth all in all, must carry in itself a constitution of its own, as really objective and enduring, to say the least, as the course of nature, on which as a basis it is made supernaturally to rest. The ancient Gnosticism, however, had no knowledge of any such organic, historical Church. Its associated Christianity was something of a quite different nature; made up of an election of living units, the pneumatic order of human spirits, each attracted for itself towards Christ, and all uniting by aggregation only to form the idea of his kingdom. As the Savior himself had no real being in the world, stood among men only in the form of an unsubstantial phantasm, or in the show of a human life which was after all but the sign or symbol of his invisible nature, not the very presence of this nature itself; it was not possible of course to attach any different idea of reality to the new life which he introduced into the world. The Church must become as Docetic and idealistic as her imaginary head.

And so in the case of all later manifestations of the antichristian spirit. With the course of time, we find it consenting in appearance to yield the first point; it affects to believe and confess that Christ did once come in the flesh; an *event*, far off in the dim distance of the past, and in this way much as though it belonged to another world; but its original character is only the more strongly asserted, with all this, in the view it continues to take of the Church. Nay, it fights against the idea of a real Church, Antichrist as it is, as though the honor of the true historical Christ must necessarily be made to suffer by admitting its claims. Out of zeal for what Christ *once* was in the world, it madly seeks to turn his whole presence in it since into the character of a mere ghostlike abstraction. The Church, in its estimation, is the form only in which a certain system of thought, feeling, and action, produced by the gospel, is accustomed to make itself known, in conformity with our general social nature. In the end, accordingly, it resolves itself into thin air.

The whole Sect system shows here its true character; for it turns throughout on the assumption, that Christ has no real Church in this world; but only an invisible spiritual Christianity, which men are at liberty to arrange and shape, by the help of the Bible, according to their own pleasure. Schism, as such, has no faith in the holy catholic Church; holds the very word for popish, and the thing itself no better than empty wind; save as it may be taken to mean its own figment of a Church, which exists objectively in the clouds only, or at best in the Bible, and subjectively in such developments of piety as are supposed to square properly with this rule.

Fourth Mark.

This want of faith in the Church, as the presence of a real divine life in the world, reveals itself always in a low view of the *ministry* and *sacraments*, and of Christian *worship* generally. If the Church be not the depositary of supernatural powers, made objective and constant in the world under this form, it is not to be imagined of course that the organs and functions of the Church can carry in them any greater value or force.

It is characteristic of Antichrist accordingly, under all forms, to undervalue the true idea of the Christian ministry, and to sink the character of all church services and institutions to the level of our common human life; at the very moment, it may be, when it is pretended to exalt them, in another view, to the highest spiritual dignity. All Sectarian Christianity, in particular, is clearly distinguished by this mark; as any one may see from the history of past sects, or by considering the character in which sects appear in our own time. They make little account of any outward ordination; because it is the Spirit that qualifies all true ministers for the sacred office; and *their* ministry must be God-sent, not manufactured by man. The office in this view, however, comes to no real union with the man on whom it seems to rest; and the consequence is, that all ends at last, for himself and for others also, in the strength which may happen to belong to him in his simply natural capacity and state. The ministry is shorn thus of its true divine sanctity, and all ministerial functions undergo a corresponding degradation.

The same dualistic view prevails also in the case of the sacraments; sundering the visible from the invisible; overthrowing the idea of sacramental grace entirely. The spirit of Sect universally shrinks from the acknowledgment of any objective efficacy, either in Baptism or the Lord's Supper. It finds an immense difficulty in admitting the sacraments to be at all a special mode or form of grace, in which the divine force of Christianity is brought near to men, as something different from the exhibition which is made of it in the mere word; not reflecting that it would be equally difficult, in all probability, to admit the presence of any such special divine force in the person of the Redeemer himself; were he now outwardly among us, as in the days of his flesh. Faith in the sacraments, and faith in a real Christ who is come in the flesh, go hand in hand together. Sects clearly betray their rationalistic, Gnostic spirit, by making the Lord's Supper to be a simple sign or monument, and denying all power to holy Baptism. Their sacraments are Docetic, fantastic; all spirit, borrowed from the region of clouds; only to prove at last all flesh, having no reality save in the worshiper's brain. Hence a tendency, on the part of all sects, as such, to set aside the sacraments altogether, or at least to change their character into an entirely new sense. The Baptistic principle, in particular, may be said to lie involved in their whole theory of religion. Infant baptism has no meaning for those, who have lost all faith in the idea of sacramental grace.

The true idea of worship also will be found wanting, in the same circumstances, to the same extent. To be unsacramental, is necessarily to be at the same time unliturgical. The power of Christian worship consists in this, that the worshipers be filled with the sense of a common church life, and present themselves in this consciousness as a living sacrifice to God. Its whole conception requires that it should move in the sphere of the objective, and not fall over to the sway of simply individual thought or feeling. But we all know, how completely the spirit of Sect serves to reverse this law. Sects have no sense for the objective and liturgical in worship; hold all this rather to be at war with the idea of devotion; and aim accordingly, on principle, to clothe the entire service of God as much as possible with just the opposite character. Their hymns, and the tunes to which they are sung, their prayers, and of course also the whole tone of their preaching, bear the same impress of extreme subjectivity. This is supposed, indeed, to constitute their highest excellence and worth; as it seems to place the worshiper in direct personal juxtaposition with the spiritual world itself, and carries with it oftentimes a great show of earnestness and life, in its own form. But the transition here again is most easy, nay, most necessary, as all experience proves, from the region of clouds downward to the region of clods. All Sect worship, fanatical and extravagant at first, sinks finally into the dullest routine of empty ceremony. Sects as such, we may say rather, have no worship, in the only true sense of the term; and can hardly be said to know at all what worship, as a divine liturgical sacrifice, means.

Fifth Mark.

The antichristian spirit reveals itself still farther, in the way of contempt for all *history* and *authority*. It is not possible to believe in a real Church at all, if we do not recognize in it the continued presence of the same divine life, or new creation, that was originally introduced into the world by the incarnation of Jesus Christ. In the character of a supernatural fact or entity, actually at hand in the world's life, and as something different in this respect from a mere theory or conception, the Church *must* exist as the BODY OF CHRIST objectively and permanently, in the world, under the form of history: not here to-day and gone to-morrow; but always here, according to Christ's own solemn promise: not in the way of dead, monotonous tradition; but in the way of a true organic life process, reaching forward continually, through all ages, to its full proper consummation at the end of the world. In the very nature of the case, then, the individual must be bound by the general, the part by the whole: not blindly or slavishly, of course; but still in such a way, that no rupture or chasm between the two may be endured, as though the individual could be true by itself, in any original and independent form, apart from the organic whole to which it belongs. Hence the idea of Church authority, and sound ecclesiastical tradition. Faith in a real Christ, felt to be always in the Church really to the end of the world, will make it impossible for Christians to undervalue and despise either the present Church or the Church of past ages.

In proportion, however, as the sense of such a new creation in Christ Jesus, as the fact of the incarnation implies, may be wanting, this catholic feeling cannot be expected of course to prevail. When the objective Church, present or past, is no divine *fact* for faith (as in the Creed), how should it be expected to control and rule in any way the particular Christian consciousness? The particular Christian consciousness in such case, if Christian it may still be called at all, is necessarily sectarian and schismatic—*ruptured* from the life of the Church as a whole. It belongs accordingly to the very constitution of *Sect*, on the other hand, that it should ever be thus a foe to all history and authority. Sects, in proportion as they *are* sectarian, are disposed to stand upon the right of private judgment and individual freedom; and entertain, in particular, a sovereign contempt for the "Fathers," and for Church antiquity in every shape.*

Sixth Mark.

Such affectation of *individual freedom* is itself again worthy of being noticed, as a separate mark or feature of Antichrist.

Christianity proposes, indeed, also to make men free. "God hath not given us the spirit of fear," says the apostle, "but of power, and of love, and of a sound mind." Christ may be denominated emphatically the principle of all freedom; and religion, as derived from him, is any thing but a law of blind obedience, either for the understanding or the will. But for this very reason, it is not something to be produced or determined in any way, by the mind or will of men singly considered. Its form is *not* that

---

*It is hardly necessary to say, that this claim to absolute independence on the part of sects, is sheer pedantic affectation, when all is done. The thing itself is absurd and impossible. It lies in the constitution of our nature itself, that individual life and thought must be bound, in some way, by what is general. If then we refuse to acknowledge and honor authority under its legitimate form, we do not become free; we only accept authority under some form that is false. All true freedom holds in the bosom of true authority, as all bondage begins where the orbit of law is forsaken. To be subjective supremely, is to be supremely weak. Your blustering braggadocio is always a coward. The man who is forever bent on having his own way, is sure to go forever wrong. Sects are always palpably unfree, in proportion as the sect spirit forms their prevailing character. They disown antiquity, to make room for their own upstart history of yesterday. They refuse all reverence to the catholic Church, that they may do servile homage to some miserable fragment of the Christian profession in its stead. They have their "fathers" too, and their "traditions," as all the world knows; and none bow down more blindly to the spiritual rule they have been pleased to set up for themselves, in their own way. This, in fact, is the very curse of sectarianism, that while it professes to make men free, it teaches them to become slaves; cuts them off from the main stream of Christianity; carries them into a corner; thrusts aside the *church* consciousness for the *sect* consciousness; contracts the horizon of their theological vision to the measure of its own small canopy, no bigger in some cases than a common umbrella; and then urges them, *thus bound*, to look forth contemptuously on all the rest of the Christian world, with true Chinese vanity, as barbarian and unfree.

of the single reason, or of the single will, as such; it carries in itself always a general character. *My* reason can be rational here, only as it admits the Christian reality under this form; *my* will can be free here, only as it freely consents to be bound by the objective life which it is thus required to enter. Christianity knows nothing of a purely subjective freedom, in any view. All individual reason, and individual will, *must* be bound, in order to be either rational or free. Authority, therefore, is just as necessary a constituent of religion as liberty itself; they are opposite poles only of one and the same life.

This, however, the antichristian spirit can never understand or allow. It is by its very nature, particularistic and subjective. It finds the measure of all truth and right in itself, and not in Christ or the Church. Christianity starts, of right, in faith; receives its contents primarily in the way of creed, as exhibited in the person of Christ; its maxim is, *credo ut intelligam*, I believe in order that I may understand; only as it is first merged thus in the sense of the new creation as a divine present reality, may the reason of the individual subject be trusted at all, in its endeavors to apprehend what this creation means. But the spirit before us reverses this rule. Plainly expressed, its maxim is, *intelligo ut credam*, I must see and know in order that I may believe. It makes itself the last standard of truth, and is prepared to acknowledge Christ, only when He is found to suit its own preconceptions.

The pretension indeed is too monstrous, to be openly admitted in this barefaced form. It is cloaked accordingly, for the most part, with a show of subjection to the authority of the *Bible*. Antichrist (Matt. IV. 6) is ever ready to urge an "It is written," in favor of his own cause. He makes a merit of obeying God, in this way, while he tramples under foot all merely human authority. So it is characteristic of the Sect mind universally, as we all know, to make a pedantic parade of its love for the Bible. Your thorough sectarian is apt to rail out against old creeds and confessions; he is not to be bound thus, by the judgment of any man or body of men; others may lean on such human props; but the simple Bible is enough for *him*, and to no other testimony or law can he consent to appeal. He will not hear the Church; for that, he tells us, is the voice of man; but in the Bible God speaks, and he is willing to give it an obedient ear. He has faith in the Bible, but no faith in the Church; the fact of the written Record, he can embrace as truly supernatural and divine; but challenge his homage, in the same way, to the fact of Christianity itself, as a divine supernatural reality, subsisting in the life of the Church through all ages, and it is well if he do not scorn the thought as no better than gross superstition.

All this show of respect for God's Word however, is of no force whatever to invalidate what has just now been said of the false freedom of the spirit in question. It is only a plea, as already intimated, to excuse the arrogant assumption of superiority to all objective general authority whatever. With all his talk of following the Bible, the sectarian means by it simply, in the end, his own sense of what the Bible teaches. The Bible must be interpreted in some way; in order to enter any living mind, it must pass through a living medium of thought already at hand; for the undeveloped soul, it can have no meaning. An absolutely *immediate* use of it without all intervening preparation, is out of the question. If the medium at hand be not the product of educational or traditional faith, the mind of the Church handed over to the individual subject, it will still be there as the particular mental frame at least of the subject himself, the product it may be in part of mere fancy or caprice, but always something different, of course, from the Bible itself, whose sense it is called to explain. The sectarian then never comes to the Bible without a medium for converting it into thought and life; but instead of admitting the mind of the holy catholic Church, as it has stood from the beginning, to circumfuse his private thinking, in a free way, he affects to have no confidence in this whatever, and brings his own separate subjectivity to the case, under some other form, as though this were all that he needed to master the glorious world-revelation here laid at his feet.

Nor does it mend the matter at all, to plead here the promised guidance of the Holy Spirit. The question still returns, *How* are we led by the Spirit into all truth? Christianity is a whole, first in Christ and then in the Church, which it must ever be fanatical for me to think of grasping, as an isolated particle simply in its general life. This fanaticism however belongs to the Sect spirit, in its very constitution. It will have it, that both the Bible and the Holy Ghost are for the individual in such a way as to exclude all intermediate authority. All comes back finally to the form of mere individual judgment and will. The Bible and the Holy Spirit against the whole Church, is the plausible cry; but it comes always to this in the end: MY sense of the Bible against the sense of the whole world besides. In riding the Bible with such pedantic parade, each sect rides in fact only its own theological hobby, in the Bible's name; while the individual ME is arrogantly exalted (*Antichrist*) above all that is divine either in the Church or Bible, as though it were the source of Christianity itself, and Christ could have no being objectively in this world, save by its sovereign permission.*

---

*Here is a fine opportunity for the Sect spirit to make a false issue, in its own favor, against this very tract; as it has already done, in fact, over and over again, in opposition to the writer, in other cases. The tract, it will be said, is not willing to acknowledge the Bible as the rule of faith, but seeks to bring in a law of blind tradition in its place. The charge, however, is hypocritical and false. Hypocritical, because all sects do themselves make use of tradition, in the interpretation of the Scriptures; the poorest among them having some poor scheme of doctrine handed down from its own yesterday, *through* which, as a medium, its sense of God's word is always taken. Hypocritical again; because no sect is willing to acknowledge the Bible as interpreted by other sects; which it ought to do, if its

Seventh Mark.

Another mark of this schismatic spirit is found in its tendency to *hyperspiritualism*. Christianity is emphatically a spiritual religion; but it is at the same time real, and in this respect conformable to the actual nature of man. It is the spiritual in true union with the natural, as the necessary basis of humanity, and a necessary element also in its constitution. Its Christ is one who has come in the flesh. Gnosticism will know only of a Christ who comes in the clouds, or which is the same thing, in the human brain. It claims to be in this way spiritual, in the highest degree; pneumatic, and not psychic; impatient of all contact possibly with our common earthly life. So through all phases; the spirit in question is always the same; swimming in empyrean heights, in such way as to lose all substantial hold upon the earth. Rationalism and sectarianism are both alike at this point; zealous for spiritual religion in opposition to a religion of forms.

All sects in particular boast of having the spirit, as they call it, in extraordinary measure; and affect to be more or less independent of outward ordinances in this way. They need, as we have seen, no outward historical Church, no real sacraments, no objective worship. Christianity is for them a matter of purely inward particular experience; a supernatural illapse of life upon the single subject, with or without means, as God may see fit. All is spiritualistic; rising in this form oftentimes to the region of seeming inspiration or ranting frenzy; but still fantastic, always unsubstantial and unreal; with the necessity of cooling down ultimately into the form of frigid rationalistic abstraction.

---

own maxim were sound; but each one insists that it shall be taken only in the particular sense that appears to suit itself; while all join notwithstanding in the convenient cry: Great is *Private Judgment*, the Diana of the Sectarians! The charge, moreover, is false; we do not undervalue the Bible in favor of tradition, and we do not question the right of private judgment in its true form. All blind outward mechanical authority, in the interpretation of the Scriptures, as taught by Rome and practically allowed in a different form by the SECT ANTICHRIST, we disown with our whole heart. But for this very reason we own no private judgment, as worthy of trust, that is not organically comprehended in the life of Christianity as a whole. We will not endure licentiousness and self-will for the true liberty wherewith Christ hath made us free. We accept the Bible as God's word; but we see in the Church also the perpetual presence of a divine fact, from which that word may never be sundered without peril to the truth; and we hold for little better than infidel cant, all veneration men may pretend for what is written, that is palpably coupled with no corresponding veneration for the mystical life of the Son of God, in its historical form.

Eighth Mark.

This brings to view another most significant and far reaching feature of the antichristian spirit, namely the hopeless, helpless *dualism*, that characterizes its whole theory of the Christian life. God and nature, this last completed in man, come to a true union only in Christ. His theanthropic person is the form itself, in which the divine and human are brought to a real inward reconciliation. Apart from this fact, we can have only pantheism or dualism, or an unsteady oscillation rather between both. But this fact Antichrist rejects. So far as the spirit prevails then, it will not suffer the two worlds which Christ represents, to come to a true, inward, historical reconciliation, at any point. The union remains throughout, external, mechanical, abstract, and fantastic; having its pattern at best in the Nestorian Christ, where each nature is made to exclude the other, in such way as to exclude at the same time the idea of a common personal life. All is dualistic. A violent, abrupt chasm, is made to sunder the earth from the heavens, man from God, the world of nature from the world of spirit; and all attempts to bridge it over resolve themselves into Gnostic dreams, that bring the mind no sense of reality or truth.

It is wonderful how far this criterion is found to hold, in the religious thinking of Sects, and of all who are infected in any way with the old Nestorian view of Christ, after the manner, we may say, of Sects generally. In proportion as the person of the Savior is divided for their consciousness, the heavenly nature floating over the human merely without the conjunction of a real common life, the same character of unreality may easily be felt to reign also in the whole view which they take of Christianity. The visible and invisible come to no true union, in their sacraments and worship. Their idea of the Church is dualistic, making it, finally, a phantom. The relation of the new creation to the old, is felt always to be abrupt, violent, chasmatic; as though the first stood in no organic connection with the last, but were only joined to it in an outward way. Christianity is not viewed as the form in which the world itself becomes finally complete; the resolution of the inmost secret of humanity; the last scope of all God's ways in the vast process of creation. It is a factitious system, rather, the product of infinite skill combined with infinite love, mysteriously superadded to the constitution of the world's proper life, for the purposes of redemption. It is above this life, beyond it, over against it, as another order of existence; but comes to no real reconciliation with it, by taking it up in its own sphere, and penetrating it with its own divine power.

The idea of any such inward marriage between Nature and Spirit, the millennium of creation, is wanting to the Gnostic altogether, and can never come to any full acknowledgment in the mind of the Nestorian.

Your sectarian consciousness may bind them together, by a sort of outward tie; but it has no power to make them one; unless it be in the way of reducing the distinction itself to a nullity, by making one side to be all and the other nothing. It owns the supernatural; but, in doing so, wrongs the natural; wrongs both; makes the supernatural to be magical only, and flings a dark Manichæan aspect over the world in its common view.

Sects disown history. To them the past is no womb of the present in the life of the Church. *Their* Christianity is always τὸ διοπετές, direct from the clouds. (Acts XIX. 35.) Sects have no faith in organic grace; a power involved in the actual constitution of the Church, historically considered, for the accomplishment of its own ends; no faith in baptism or educational religion. Conversion, for them, is ever something abrupt. And the spiritual life that follows, carries always the same character. It is bound to particular seasons and occasions, and comes to no steady union with life as a whole. The religion which affects to storm the heavens in the social conference to-night, has no power, and, as it might seem, no disposition, even, to sanctify the counting room or shop to-morrow. It is made up of two lives—one pertaining to this world, and one pertaining to the next, between which it moves dualistically, with scarce an effort to bring them together. Sect piety is ever like the legs of the lame—unequal, unsteady, and full of contradiction.

Christianity, in its own nature, is world-embracing, and seeks to sanctify to its own use every sphere of the world's true and proper life. It is universally characteristic of Sects, on the contrary, that they admit no such catholic view of its nature, but are disposed rather to look with dark, malignant glance on the whole natural constitution of the world as something intrinsically bad. Science, art, politics and social life, are, for the genuine Sectarian, always more or less profane. His Gnostic Christ dooms him to perpetual imprisonment, gloomy and sad, in the labyrinth of a Manichæan world.

Ninth Mark.

The antichristian spirit, having the character, and occupying the posture, which have now been mentioned, cannot fail to show itself *fanatical*. The subjective can never be calm, quiet and strong, except as it is borne upon the bosom of the objective. The spiritual has no reality for man, except as revealed and apprehended in organic union with the natural. The dualistic consciousness of the Gnostic race must ever be in itself a consciousness, at bottom, of weakness and falsehood; associated, as we have just seen, by a sort of inward necessity, with a tinge of Manichæan malignity towards the world. But all this in religion, is the very conception of fanaticism itself. It belongs, then, to this spirit, as all history, at the same time, abundantly shows, to reveal itself in this way.

It is, by its very constitution, restless and violent, extravagant and prone to extremes.

Sectarianism is always fanatical; either in the way of wild excitement, or quiet bigotry and prejudice; which are different stages only of the same moral disease. It affects to be strong, and yet has no strength in fact. Its earnestness runs into passion; in which form it becomes necessarily more or less unnatural and excessive; with the certainty of ending, sooner or later, in self-exhaustion and collapse. It is only the catholic Christianity, resting in the faith of divine powers objectively present, through Jesus Christ in the Church, that can be at once profoundly earnest and profoundly calm. The religion of Sect can never have the same character. It is unquiet, irregular, spasmodic; substitutes feeling for faith; moves always by impulse and effort; runs into excesses; alternates between extremes. Its image, at best, is the whirlwind or mountain torrent, the very violence of whose action is a symptom of their own transient nature, and an argument that their strength itself is something hollow and unreal.

Tenth Mark.

Antichrist is known still farther as a spirit of endless *division*. Christianity, as the deepest life of the world, is necessarily universal and catholic. In Christ Jesus there is neither circumcision nor uncircumcision, but a new creation, in which all other distinctions are abolished or reconciled. The Christian consciousness, as such, cannot allow itself to be subordinated to any other consciousness; for this would imply that Christ is not the last fundamental fact in the world's life. Any consciousness, on the other hand, that stops short of this fact, that does not move truly and really in the sense of what is comprehended in the person of Christ, as the Word made flesh, must necessarily be particular and incomplete; and if, with this character, it still affect, notwithstanding, to be the Christian consciousness itself, it must show itself, of course, to the same extent, uncatholic, also, and schismatic. Where the sense of a real Christ is wanting, there can be, as we have seen, no sense of a real Church; the new creation resolves itself into a world of phantasms and dreams, or, at best, into a system of spiritual verities, which men are to appropriate only in the way of thought and feeling; all is subjective, and for this very reason dependent finally on the mind of the subject for its particular form. A spiritualistic, subjective Christianity, may be said to carry the idea of schism in its very constitution.

Our modern Sect system, therefore, is but a fair revelation of the true character of this spirit, as it has prevailed from the beginning. It divides Christ on principle; in full correspondence thus with its own theoretical counterpart, rationalism; to which, in like manner, Christ is no original, universal fact, with which all Christian thinking is required to begin, but a mere theorem or problem, rather, for the exercise of thought in a different way.

Sectarianism goes throughout on the assumption, that there is no holy catholic Church in this world, one and universal, by its very conception, as the person of the Savior himself; but that the Church is simply what men may choose to make it, for their own accommodation, in conformity with the general law of their social nature. Men have a right, it is pretended, if they are not satisfied with the Church as they find it, to secede, and form a new organization more to their own taste, or the Church may rend itself into two bodies, with more or less violence, and each continue to be as much a Church as before. The principle in this way becomes one of unlimited division; if it be proper to have fifty Sects, we may as easily allow five hundred or five thousand; it follows, at last, that any congregation, or fragment of a congregation, is competent at any time to erect a separate standard in the name of the Church, and carry away with it all the powers that this divine constitution may be supposed to comprehend.* But is not this palpably to overthrow the idea of the Church entirely—transferring it to the clouds, or sinking it to the character of a mere abstraction?

The Sectarian consciousness can never be a true Church consciousness; as the particular can never truly stand in the place of the general; but necessarily becomes false by any such pretension. Ordinarily, indeed, Sects do not lay claim to the character of universalness. Their consciousness itself is such as excludes the idea of catholicity or church *wholeness*. They may be exclusive; are so at bottom always; but their exclusiveness is that of party, based on the sense of some subjective distinction, not the homage which faith renders to the objective fact of Christianity itself. Hence Sects commonly allow, that the Church is more comprehensive than *their* particular communions. They claim to be, each for itself, not the only way, but simply the best way, to heaven; not *the* Church, as though there were no other; but only *a* Church, or, as the thing more readily expresses itself, a society, connection, or religious *persuasion* rather, in which is collected the cream of true religion, with due allowance for something at least of the same life, to show itself also under other forms. In all this, however, there is vast contradiction. The Sect consciousness owns itself for something less than the whole, and still requires the whole to do it homage, as though it were universal and

---

*Mr. Rupp, in his "Original History of the Religious Denominations, at present existing in the United States," 1844, gives us a list of between forty and fifty sects, which are here allowed to represent their own faith. But this, it seems, was much short of the truth, at least as it stands now. The same gentleman has issued proposals lately for a new work, to contain "authentic accounts of upwards of *seventy* religious denominations, associations and sects," belonging to the fruitful history of our country.

supreme. Christianity is allowed to be deeper and broader than itself, and yet it is treated, in fact, as a subordinate sphere of life. The Sect consciousness is not borne and carried into the Church consciousness, but by its very nature affects to be itself the bearer rather of this last; a clear, practical solecism, which of necessity upsets the conception of a real, objective, holy catholic Church altogether. Sects profess to honor the universal Church, but it is perfectly plain that they honor themselves a great deal more. They acknowledge and exclude one another at the same moment. They are not co-ordinate departments of the same one Christian life; the distinction which divides them, is stronger than the bond that should hold them together. So far as they may seem to come together at all, it is not by entering into the sense of the Church as a real whole, of which they are only parts, but by setting aside altogether the idea of any such Church, Sects may enter into an alliance or league *as* Sects; but such union is no Church, and the catholicity thus pretended is itself but wholesale schism in disguise. It belongs to this antichristian, no-church spirit to rend asunder and divide, while it has no power whatever to heal and make whole. It is constitutionally schismatic, and may be known and distinguished by this mark, all the world over.

Eleventh Mark.

Another feature of the spirit in question may be found in the tendency it has always to *end in the flesh*. Theoretic Gnosticism falls over easily into the sphere of Ebionism. Manichæan strictness readily runs into Antinomian looseness. Ecclesiastical history abounds with exemplifications of this general truth. "Hyperspiritualism is ever fleshly pseudo-spiritualism; that is sure to fall back sooner or later, impotent and self-exhausted, into the low element from which it has vainly pretended to make its escape. Anabaptism finds its legitimate, natural end in the excesses of Munster; as Mormonism in the like excesses of Nauvoo. What a difference apparently between the inspiration of George Fox, and the cold infidelity of Elias Hicks. And yet the last is the true spiritual descendant of the first. The inward light of the one, and the light of reason as held by the other, come to the same thing at last. Both contradict the true conception of religion. Both are supremely subjective, and in this view supremely rationalistic, at the same time." In its highest flights, the religion which affects to be all spirit, remains intrinsically bound to the earth; it has no objective support, either for its speculation or its devotion; what it pretends to lean upon is no divine reality beyond itself, but a Gnostic fiction, merely sprung from its own womb: all ends at last in the farce of sheer, helpless subjectivity, a grinning parody on the lofty epic which has seemed to go before.

Fanaticism has a tendency always to become rationalistic in doctrine, and licentious in practice. Sectarian piety is characteristically inconsistent and unsteady. All spirit in one aspect, it is all flesh in another. It mounts towards heaven to-day, only to flounder in the mud to-morrow. Sects themselves continually change their character in this way. They start in the clouds, but invariably fall prone at last upon the earth. Their life, in due time exhausts itself, by its own action; their fervid heat grows cool; their spiritualism subsides into fleshly form, a sort of conscious lie, that merely apes its former self; and each appears as the effete residuum only, or at best the monumental petrifaction of the high-wrought enthusiasm that formed its original being.*

Twelfth Mark.

The last characteristic of Antichrist we shall notice, is presented to us in the form of *false theology*. As we have already seen, the spirit involves a fundamental heresy from the start; and, however this may be brought to conform subsequently, in terms at least, to the established orthodoxy of the Church, it will be found to carry in itself always the same principle of falsehood, which cannot fail to make itself felt in the way of more or less refined error, throughout the whole structure of theological thought into which it is allowed to enter. Christianity as a science, involves a doctrine of God and a doctrine of man. These become one organically in the doctrine of the God-man, Christ. Anthropology and Theology both become complete, only on the basis of Christology. A false christological theory, then, though it be never so refined, must always vitiate the view that is taken at the same time both of the nature of God and the nature of man, imparting thus a secretly heterodox character to the whole theory of religion. The theanthropic fact, revealed in Christ's person and perpetuated in the Church, is the key, the only key, that unlocks the hidden mystery of the world. Turn this into a Gnostic phantasm, or Nestorian abstraction, and, all theology becomes to the same extent uncertain and

---

*The moral *dishonesty* of the Sect spirit deserves here particular notice. The part assuming to be the whole, and turning in its life thus on some egotistic principle rather than the sense of an objective reality in religion, becomes necessarily false in the same measure to the truth itself. All *parties*, as such, are constitutionally dishonest, whether in politics or religion. Godly simplicity and true catholic feeling, go hand in hand together; while the whole tendency of Sectarianism is towards a sort of low calculating policy, that thinks to carry its own ends in religion, just as it follows its private interests in the world. It is truly humiliating, to look round on our Sect system as it stands and see how widely it has come to be infected with this bad spirit. *Jesuitism*, under a Protestant cloak, is every where more or less at work, in the way of misrepresentation, false pretence, and cunning intrigue. So long as any Sect has the feeling, that all other Christianity, past or present, is to be tried by its own small measure, as the absolute perfection of truth, how is it possible that it can have either the disposition or the power to be just towards any Sect besides?

unreal.* The antichristian spirit is necessarily heretical as well as schismatic.

Sects have no true theology. They are prone always to undervalue it in any form, as having a secret consciousness that for *them* it is in fact nothing. And in such shape as they have it, we find it to be always a system of mechanical abstractions, as barren for the understanding as it is cold and jejune for the heart. All runs out into a scheme of invincible dualism; man here, God there; two worlds, set over against each other, in the way of everlasting abstract opposition; all communication between them magical only and fantastic, not historically real; the incarnation a divine *avatar* simply, in human shape; the Church, an idea; its sacraments, signs; the Bible, an aerolite, shot from the skies; the whole process of salvation, a sort of divine legerdemain, wrought in the soul by the help of invisible powers; all resolving itself at last, some outward supernatural apparatus only excepted, into marvelous coincidence, at almost every point, with the grossly subjective, neological theology of the mere Socinian or Deist, from which the idea of the supernatural is banished altogether.

IV. THE SECT PLAGUE AND ITS REMEDY.

Other marks or features of Antichrist might be traced, if it were necessary, in the general character of the Sect system. Enough has been exhibited, however, to identify its bad origin and nature. With all its pretensions to Christian sanctity, we find it to be at war throughout with Christ and his Church. Tried by the rule of St. John, it is not of God, but a spirit of falsehood and delusion only, which we are bound to hate and oppose, whenever it may come in our way.

---

*No theology can be profound, that is not to the same extent catholic. The first condition towards a genuine interest in the science, is emancipation from the power of Sect; not indeed in such a way as to cease to be confessional, for that would be to break with history at the same time; but so as that this shall be turned into the medium simply, of communication with the objective whole of Christianity, as a divine reality in Christ and the Church. Sectarianism as having to do with a fragment of this reality only in its own life, (partial and unhistorical by its very constitution,) can never rightly master the whole of it in the way of knowledge. Its theology runs into a system of notions and abstractions:,with polemic exclusion of all beyond its own sphere. True theology is not so much polemical, in this way, as comparative and ironical in the form of historical symbolism. Sects, as such, take little or no interest in the objective mystery of Christ and the Church. They are apt to consider the christological question, the subject of the sacraments, and all church ideas, comparatively barren and insipid; having more taste, naturally, for their own particular shibboleths; and not remembering that all Christianity starts in the realities of the creed, and is of no force any farther than these continue to be felt in the way of faith. There can be no surer mark of a poor theology, than this; that it has no earnest sympathy with the idea of the Church, as a divine historical reality grounded in the constitution of Christ's person.

This judgment must not be taken, of course, as an indiscriminate denunciation of all denominational or confessional distinctions, in the Church. What we have in view all along, as before remarked, is the Sect *mind*, without reference to particular organizations or societies, through which it may be revealed.

We have no right, in the first place, to put all ecclesiastical organizations on the same level, as regards church character. There is a difference between the idea of a denomination or confession, and that of a mere party or sect. It may be difficult to explain it clearly in theory, and still more so to apply it practically to existing religious bodies. But the nature of the case requires that it should be admitted; since we must otherwise allow the Church to be nothing, over against the principle of unlimited individual caprice; and all serious Christians, no doubt, have some sense of the distinction, as reaching into actual life. A denomination or confession forms a component part of the one universal Church; separated from the general body, by inward necessity; representing for the time a certain essential side of the common Christianity, which must otherwise have been undervalued and wronged; with the prospect and hope of a final re-integration of the interests thus divided, into their proper catholic unity. A Sect, on the other hand, stands in no such organic connection with the Church as a whole. It is the creature in full of private wilfulness and caprice, not the growth of the true Church life itself. It affects to be a perfectly original, and perfectly complete Christianity, by itself; and involves in fact, if not in open profession, a rupture with the entire consciousness of all the Christian world besides, as something defective and false.

According to this distinction, Sects as such are always evil, and every man is bound to shun them, as he values his own salvation. We may not say the same thing, however, of religious denominations. In the present state of the world, they may be justified, as being at least relatively necessary, in the great historical process, by which the Church is carried forward to its appointed end. Since the Reformation, in particular, the Church has fallen unavoidably into the form of more or less rupture with itself; so as to appear divided into different confessional organizations; without still losing, on this account, the internal oneness of its life as a whole.

In the next place, however, we must distinguish also between Sect feeling and Church feeling, in the bosom of denominations themselves. We cannot admit the presence of a true Church feeling, to any extent, in strictly Sectarian bodies; they are schismatic by their very constitution, and all who belong to them partake necessarily more or less of the same spirit. But it is quite possible, on the other hand, for Sect feeling, as well as Church feeling, to prevail in regular churchly denominations. It does not follow, then, that a denominational position may not be liable to exception here, simply because it can be vindicated as necessary and right in the actual state of the Church. It may be occupied, notwithstanding, with a spirit that is wholly Sectarian and schismatic. Denominational zeal, indeed, is ever ready to degenerate into the low bigotry of Sect; which of course, however, in such case, can be no more entitled to respect, than if it were found in open connection with the most unchurchly self-constituted organization in the land.

In admitting moreover the necessity of confessional distinctions, we do not allow them to be good and desirable in their own nature. They are relatively good only, as serving to open the way to a higher form of catholicity than that which they leave behind; whilst in themselves absolutely considered, they contradict and violate the true idea of the Church, and are to be bewailed on this account as an evil of the most serious magnitude. This divided condition of the Christian world is, at best, like the unsettled state of God's ancient Israel, during the wanderings that intervened between the Red Sea and the river Jordan. The wilderness was something better than the bondage of Egypt, for which it had been exchanged; and it had vast value, in the way of preparation for the land of Canaan, which was to be reached, finally, as the end of its weary trials. But still it was a sterile, howling desert, when all was done, and it must have argued an utter want of faith in God's word, for any to have taken up their rest in it as the land of promise. Just so in the case of our religious denominations. Allow them to be the necessary result of the Protestant movement, still they belong only to the *movement* as such, and not at all to the ulterior order in which this is required to become complete. In this view, it involves no contradiction whatever, to occupy a denominational position in the Church, as something which is made necessary for the time, by the general calamity of the age, while, notwithstanding, we pronounce the whole denominational system an abomination and abuse. Only as we do so, indeed, can any such position be justified as transiently right; for in no other view can it be reconciled, with a true catholic sense of the proper unity and universality of the Church. We have no right to acquiesce in the system, as ultimate and normal, in any sense, for Christianity. We have no right to be reconciled to it, even for a single day, except as a painful, though it may be needful, transition stage, confused and chaotic, by which we are to be conducted over to a higher order of Christian life. Our very patience in the case should include an impatient *How long, Lord?* silently breathed into the ears of Zion's King. To say of the wilderness, This is our home, and we will seek no other, is to be at once in spirit unchurchly and schismatic. The system does violence to the true idea of the Church, tends to subvert it fundamentally; and we are bound to endure it, whilst it must be endured, only as an acknowledged misery, with steady protest against its power, and an honest desire to have it brought to an end.

As thus wrong in its own nature, and leading over at once to the life of Sect in full, the moment it comes to be acquiesced in as right and good, the denominational or confessional system is not to be distinguished practically, in the end, from the Sect system itself in its worst form. The two flow together as the power of a single evil. In our own country especially, as the Church now stands, this is palpably clear. Our denominational Christianity is fairly responsible for all the mischief of our Sectarian Christianity. We have full right to speak of the whole indiscriminately, as the *Sect plague* of our age and nation.

It is one of the favorable indications of the time, that few are willing now to stand forward as the open and formal apologists of the Sect system. Not many years since, this was quite common. New Sects were publicly proclaimed a blessing to the Church. They served, it was said, to separate discordant elements in its constitution; to provoke to good works; to act as a system of mutual checks and balances, in its general organization; to increase its efficiency, by a proper division of labor. In this view, it was fashionable to speak of them as the legitimate form of Christianity itself, which as such might be expected to reach forward, with full force, into the period of the millennium; when the Church is to appear "fair as the moon, clear as the sun, and terrible as an army with banners."* Happily, we say, all this has in a great measure passed away. Our general sense of the evil of the Sect system is still, no doubt, most unequal to the truth, and we find it still practically and indirectly justified on all sides; but the feeling seems to have fastened itself on the inmost consciousness of the Christian world, that it cannot be vindicated as the normal order of the Church, and that Protestantism can never accomplish in full its high mission, till the divisions to which it has given birth shall have been brought to an end. The late "World Convention" at London, though it has issued in smoke, as might have been expected, deserves to be kept in view always, as a most significant fact, in this view. It stands as an open confession, we may say, on the part of the whole Protestant world, that its present division into Sects is a grand and crying evil, and that it has become one of the first necessities of the Church, if not indeed the very first, to bring the wholesale schism to an end. Such plainly is coming to be, more and more, the general feeling of the age. In different quarters, and from different points of view, the idea of the Church is waking into new force in men's minds, and producing a more or less uneasy

---

*A very favorite way of representing the subject, at one time, was to compare the different denominations to the several different kinds of soldiers that go to make up a regular army. More beautiful is the illustration (the last we have seen of the sort,) brought forward in connection with the late "Christian Alliance" movement by a distinguished orator from the Established Church of Scotland, making the several denominations to be so many chords, whose combined music constitutes the harmony of the one, holy, universal Church! Alas, that so pretty a fancy should have so little truth in fact.

apprehension of the great Antichristian falsehood with which we are surrounded. In all this, of course, we have much reason to rejoice; since the first condition of effectual help, in this case, is the oppressive sense of want. They that be whole need not a physician, we are told, but only such as are sick.

It is a wonder, indeed, that any could ever be carried so far out of the way, with the New Testament in their hands, as to plead for the Sect system on principle. It stands plainly in broad contradiction to the teaching of the Apostles, and the express will of Christ. The sense of the whole Gospel on the subject, may be said to be summarily comprehended in that memorable, and deeply-touching prayer: "Neither pray I for these alone, but for them also which shall believe in me through their word; that they all *may be one*; as thou, Father, art in me, and I in thee, that they also may be one in us; that the world may believe that thou hast sent me."

But it is not simply particular declarations of Christ and his Apostles, that are contradicted by the Sect system; it is opposed to the whole *idea* of Christianity and the Church. This we have endeavored to show in the present tract. Christ is the last and deepest principle of humanity, which as such is required to take up the *whole*, in the way of organic unity, into the new order of life, thus introduced into the world. The idea of a nation or state is not thus universal, because it is based on nature primarily, which as such always implies distinction and multiplicity; there may be many nations without any sort of violence to the conception of man. But the idea of the Church can bear no such rupture; it is universal necessarily, as being in truth the only proper expression of man's universal life itself. To such universality, as we have already seen, neither Paganism nor Judaism, in themselves considered, had any power to come. Christ is the true sense of the world, the absolute religion of man, in which all previous forms of consciousness are required to pass forever away. Christianity, as springing from him in the Church, may indeed still admit distinctions; but only in such a way, as the body may have parts, continuing itself to be, notwithstanding, the one true and only whole, in which all are carried and included as a single life. It can endure no such rupture as violates the organic oneness of its own nature. Christianity must be the deepest and most universal form of life, the trunk consciousness, if the word may be allowed, to which all spiritual distinctions besides, Greek, Jew, male, female, bond, free, &c., stand related simply as diverging branches that spring from the same tree. This indubitably is the true *idea* of Christianity; and it is this idea rather than any formal statements on the subject in the New Testament, which conducts us finally to the article of the "One, Holy, Catholic Church," as it has stood in the Creed of the whole Christian world, from the beginning. No one can enter far into the consciousness of what Christ was and is still, without feeling the authority of this article. To deny it, is virtually to fall back to the standpoint of the world as it exists on the outside of the Christian mystery. It is to be entangled again in the old Gentile consciousness, or in that of the Jew.

Into this condemnation our Sect system, under its present reigning form, most evidently runs. We may imagine, indeed, an *organic* system of sects, by which the general Christian consciousness might fall asunder into so many confessional branches, that should continue afterwards to integrate each other, without prejudice to the unity of the whole. But such is *not* the order that here actually prevails; and it needs but little reflection to see that the system, left to itself, can never be brought to assume practically any such form. Our Sects are in no sense whatever component parts of a common organic whole. No one can dream that the Christian consciousness, as concerned in their production, has required, by any sort of inward necessity, just so many, and no more, to express in full its own meaning. That notoriously is not the principle at all that lies for the most part at their foundation. To a great extent, they owe their existence to no truly objective interest whatever, but to self-will, passion, accident, and caprice. The causes of split, in most cases, are not a whit more important than other matters which have led to no such result, only because no personal references have come in to push them into similar consequence. The system, in this way, includes in itself no law or norm for its own regulation; no internal reason, to which an appeal can be legitimately carried against the rise of new sects. No one can say to it, "*Thus* far shalt thou go, but no farther." If it be right to have five Sects, why not fifty? and if fifty, why not five hundred? If a thousand congregations, wilfully erecting a new ecclesiastical standard, can, as a matter of course, carry with them the full life of the Church, why may not a single congregation, or the half or fourth part of a single congregation, do precisely the same thing? Why, indeed, may I not constitute my own family into a separate "denomination," and have no more to do, ecclesiastically, with the rest of the world afterwards than the Methodists have now with the Presbyterians, or the Covenanters with the Seceders? The system flows forward irresistibly towards a perfectly atomistic independency, and has a tendency thus, from the start, to prostrate completely the whole being, as well as the whole idea, of the Church.

It is a striking, though most sad, illustration of the inward falsehood of the Sect system, as now described, that in most cases the original grounds of separation, with the bodies thus divided, have lost, to a great extent, frequently indeed altogether, the interest which they had in the beginning; while notwithstanding the door remains just as much closed as ever, in each case, against reconciliation and union. Witness the fragments of the Scotch secession, mechanically transplanted to this side of the Atlantic. Witness the old antagonism of Lutheran and Reformed, as still kept up in the American German Church, while yet the Lutheran Confession, for the most part, has utterly surrendered its own original principle, and swung clear over the Calvinistic line itself on the opposite side. Is Methodism any longer faithful to its first idea and design? And then as regards the mass of our more upstart native Sects, how few of them, if they ever had any intelligible, distinctive theory to begin with, can be said to know or seriously care what it was, at the present time? It is the curse of sectarianism indeed that it cannot be truly historical; whilst, at the same time, history is the only enduring form of life; "das Fertige ist das Todte,"—what is *done* is necessarily also dead. The Sect life, sundering itself from the general consciousness of the Church, (uncatholic,) may start with vast show of spiritual freshness and vigor—like a divergent stream from the Euphrates or Tigris—but only, if it continue in such separate course, to lose itself ultimately in the sand, or settle into some stagnant pool, from which it can never afterwards accomplish its escape. The spirit expires gradually, in the arms of its own letter; the old terminology degenerates into sheer cant; and in place of the living witness that once gave utterance to some divine reality in the denominational creed, we have before us, finally a grim statue, or life-aping automaton at best, that simply parades in dumb show a sense which it has no longer any power to understand. It cannot be concealed, that into this judgment of Lot's wife our Sects, at least in a large part, are fast falling at the present time. And yet all this facilitates not, in the least, their return to any sort of catholic unity. There they stand over against each other, their original meaning for the most part gone, and yet they have no power in the world to come together. The system possesses no principle of cure or help, in its own nature. It has no tendency whatever, however remote, towards true catholicity. It is the very opposite of all organic Christianity. It is absolutely impotent to build up or unite, and mighty only to divide and destroy.

It is perfectly idle, in these circumstances, to remind us of the *invisible* hand, by which after all the true children of God, in the midst of all these divisions, are secretly drawn together. It is possible, no doubt, for this to prevail to some extent over the difficulty here thrown in its way. We are bound indeed to rejoice in the conviction, that there are at this time among our different denominations, very many truly catholic souls, in which habitually the sense of denominational peculiarity is kept subordinate to the sense of church wholeness, and whose full tendency is towards the great millennium, the "Church of the Future," in which our existing captivity shall come finally to an end. But it is altogether plain, at the same time, that the exercise of such catholicity, as things now stand, is by no means easy; it runs against the natural bent of the Sect system itself, and can be maintained only with much self-discipline and prayer. And it is equally plain, that it has no place whatever in the mass of our Sect religion. It will not do to say: See how these Sects love one another, in the face of all their rivalry and outward separation! The "invisible" unity, we are told, is something deeper and stronger, than the denominational lines and landmarks that challenge the eye of sense. But if it be so, why should it not have force to make itself visible? Or is it only that which is comparatively weak and partial, in our interior life, that can be expected thus to clothe itself with corporeity and outward form? Alas, there is palpable contradiction, and gross hypocrisy, in the whole pretence. It is not possible for a true *Church* consciousness to exist, as the real ground-feeling of our religious life, the *whole*, of which all other forms of this life are only parts, without struggling at least towards a corresponding revelation of itself in an objective and visible form. To make the One, Holy, Catholic Church, a sheer invisibility, is just to convert it into an idealistic, Gnostic abstraction. Why not remand the Sect consciousness itself, into the same shadowy realm? Why not give us an invisible Lutheranism, Presbyterianism, Methodism, as well as an invisible Church Catholic?

It will not hold. Our sects, as such, do not love each other, and are not inwardly bound together as the case requires, by a force that is deeper and stronger than that which keeps them apart. With all of them, the Sect consciousness is something deeper than the Church consciousness, the sense of the universal is overpowered by the sense of the particular. An occasional shaking of hands fraternally on the platform of a Bible Society, or a melting season of promiscuous communion now and then around the sacramental board, fall short immeasurably of the true idea of catholic unity. There may be no open controversy. That belongs only to the first stage of the process; the heat of which after a short time, is found to cool down into a comparatively quiet form of hard, stiff tradition. But this want of controversy is itself, in such case, a sign commonly, that all real communion has come to an end, between the now mutually tolerant bodies. They have entered into different theological and ecclesiastical worlds, in which each has lost the power, to a great extent, of understanding the rest, or taking any interest in their affairs. Look at the "organs," as they are called, the religious papers and reviews, of the several denominations, which represent and rule at the same time, the various currents of their life. What a melancholy isolation of interest, in each case more or less, to the one narrow island which measures the horizon of the single sect. Some reference there may be occasionally to foreign ecclesiastical facts, in the way of passing news. But how little of broad, generous sympathy, with the affairs of God's kingdom as a whole. How little concern or power apparently, to forsake at any time the simply sectarian stand-point, and enter with hearty zeal into the cause of the universal Church, as a reality of infinitely more account than any fragment of it under a denominational form. Our Sects acknowledge one another indeed, for the most part, as true churches; a virtual confession, of course, that no one of them is complete by itself, and that they must flow together in some way, to be all that is comprehended in the idea of Christianity. But practically, all this is every day denied again and forgotten. Each affects, in fact, a measure of self-sufficiency and self-satisfaction, that leaves nothing to be sought or expected, in the way of complement, from abroad. All its thinking and working are conducted on the principle, that its mission is simply to carry out perpetually the sense and purpose of its own separate organization; precisely as though this were the true wholeness of Christianity, that must in the end swallow up the entire Church; without the least concern, as it would seem, to have the several confessional tendencies reconciled and united in a higher life, which may be found to be thus the universal truth of them all. The relation is one of mutual repulsion only, and exclusion.

This contradiction lies in the very nature of the system itself. Every Sect so far as it may have any part whatever in Christian truth, is necessarily exclusive, whether it openly assume such character or not. And the reason is simply this, that the idea of the Church, as such, is necessarily universal. It implies the *whole* of the new heavenly creation it is employed to represent, with the rejection of all besides, as lying out of its sphere. All true catholicity is thus, at the same time, in the highest degree exclusive. It rests in the Church, as the one universal and *only* form of the new creation in Christ Jesus. It is not possible to sunder this character from the idea of the Church; and so it follows, that Sects in pretending to carry the full life of religion along with them, under this form, into their separate organizations, are always urged secretly to assert an exclusive Christianity in their own favor. A body which thus claims to be *a* Church, independently of all the rest of Christendom, is bound indeed, in inward consistency, to hold itself as *the* Church; since catholicity is felt to be just as necessary an attribute of such pretension, as holiness or divine authority. That is the most consistent sectarianism then, by all means, which openly unchurches all beyond its own pale, doing homage thus to the principle of true Church catholicity, while it turns it into open caricature. In a quiet way, all sectarianism *means* just the same thing in fact as long as it retains in itself any faith or life. It is the part, affecting to take the place of the whole; Antichrist usurping the attributes and prerogatives of Christ; in its best form, the old Jewish consciousness, with its narrow prejudices, substituted for the law of the spirit of life in Christ Jesus; or in the way of escape from this again, only the old Gentile consciousness, made tolerant and comprehensive, by true ethnic indifference to the whole idea of the Church. In this last case particularly, Sects find it much more easy to bear with one another, in their own division, than to brook the thought of their passing away in the power of a deeper life. Just as the different religious of ancient Rome, could seem to walk lovingly arm in arm together, as long as each made room politely for the territorial rights of the rest, but were roused to common wrath against Christianity, for claiming to be the absolute and universal truth of all religion; so there is nothing which is more sure ordinarily to provoke the displeasure of our liberal and loving Sects, than the claims of the one catholic Church brought near to them in any sensible way. It is very remarkable too, that those precisely which are most full of universal brotherhood pretension, in this ethnic style, are the most quick to show their true shape, when touched by the Ithuriel spear of which we now speak. So long as it rests in anniversary speeches, it may do well enough: but let it come to true catholic *ideas*, begin where you please, and all this sweet patience is over. The Sect spirit *knows* itself to be the opposite of the genuine Church spirit; no better than a solemn lie, in truth, which has crept into its place; and the voice of the Church, even, afar off, falls upon it always like the sound of its own death warrant. Sects, as such, cannot love the Church.

We cannot pretend here, of course, to notice in detail, the mischievous results of our Sect system, as they are made to surround us from day to day in its actual operation. They stare us in the face, from all sides. The marks of Antichrist, as already described in this tract, have not been derived from mere theory or speculation. They are a transcript simply of forms of life, that can easily be recognized in every direction, as the legitimate fruit of this evil. In the midst of our more respectable denominations, there are widely extended developments of the Sect life, which all these unite in condemning as hurtful and false; developments, which must be regarded as involving a total and fatal rupture with the proper Christian consciousness, as embodied in. the idea of the Church. Vast multitudes, in this way, would seem to be left, by such false connections, without a ministry and without sacraments altogether, or at least in a state of most precarious uncertainty and question with regard to so great a point. For all this, however, the system as a whole is fairly responsible; since, as we have seen, it carries in itself no principle of limitation on the side towards schism, but tends rather, by obliterating all proper church feeling to encourage the imagination that any Sect, however upstart and wild, is just as much of a Church as another. And then under its more respectable forms themselves, we need not be told how sadly the spirit in question is found to pollute and mar, on all sides, the fair face of our general Christian profession. Not only, as before said, are our Sects egotistically sundered from one another in their inward life; each trying and pretending to be a whole Christianity, which it is not, and never can be, in fact; but this disjunction takes necessarily also the character of rivalry and conflict. Not in the way of zeal now commonly for confessional doctrine and testimony; *that* has become in a great measure quiet; possibly renegade to its old faith; but with the spirit of mere clique or party, selfishly wedded to the authority of its own name. Most of our Sects at least, are no longer "confessions" at all, but ecclesiastical corporations simply, bent on their own outward prosperity and aggrandizement. So they press and rub each other, with constant unpleasant collision, in all their movements. Their activity for God's glory and the salvation of souls, takes the form of competition and strife. Even the holy cause of "revivals" itself, is desecrated to party ends. Different interests in business and trade are not more thoroughly divided, than are these different interests in religion, in every town and village throughout the land. Ordinary political parties show themselves just as much capable of common sympathy and mutual toleration; for *their* jealousies and animosities can sleep too, when the heat of some angry "campaign" has been passed, and fanaticism sinks exhausted into the arms of silent bigotry. The charity which "rejoiceth not in iniquity, but in the truth," reigns not in the relations of Sects. It is not as in the case of the natural body, where "the members have the same care one for another; and whether one member suffer, all the members suffer with it; or one member be honored, all the members rejoice with it:" but every one finds rather a secret satisfaction in the calamities of the rest, and is moved with secret envy at their prosperity. The loving harmony of different Sects in the same place, forms, we all see, not the rule but the exception, and is for the most part a band which the lightest breeze can snap asunder.

How indeed should it be otherwise? The Sect life *must* affect to be a full Church life, and cannot possibly prosecute its own supposed mission, in this form, with any sort of earnest zeal, without becoming in some way exclusive and aggressive. Here, for instance, is a new village of a thousand or fifteen hundred souls, in the far West. A single church and one faithful pastor, would be amply sufficient for all its spiritual wants. It has already perhaps two distinct congregations, acknowledging each other as evangelical and true churches. But there is a portion of "material," that does not exactly belong to either; and soon accordingly, we have an effort to establish two or three additional chapels, each floating a new sectarian banner, brought thither by missionary activity on the part of so many different ecclesiastical bodies, which feel themselves bound in consistency, to push their own denominational "interest" into every nook and corner of the land. The five Sects thus struggling to keep foot on ground, broad enough only for the use of one, can never abide in true amity and love. Each is doomed, by inward necessity, to resist and undermine as much as possible all the rest. Alas, how fares it with all the sweet graces of the real Christian life, in such a case? Need we carry out the picture, in order to make it felt in the full measure of its unloveliness? But now that western village is only a naked revelation of the necessary working of the Sect spirit, latent if not overt, all the world over. Its natural and legitimate fruits, are those of the flesh only, and not those of the Spirit. Talk of its incidental advantages, its unhallowed rivalries and emulations *overruled* of God for good! The very thought, if employed to palliate the abomination, is profane. It belongs to the slang of the same ecclesiastical radicalism, which under a still lower form of thinking, would persuade us that temperance societies, mutual insurance fraternities, and other such schemes of moral utilitarianism, may safely be trusted to do the high work of Christ's one, Holy, Catholic Church. Worst of all, in this way, the sense of religion is itself blunted and its whole theory converted into falsehood. An unchurchly theology can never be rich and deep; and it lies in the very nature of the case also, that an unchurchly piety must be always more or less unsymmetrical and unfree, if not absolutely a harsh parody upon its own name. Sect religion can show itself pure and strong, only by rising with inward effort, above its proper native sphere. Remaining in this sphere, its tendency is always to run into pedantry, hypocrisy and cant.

After this review of the general misery comprehended in our reigning Sect system, we are prepared to notice in conclusion its proper REMEDY.

It will be seen at once, of course, that we have no sympathy whatever with those who imagine that all which is wanted here, is the violent overthrow in any way of outward denominational distinctions, as they now stand. We wage no crusade against Sects, in this form. Of what avail would it be to strike all of them dead at a single blow, if the Sect life be left still in force, ready to sprout forth into new similar creations the next day? Such merely negative destructional opposition to Sects, is itself necessarily sectarian also in its very constitution, and call only issue at best accordantly in some new *no-sect* Sect, which is likely to be as narrow and rabid in its own way, as any of the rest.*

Just as little can we make common cause, with those who make the idea of catholicity to consist in a certain liberality, which shows itself indifferent at last to all religious distinctions, and overcomes the Sect consciousness by bringing it to dissolve simply in the sense of our life as a mere natural whole. Here, as before, the process of reconciliation is wholly negative and destructional; it surrenders, so far as it may prevail, the positive substance of Christianity, and lands us in a unity, which is the mere show of truth and faith, without their power. Against such spurious catholicity, often like an angel of light, we have need to stand constantly upon our guard. Caricature as the Sect life always is of the true life of the Church, it still involves at bottom some apprehension of a positive new creation in Christ Jesus, which as such must needs be exclusive in order to be really catholic; and this, in any case, is something better than the "liberal Christianity," that in giving up the caricature parts also with the

---

*Witness the sect of the "Christians," as they call themselves, in the West, the "Campbellites" or "Disciples of Christ," the "Church of God," as founded a few years since by John Winebrenner, &c. All these agree, in casting off creeds and tradition, and going back to the Bible. That is, they are absolutely unhistorical; and for this very reason their pretended catholicity has no contents or substance whatever.

idea of the Church itself, and becomes universal only by including nothing.

Equally plain is it, however, that no faith is to be reposed in the dream of any thing like a free construction of catholic unity, by counsel and compact, among the different Sects themselves. To think of their ever consenting to merge their existence in a new common church organization, would be, of course, perfectly extravagant. Every Sect has power to multiply its own bad life, like the polypus, by new sections and slips; but no single two of them, it seems, have a way of full organic power to come together again, in the way of full organic union. In this aspect, the system offers no hope for the future, but a prospect only of blank despair. The most to be expected from it, then, would be, an outward federal union of Sects, leaving each to its present independence, with some loose covenant and creed to represent the whole. But such a confederation, could it be made real, would be no Church; so far as this conception might continue to have force, it would remain bound only to the separate Sects as such. And, who may not see, that in the very nature of any such transaction, the Sect consciousness is left to assert throughout its own supremacy over the sense of the Church, something more wide than itself? It is just like the French Convention of Jacobin memory, after the prostration of throne and altar, legislating into authority the existence of a "Supreme Being!" The Sects here, in solemn parliament assembled, each fully persuaded of its own indefeasible sovereignty and power, undertake to create a universal Church; not fully sure, indeed, whether there *be* any Holy Catholic Church, in the sense of the ancient creed; but honestly minded, at all events, to bring something of the sort to pass, if God so please, and then see how it will work. But what is all this, less than an impudent affectation, of mastering the Church consciousness, into base subordination to the Sect consciousness, and making the *whole* thus to be the mere creature of its own parts? Every such pretension is systematic and uncatholic in its very nature; and so far as it may ever prevail, runs out necessarily into the same merely indifferentistic liberalism which we have already noticed. Nothing is more easy or common than the union of such false catholicity, in one aspect, with the full bigotry of Sect in another.* They belong to the same general sphere; different sides, only, of the antichristian life; the Gentile consciousness and that of the Jew, playing into each other for self-support, with equal wrong on both sides to the mystery of the one universal Church, as constituted and revealed in Jesus Christ.

---

*It will be remembered easily, that the bodies which showed themselves most forward and active in the movement of the late World Convention, were those precisely which, in their general character and spirit, are known, on all hands, to be the most violently unhistorical and sectarian.

We have no hesitation, then, in saying, that all redemption from the power of the Sect plague, must begin with a revival of true and hearty faith, in the ancient article of ONE, HOLY, CATHOLIC CHURCH.

The idea of the Church, in the first place, is the only effective measure of schism. It is to this, precisely, what the moral law is to the conception of sin. Where there is no law, we are told, there is no sin; the sense of the last springs only from the sense of the first. So, where there is no Church, there can be no schism; no proper apprehension of it, at least, where it may prevail in fact. As long as men are disposed to deny the existence of one catholic Church, or to place it in the clouds merely as an invisible abstraction, or to substitute for it the negation and shadow of a simply ethnic brotherhood, it must be in vain to preach to them the evils of division and schism. They can have, at best, only a partial conception of their nature, and will not be engaged, of course, to put forth any strenuous desire or effort after deliverance.

This, plainly, is our prevailing state at the present time. We talk of the necessity of Christian love and union, and see to some extent the misery of our sectarianism; but still we seem satisfied in general, notwithstanding, to abide in the present system, as on the whole necessary and good. It is attended with no painful sense of schism, as necessarily involved in our divisions themselves. It is hard, oftentimes, to say precisely what this old ecclesiastical term signifies to our minds. No Sect, as such, can make any effective protest against the position of any other, as schismatic; for, in the very nature of the case, it can have no objective rule or measure to appeal to, that is any broader than its own Sect consciousness itself. But the consciousness of one Sect, in this view, is just of as much authority as that of another. And so it comes to pass, that men feel themselves, for the most part, free to act in Church matters as they please. To quit a Church connection, once viewed even in the Protestant world as a most solemn thing, is now regarded very much as a simple change of residence; it is simply to pass from one Sect over to another, which belongs as much to the Church general as that which has been left behind. In the same way, ecclesiastical privileges are shorn of their value, and ecclesiastical penalties of their proper weight. It is hard to make any body feel that there is the slightest danger of getting out of the Church, so as to have no true ministry and no true sacraments, in any sort of nominally Christian society. Such account of ordinances is treated as, at all events, no better than superstition. Few seem to have the least fear of schism, if only they can lay claim, in their own way, to the Bible and God's Spirit. And the reigning Church sentiment, even with the more regular denominations, is such as to countenance in full this sad delusion. The Sect mind, stopping short of all true Church consciousness, can never, under its most respectable forms, administer any potent rebuke to the spirit in question. It is involved always in the same condemnation. It has no hearty faith itself in the Church; and how then can it so speak as to infuse any such faith into others?

The only help here, it should be clear, is in the general resuscitation of a sound Church feeling, as something deeper and more comprehensive than the feeling of Sect. Let this wake into life, to some proper extent, and it would be of more force to stem the course of sectarian fanaticism in a short time, than long years of argument and testimony exhibited in our present state. No one would think then, of vindicating our Sect system, as the ultimate and normal order of Christianity; but all must feel themselves bound to condemn it, and to mourn over it, as a captivity to the iron reign of schism, with longing anticipation of the day when God shall happily bring it to an end.

And so again, it is only by the force of such resuscitated faith in the Church, in the second place, that the way can be opened at all for any return out of this bondage, into the land of true catholicity and peace. It requires, surely, no very deep reflection, to perceive the force of this proposition. The Sect consciousness, as such, can never bring men beyond its own sphere; can never lead them into the clear knowledge of the Church, and of course still less into its full life. All this must come from a different quarter, the living apprehension namely of the idea of the Church itself, as an objective reality in the world.

For it will be observed, that we speak throughout of the catholic Church as an object of *faith*, which in this view must be regarded as something at once supernatural and real. So it is exhibited to us in the Creed. It is not a mere notion, or abstraction, or subjective creation of the human mind, in any form; but includes in itself an objective being, as we have seen, no less real and abiding than the person of Christ himself, from which it starts. This it is, precisely, that makes the great difference between spurious ethnic catholicity, as exhibited to us in world conventions, or mere stage displays, and catholicity under its genuine form. The first holds only in the region of natural thought and feeling, and disturbs not necessarily, in the least, the inward habit of the Sect mind from which it springs; to admit the existence of a Holy Catholic Church, in such a case, is no more than to admit the existence of a British Parliament, or in American congress, or the authority of what is called the command of law in both countries. But the other stands in faith, whose very nature it is to mould the consciousness of its subject into the form of its object; and having this form, of course it must necessarily require the Sect mind to give way before the power of the deeper life which is thus made to take its place.

And here we may see, at once, the vanity of the plea, which is sometimes urged against all faith in a real Church, that we are not able to point out clearly its external form, in the history of the world, in such a way as to cut off all cavil; as well as the falsehood of the position sometimes taken by Sects, that the first step needed towards catholic unity, is to make out satisfactorily some plan or scheme, to which the parties may then jointly agree as suited to secure this object. Every such thought, however, plausible as it may appear, virtually denies the Church to be any object of faith whatever, and converts it from the start into an object of mere sense or natural ratiocination. *Show* us the Church, say the sects, and it sufficeth us; but to what can all homilies on the subject of catholicity and schism amount, so long as you are unable to mark out any door of escape from the present evil? Most plausible certainly, but at the same time sophistical and false. For is not this, palpably, to place in question the reality of the Holy Catholic Church altogether, as an objective supernatural fact, in the sense of the ancient Creed? The catholic Church is a *mystery*, in the sense of the Creed, just like its other articles, which as such is to be apprehended primarily by faith, and *not* in the way of intelligence. It does not, of course, exclude intelligence, as this is not done either by the article of the incarnation; faith is not blind here or slavish: but it is the necessary form of access, in the first place, to the object of knowledge. As springing not from ourselves, but from abroad, and under a supernatural character, this must be brought nigh to us, by faith, as a divine reality, before it can be understood. To put intelligence before faith, here as elsewhere, is just what we mean by rationalism. The conception of a Church to be manufactured by the Sect mind, enthroned for the time as the higher power, called to sit in judgment on its claims, is itself an infidel absurdity. As well pretend to construct, in the same *ab extra* way, the mystery of the incarnation, before surrendering the soul, by faith, to the power of the fact! Jesus Christ authenticates himself. And so it is, with the mystery of the Church. It must overwhelm our inward consciousness first, with its own objective force as a necessary result from the great Christological fact itself, in order that it may come to right revelation subsequently in the sphere of thought and outward life. It is not necessary at all, that the full contents of the article should be at once in our view, to allow the complete exercise of such faith. Peter's confession: "Thou art the Christ, the Son of the living God!" carried in itself in truth, potentially, the whole sense of the Apostles' Creed, though with no insight of his, at the time, into the several articles of this, as afterwards evolved from its bosom. And just so, we may have a true faith in the article of the One, Holy, Catholic Church, while yet most incompetent, in our own minds, to estimate, in full, the terms and conditions under which it may be required to manifest itself in the world. Such faith does not turn primarily on the presence of the Church, as a given corporation accredited by outward seal, but on the idea of Christianity itself, as necessarily requiring this constitution to make itself complete. Not only the word of Christ, but his life, demands its presence. The article flows forth, with inward necessity, from the Christological mystery itself. To stand in the full sense of this, as the fact of a new order or life made originally permanent in the world, is to have the reality of the Holy Catholic Church, at the same time, actually at hand also as a part of our creed. The reality, in this case, is no mere notion or shadow, but a true divine object, apprehended by faith; and the consciousness which springs from it is something far more accordingly than the hollow, negative catholicity of Gentile unbelief; it is the sense of such wholeness as belongs to the positive life of Christianity itself.

With such objective, historical being in the world, as this faith implies, the Church of course is no abstraction. Its existence is concrete, and its attributes are determined by its constitution. Still its revelation is a process, in the course of which wide room is found for the actual and the ideal to fall asunder. In these circumstances, all may be said to turn on the presence of such a sound Church consciousness as is now described. It is from this alone, that all catholic ideas must flow; and in virtue of it only, can they ever be brought to take form in actual life.

Let no one say or think then, that it amounts to little to insist upon faith in the Church itself, as the most necessary remedy for the Sect plague, which now afflicts our Protestant Christianity. We come here at once to the ground-cause of the plague itself, which all may see to be the reigning want of such faith, in the form now described; and it is plain, that until this be in some measure removed, no other palliative or help can be of much avail. What can well be more preposterous indeed, than to aim at catholic unity without being fully persuaded that it is any thing more than a dream, or to treat the Church as a mere *hypothesis* in the first place, in order to test the possibility of bringing it to pass! Are the articles of the Creed, then, to be taken in the way of experiment? Are the great verities of the new creation so many problems to be solved, or theorems to be demonstrated, before we can yield to their authority as true? Can a genuine Church consciousness ever grow forth from the power of the Sect mind, however large and free in its own more narrow sphere? Take the ground, that the Sect-mind is itself a true Church-mind, that the Church, in any whole view, is an abstraction only, which need never become visible, or that we can have nothing to do with it properly, in any different light, till it has resolved itself into some tangible case, whose merits we can then canvas and decide upon in an outward way; approach the subject, we say, in any such style as this, and it is clear that all the interest we may take in it, must come to nothing in the end. What we need to start with is the sense of catholicity itself, "faith in the mystery of one universal historical Church," and the felt power of old catholic ideas as we find them reigning in the ancient Christian world. It cannot be disguised, that a wide-spread hostility prevails towards these ideas themselves, and not simply towards the abuses into which they may have been run by the Church of Rome. So long as this is the case, there can be no honest care or concern for Church unity. These catholic ideas are not arbitrary or accidental; they form the necessary outbirth of a true Church life; and to refuse them their proper honor, is of itself to do homage always to the spirit of Sect as a higher power? Only as such feeling gives way before the sense of Christ's one universal Church, and room is made thus for true inward sympathy with catholic ideas, may we hope at all to understand or settle satisfactorily, the questions involved in the restoration of our present captivity. Faith in the Church is not of itself all that the case requires; but it is the first and greatest thing, that must open the way for all ulterior counsel and action; and it is worse than idle to prate sentimentally of our good purposes, in its absence. Half of our Sects would be at once dissolved by it, like mists before the rising sun; while the field of division and debate, among the rest, would be narrowed to less than half its present dimensions; and, in the distance at least, would be seen rising, to the fond vision of hope, the glorious one catholic CHURCH OF THE FUTURE, as the praise, and joy, and glory of the whole earth.

CATHOLIC UNITY

John W. Nevin's sermon, "Catholic Unity," preached at the Triennial Convention of the German and Dutch Reformed Churches in 1844, was revised and published, at the request of the author, as an appendix to Nevin's translation of Philip Schaff's The Principle of Protestantism as Related to the Present State of the Church *(Chambersburg, Pa.: Publication Office of the German Reformed Church, 1845), pp. 193–215. It replaced an extended excerpt of the sermon published in the original German edition. In this final version, Nevin added notes proving definitively his assertions about the Protestant reformers' theology of the Eucharist.*

CATHOLIC UNITY;

A sermon delivered at the opening of the Triennial Convention of the Reformed Protestant Dutch and German Reformed Churches, at Harrisburg, Pa., August 8th, 1844.

BY REV. JOHN W. NEVIN, D.D.

Eph. IV. 4–6.—*There is one body and one Spirit, even as ye are called in one hope of your calling; one Lord, one faith, one Baptism; one God and Father of all, who is above all, and through all, and in you all.*

This is the image of the CHURCH, as delineated by the hand of the inspired Apostle. In the whole world, we find nothing so resplendently beautiful and glorious, under any other form. The picture is intended to enforce the great duty of charity and peace, among those who bear the Christian name. In the preceding part of the epistle, Christ is exhibited as the end of all separation and strife to them that believe, and the author of a new spiritual creation, in which all former distinctions were to be regarded as swallowed up and abolished forever. Reference is had in this representation primarily to the old division of Jew and Gentile; but in its true spirit and sense, it is plainly as comprehensive as humanity itself, and looks therefore directly to every other distinction of the same sort, that ever has been or ever shall be known in the world. Christianity is the universal solvent, in which all opposites are required to give up their previous affinities, no matter how old and stubborn, and flow together in a new combination, pervaded with harmony only and light at every point. "In Christ Jesus, neither circumcision availeth anything, not uncircumcision, but a new creature." "Those who were far off, are made nigh by his blood." "He is our peace, who hath made both one, and hath broken down the middle wall of partition between us; making in himself of twain one new man." In him, all spiritual antagonism among men is subverted. The human world is reconciled first with God, and then with itself, by entering with living consciousness into the ground of its own life as revealed in his person. Such is the idea of the Church, which is "the body of Christ, the fullness of Him that filleth all in all." And now at length, passing from doctrine to practice, the Apostle calls upon those to whom he wrote to surrender themselves fully to the claims of this exalted constitution. "I therefore, the prisoner of the Lord beseech you, that ye walk worthy of the vocation wherewith ye are called. With all lowliness and meekness, with long-suffering, forbearing one another in love; endeavoring to keep the unity of the Spirit in the bond of peace." Such a temper, and such a life, are necessarily included in the very conception of the Church, as here described. "There is one body and one Spirit, even as ye are called in one hope of your calling; one Lord, one faith, one Baptism; one God and Father of all, who is above all, and through all, and in you all." He does not say, *Let* there be one body and one Spirit, as simply urging Christians to seek such agreement among themselves as might justify this view of their state; but the fact is assumed as already in existence, and is made the ground accordingly of the exhortation that goes before. There is one body and Spirit, and *therefore* are ye bound to keep the unity of the Spirit in the bond of peace. The unity of the Church is not something which results first from the thought and purpose of the vast membership, of which it is composed; but on the contrary, it is the ground out of which this membership itself springs, and in which perpetually it stands, and from which it must derive evermore all its harmony, and stability, and activity, and strength.

From the beginning, this great truth has dwelt deep in the consciousness of the Christian world. Through all ages, and in all lands, that consciousness has been uttering itself as with one mouth, in the article of the creed, *I believe in the Holy Catholic Church*. The Church is one and universal. Her unity is essential to her existence. Particular Christians, and particular congregations, and particular religious denominations, can be true to themselves, only as they stand in the full, free sense of this thought, and make it the object of their calling to fulfil its requisitions. The manifold is required to feel itself one. All particularism here must be false, that seeks to maintain itself as such, in proportion exactly as it is found in conflict with the general and universal, as embraced in the true idea of the body of Christ.

I propose to consider, in the further prosecution of the subject at this time, *first*, the Nature and Constitution of the Holy Catholic Church, in the view now stated; and *secondly*, the Duty of Christians as it regards the unity, by which it is declared to be thus Catholic, and holy, and true.

I. *We are to consider the Nature of* CATHOLIC UNITY, *as comprehended constitutionally in the idea of the Christian Church.*

Unity does not exclude the idea of difference and multiplicity. Indeed it is only by means of these, that it can ever appear under an actual, concrete form. Where the one does not carry in itself the possibility of separation and distinction, it can never be more than a sheer abstraction, an absolute nullity. The idea of oneness, however, does require that the different and the manifold as comprehended in it, should be in principle the same, and that all should be held together by the force of this principle actively felt at every point. Such is the unity of the Christian Church. It is composed of a vast number of individual members; but these are all actuated by the power of a common life, and the whole of this life gathers itself up ultimately or fundamentally in the person of Jesus Christ. He is the principle or root of the Church; and the Church through all ages is one, simply because it stands, in the presence and power of this root, universally and forever.*

Every Christian, as such, is the subject of a new spiritual life, that did not belong to him in his natural state. This is in no sense from himself; for that which is born of the flesh, is flesh, and cannot be cultivated into any higher character. Only that which is born of the Spirit, is spirit. The Christian has his life from Christ. He is not only placed in a new relation to the law, by the imputation of the Savior's righteousness to him in an outward forensic way; but a new nature is imparted to him also, by an actual communication of the Savior's life over into his person. In his regeneration, he is inwardly united to Christ, by the power of the Holy Ghost, and thus brought within the sphere of that "law of the Spirit of life," by which in the end the "law of sin and death" is overpowered and destroyed in all them that believe. A divine seed is implanted in him, the germ of a new existence, which is destined gradually to grow and gather strength, till the whole man shall be at last fully transformed into its image. The new nature thus introduced is the nature of Christ, and it continues to be his nature through the whole course of its development, onward to the last day. The believer has indeed a separate individual existence; but his existence has its ground in the life of Christ, just as in any other case the individual begins at first and stands always afterwards, in the force of the generic nature to which it belongs. His sanctification does not consist in his being engaged simply to copy the excellencies of Christ, as a man might admire and copy the character of a Moses or a Paul; but it consists in this, that the very life of the Lord Jesus is found reaching over into his person, and gradually transfusing it with its own heavenly force. The old nature is not at once destroyed; but the new nature of Christ is inclosed in it, as the papilio in the folds of the chrysalis, and in due time this last must triumph over the first entirely, leaving it behind as an empty sepulchre in the final resurrection. Thus emphatically, Christ and the believer are one. Because I live, we hear him say, ye shall live also. He that is joined to the Lord is one Spirit.

This mystical union, as it is sometimes termed, is much more strict, there is reason to believe, than is commonly imagined. There is none on earth more intimate and inward. It is real and close as the union which binds the branches to the trunk of the vine. It forms such a bond, as holds between the members and the head of the same natural body. "Except ye

---

**Incorporari* enim (ut ita loquar) nos Christo oportet primum, ut inter nos uniamur. *Calvin*, on I Cor. x. 16.

eat the flesh of the Son of Man," Christ himself has said, "and drink his blood, ye have no life in you. Whoso eateth my flesh and drinketh my blood, hath eternal life, and I will raise him up at the last day. For my flesh is meat indeed, and my blood is drink indeed. He that eateth my flesh and drinketh my blood, dwelleth in me, and I in him. As the living Father hath sent me, and I live by the Father, so he that eateth me, even he shall live by me." This is indeed figurative language; but if it have any meaning at all, it teaches that the union of the believer with Christ is not simply moral, the harmony of purpose, thought and feeling, but substantial and real, involving oneness of nature. "We are members of his body, of his flesh, and of his bones.*

This may sound mystical; but after all it is no more difficult to comprehend than the fact of our union to the same extent with the person of the first Adam. As descended from him by natural generation, we are not only like him in outward form and inward spirit, but we participate truly and properly in his very nature. We are members of his body, of his flesh, and of his bones. His humanity, soul and body, has passed over into our persons. And so it is in the case of the second Adam, as it regards the truly regenerate. They are inserted into his life, through faith, by the power of the Holy Ghost, and become thus incorporated with it, as fully as they were before with that corrupt life they had by their natural birth. The whole humanity of Christ, soul and body, is carried over by the process of the Christian salvation into the person of the believer; so that in the end his glorified body, no less than his glorified soul, will appear as the natural and necessary product of the life, in which he is thus made to participate.† His resurrection is only his regeneration, fully revealed at

---

*The passage, Eph. v. 30, with its whole connection, is very wonderful. Rationalizing commentators of course endeavor to turn it into mere sound or figure; with violence however to the entire spirit of the text as well as its letter. *Calvin* is clear upon it, and strong. The language, he tells us is not hyperbolical, but simple. Nor does it refer to Christ's general participation of the human nature, but to something more emphatic in his relation to his people. As Eve was formed form the side of Adam, and was thus a part of himself, so we are made members of Christ by coalescing into one body with him through a participation of his substance. The power of this truth is exhibited to us in the Lord's Supper, which the apostle has here in his mind. "Totum autem ex eo pendet, quod uxor ex carne et ex ossibus viri formata est; eadem ergo unionis inter nos et Christum ratio, quod se quodammodo in nos transfundit. Neque enim ossa sumus ex ossibus ejus et caro ex carne, quia ipse nobiscum est homo; sed quia Spiritus sui virtute nos in corpus suum inserit, ut vitam ex eo hauriamus."

†Carnem ergo Christi, sine ullis ambagibus, fatemur esse vivificam; non tantum quia semel in ea nobis salus parta est, sed quia nunc dum sacra unitate cum Christo coalescimus, eadem illa caro vitam in nos spirat, vel ut brevius dicam, quia arcana Spiritus virtute in Christi corpus insiti, communem habemus cum ipso vitam. *Calvin, Consens. de Re Sacram. Opp. Tom.* IX (*Amsterdam Ed.* 1667) p. 657.—Jam quis non videt, communionem carnis et sanguinis Christi necessariam esse omnibus, qui ad coelestem vitam aspirant? Huc spectant illae Apostoli sententiae (Ephes.1: 23, et 4: 15,) Ecclesiam corpus esse Christi et

last and complete. Our life now is hid with Christ in God; but when he appeareth, then shall we also appear with him in glory. The Christian is spoken of at times accordingly, as already the subject of all that has been reached in the personal life of the Savior. He is not only dead with him, but risen also, and exalted along with him at the right hand of God. This representation rests throughout upon the fact, that his life is grounded in the life of Christ, and so includes potentially all that belongs to this from the beginning.

The idea of this inward union on the part of the believer with the entire humanity of Christ, has in all ages entered deeply into the consciousness of the Church. Hence no doubt much of the favor which has been shown toward the popish and semipopish errors, in the case of the Lord's Supper. Hence too the earnestness, with which the reformers generally maintained the doctrine of the real presence in this sacrament. They saw and felt, more clearly than many of their followers seem to see and feel now, that the life of the believer involves a communion with the body of Christ, as well as with his spirit. Calvin is particularly strong with regard to this point; and some have found it hard to find any sense whatever in his language on the subject.* But after all there is no greater

---

ejus complementum, ipsum vero esse caput, ex quo totum corpus coagmentatum et compactam per commissuras, incrementum corporis facit; corpora nostra membra esse Christi (1 Cor. 6: 15.). Quae omnia non posse aliter effici intelligimus, quin totus *spiritu et corpore* nobis adhaereat. Sed arctissimam illam societatem, qua ejus corni copulamur, splendidiore adhuc elogio illustravit, quum dixit, nos esse membra corporis ejus ex ossibus ejus et ex carne ejus (Ephes. 5: 30.). Tandem ut rem omnibus verbis majorem testatur, sermonem exclamatione finit, Magnum (inquit) istud arcanum! Extremae ergo dementiae fuerit, nullam agnoscere cum carne et sanguine Domini fidelium communionem, quam tantam esse declarat Apostolus, ut eam admirari, quam explicare malit. *Instit.* IV. 17. 9.

*Dr. Dick (*Lectures on Theology,*) though of no great weight in himself may be taken perhaps as a pretty fair representative of this prevailing modern view, when he says (*Lect.* XCI,) after giving a quotation from Calvin: "I confess I do not understand this passage. It supposes a communion of believers in the human nature of our Savior in the Eucharist, and endeavors to remove the objection arising from the distance of place, by a reference to the Almighty power of the Spirit, much in the same way as Papists and Lutherans solve the difficulty attending their respective systems. If Calvin had meant only that, in the Sacred Supper, believers have fellowship with Christ in his death, he would have asserted an important truth, attested by the experience of the people of God in every age; but why did he obscure it, and destroy its simplicity, by involving it in ambiguous language? If he had anything different in view; if he meant that there is some mysterious communication with his human nature, we must be permitted to say that the notion was as incomprehensible to himself as it is to his readers." That Calvin did entertain this last "notion," there is not the least room to doubt; and as may be seen in the foregoing note, he held it to be insane (*extremae dementiae*) to have any other opinion. The view accepted by Dr. Dick, from Zwingli, he went so far as to call *profane*. He is most distinct in rejecting the idea, that the union of the believer with Christ is simply *moral*. To partake of Christ's body and blood is not merely to *believe* on him, but a mystical process which is the result of faith. Nor is it simply to appropriate his *merits*. "Excipit Westphalus, merita Christi vel beneficia non esse ejus corpus. Sed cur locutionem, qua splendide nostram cum Christo communionem

darkness in it, than is presented by Paul when he says, We are members of his body, of his flesh, and of his bones. Thus also we are taught in the Heidelbergh Catechism, that to eat the crucified body and drink the shed blood of Christ, is "not only to embrace with a believing heart all the sufferings and death of Christ, and thereby to obtain the pardon of sin and life eternal; but also, besides that, to become more and more united to his sacred body, by the Holy Ghost, who dwells both in Christ and in us; so that we, though Christ is in heaven and we on earth, are notwithstanding, flesh of his flesh, and bone of his bone; and that we live and are governed forever by one Spirit, as members of the same body are by one soul."

Partaking in this way of one and the same life, Christians of course are vitally related and joined together as one great spiritual whole; and this whole is the Church. The Church is his body, the fulness of Him that filleth all in all. The union by which it is held together, through all ages, is strictly *organic*. The Church is not a mere aggregation or collection of different individuals, drawn together by similarity or interests and wants; not an abstraction simply, by which the common in the midst of such multifarious distinction, is separated and put together under a single general term. It is not merely the *all* that covers the actual extent of its membership, but the *whole* rather in which this membership is comprehended and determined from the beginning. The Church does not rest

---

commendo maligne extenuat? Neque enim tantum dico applicare merita, sed ex ipso Christi corpore alimentum percipere animas, non secus ac terreno pane corpus vescitur." *Opp. Tom.* IX. p. 668. Nor is it enough with him to say, we partake of Christ's Spirit. "Neque enim simpliciter Spiritu suo Christum in nobis habitare trado, sed ita nos ad se attollere, ut vivificum carnis suae vigorem in nos transfundat." *Ibid.* p. 669. He will hear of nothing less than a participation of Christ's substance, soul and body: "Carnem Christi nobis edendam proponi siquis sincere et luculente tradit, ego unus sum ex numero; modum tantum definio, quod Spiritus sui virtute Christus locorum distantiam superet, ad vitam nobis e sua carne inspirandam." *Ibid.* p. 670. "In sacra sua Coena jubet me sub symbolis panis ac vini corpus ac sanguinem suum sumere, manducare ac bibere; nihil dubito, quin et ipse vere porrigat et ego recipiam." *Inst.* IV. 17. 32. It is useless however to multiply extracts. Calvin's doctrine on this point is in no respect uncertain. Nor was he singular at all in his view. It was in fact the established view of the entire Reformed Church, in the Sixteenth Century; for the bald theory of Zwingli outraged the religious consciousness of the age. "There is no controversy among us," says Zanchius, "whether the bread in the right use of the Supper be truly the body of Christ; the only question is concerning the manner in which the bread is his body." All the Reformed Confessions speak in the same strain. The *Belgic Confession*, for instance, after telling us that the mode of the communication is incomprehensible, does not hesitate, insisting still upon the reality of it as it had been previously affirmed, to employ the strong expression: "Interea vero nequaquam erraverimus dicentes, id, quod comeditur, esse proprium et naturale corpus Christi, idque quod bibimur, proprium ejus sanguinem." Those who choose to do so, may pour contempt on all this as the "obsolete mysticism of the Reformers." But such would do well at the same time to consider seriously, whether in departing from the orthodoxy of the Sixteenth Century at this point, they may not have yielded their own minds possibly to the power of a rationalizing element, which if it were rigidly pushed to its consequences could hardly stop short of Socinianism itself.

upon its members, but the members rest upon the Church. Individual Christianity is not something older than general Christianity, but the general in this case goes before the particular, and rules and conditions all its manifestations. So it is with every organic nature. The whole is older and deeper than the parts; and these last spring forth perpetually from the active presence of the first. The parts in the end are only the revelation of what was previously included in the whole. The oak of a hundred years, and the acorn from which it has sprung, are the same life. All that we behold in the oak, lay hid in the acorn from the start. So too the human world all slept originally in the common root of the race. Adam was not simply *a* man, like others since born; but he was *the* man, who comprehended in himself all that has since appeared in other men. Humanity as a whole resided in his person. He was strictly and truly the world. Through all ages, man is organically one and the same. And parallel with this precisely is the constitution of the Church. The second Adam corresponds in all respects with the first. He is not a man merely, an individual belonging to the race; but he is *the* man, emphatically the *Son of Man*, comprising in his person the new creation, or humanity recovered and redeemed, as a whole. Whatever the Church becomes in they way of development, it can never be more in fact than it was in him from the beginning. Its life is not multiplied nor extended in quantity, by its growth. Christ is the root of the Church; and to the end of time it can include no more in its proper life, however widely distributed, than what is included in the root itself.

The unity of the Church then is a cardinal truth, in the Christian system. It is involved in the conception of the Christian salvation itself. To renounce it, or lose sight of it, is to make shipwreck of the gospel, to the same extent. There is no room here for individualism or particularism, as such. An individual dissociated entirely from his race, would cease to be a man. And just so the conception of individual or particular Christianity, as something independent of the organic whole, which we denominate the Church, is a moral solecism that necessarily destroys itself. Christ cannot be divided. The members of the natural body are united to the head, only by belonging to the body itself. Separated from this, they cease to have any proper existence. And so it is here. We are not Christians, each one by himself and for himself, but we become such through the Church. Christ lives in his people, by the life which fills his body, the Church; and they are thus all necessarily one, before they can be many.*

---

*Nec vero satis est electorum turbam cogitatione et animoque complecti, nisi talem ecclesiae unitatem cogitemus, in quam nos esse insitos vere simus persuasi. Nisi enim sub capite nostro Christo coadunati simus reliquis omnibus membris, nulla nobis manet spes haereditatis futurae. Ideo *Catholica* dicitur, seu universalis; quis non duas aut tres invenire

The life of Christ in the Church, is in the first place inward and invisible. But to be real, it must also become outward. The salvation of the individual believer is not complete, till the body is transfigured and made glorious, as well as the soul; and as it has respect to the whole nature of man from the commencement, it can never go forward at all except by a union of the outward and inward at every point of its progress. Thus too the Church must be visible, as well as invisible. In no other way can the idea become real. Soul and body, inward power and outward form, are required here to go together. Outward forms without inward life can have no saving force. But neither can inward life be maintained, on the other hand, without outward forms. The body is not the man; and yet there can be no man, where there is no body. Humanity is neither a corpse on the one hand, nor a phantom on the other. The Church then must appear externally, in the world. And the case requires that this manifestation should correspond with the inward constitution of the idea itself. It belongs to the proper conception of it, that the unity of the Holy Catholic Church should appear in an outward and visible way; and it can never be regarded as complete, where such development of its inward power is still wanting. "There is one *body*," the Apostle tells us, "and one Spirit, even as ye are called in one hope of your calling." Such is the true normal character of the Church; and so far as it may fall short of this it labors under serious defect.

The Apostle does not mean to affirm however, that the want of such outward and visible unity necessarily and at once overthrows the existence of the Church. It is seldom that the actual, in the sphere of Christianity, fully corresponds with the ideal. And as a general thing, this correspondence, so far as it may be secured in any case, is reached only in a gradual way. The inward requires time to impress its image fully upon the outward. Religion is a process in the individual soul, and also in the life of the Church. Objectively considered, it is complete, and harmonious, and true to itself at every point, from the beginning; but in becoming subjective, all this may seem for a season to fail. The life of Christ in the Church includes in itself potentially from the first, all that it can ever become in the end. But it may happen that for a long time this hidden force shall be embarrassed and repressed by untoward influences, so as not to find its adequate form and action in the actual order of the

---

liceat quin discerpatur Christus; quod fieri non potest. Quin sic electi Dei omnes in Christo sunt connexi, ut quemadmodum ab uno capite pendent, ita in unum velut corpus coalescant, ea inter se compage cohaerentes, qua ejusdem corporis membra. *Calv. Instit.* IV. 1. 2. Speaking afterwards of the visible Church as carrying the title *Mother*, he says: non alius est in vitam ingressus, nisi nos ipsa concipiat in utero, nisi pariat, nisi nos alata suis uberibus, denique sub custodia et gubernatione sua nos teneat, donec exuti carne mortali, similes erimus angelis.—Adde quod extra ejus gremium nulla est speranda peccatorum remissio, nec ulla salus. *Ib.* §. 4.

Church. Thus we behold at this time the Christian world in fact, broken into various denominations, with separate confessions and creeds, among which too often polemic zeal appears far more prominent than catholic charity. Such distraction and division can never be vindicated, as suitable to the true conception of the Church. They disfigure and obscure its proper glory, and give a false, distorted image of its inward life. Still the Church is not on this account subverted, or shut up to the precincts of some single sect, arrogantly claiming to be the whole body. The life with which it is animated does indeed seek an outward revelation in all respects answerable to its own nature; and it can never be fully satisfied till this be happily secured; but as a process, struggling constantly towards such end, it may be vigorously active at the same time, under forms that bear no right proportion whatever to its wants. We may not doubt therefore, but that in the midst of all the denominational distinctions, which have come to prevail particularly since the time of the Reformation, the life of the Church, with all its proper attributes, is still actively at work in every evangelical communion. The "one body," most unfortunately, is wanting for the present; but the "one Spirit," reigns substantially notwithstanding through all communions, and binds them together as a greater spiritual whole. Joined together in the common life of Christ, in the possession of one faith, one hope, and one baptism, the various divisions of the Christian world, are still organically the same Church. In this form, we hold fast to the idea of Catholic Unity, as the only ground in which any true Christianity, individual or particular can possibly stand.

II. *Having in this general way considered the nature of that oneness which belongs to the constitution of the Catholic Church, we are prepared to contemplate, in the second place, the* DUTY OF CHRISTIANS *with regard to it.*

This is comprehended generally in the obligation of all, earnestly and actively to seek the unity of the Church, in its most complete form. We have seen that in the actual circumstances of the Church, idea and fact do not for the most part fully correspond. It is only in the way of development and process most generally, that we find the first revealing itself in the form of the second. Thus the unity of the Church, is something which is not at once realized, as a matter of course, by the appearance of the Church in the world. The actual, in fact, stands far behind the ideal. But still this relation cannot be rested in as ultimate and right. It can hold with truth, only as an intermediate stage, through which the life of the Church is constantly struggling towards a revelation, that shall be in all respects adequate to its nature. This development is not blind of course and necessary, as in the sphere of mere nature, but moral, involving intelligence and will. The Church is required to seek and maintain her own unity; and this obligation falls back necessarily in the end upon Christians as such. They are bound to maintain "the unity of the Spirit in the bond of peace," and cannot be true to their vocation, except as they consciously endeavor, so far as in them lies, to have this unity made in the largest sense complete; so that all Christ's people may be "one body" as well as "one spirit," even as they are called in one hope of their calling.

This might seem to be in some sense the great necessity of the Church. "Neither pray I for these alone," is the Savior's solemn language, "but for them also which shall believe on me through their word; that they all may be one; as thou, Father, art in me, and I in thee, that they also may be one in us; that the world may believe that thou hast sent me." Wonderful words; to be understood only by living communion with the heart of Jesus himself. If such was the spirit of Christ, the spirit of the Church must necessarily be the same. The whole Church then must be regarded as inwardly groaning over her own divisions, and striving to actualize the full import of this prayer; as though Christ were made to feel himself divided, and could not rest till such unnatural violence should come to an end. And so if any man be in Christ, he cannot fail, so far as this union may reach, to pray and work for the same object, the Catholic Unity of the Church, as the most important interest in the world.

1. It is the duty of all then, to consider and lay to heart the evil that is comprehended in the actual disunion and division, which now prevail in the Catholic Church. I say in the *Catholic* Church; because the one Spirit of Christ is supposed to pervade the whole body, notwithstanding this vast defect, binding it together through all parts of the world, with the force of a common life. But this cannot change the nature of the evil itself. It only renders it indeed the more glaring and painful. The Church ought to be visibly one and catholic, as she is one and catholic in her inward life; and the want of such unity, as it appears in the present state of the protestant world, with its rampant sectarianism and individualism, "is a lamentation, and shall be for a lamentation," until of God's mercy the sore reproach be rolled away.

We frequently hear apologies made for the existence of sects in the Church. They are said to be necessary. The freedom and purity of the Church, we are told, can be maintained only in this way. They provoke each other to zeal and good works. Without them, the Church would stagnate and grow corrupt. They are but different divisions of the same grand army, furnished for battle variously according to their several tastes, but all moving in the same direction against the common foe, and forming together in this order a more powerful array than if no such divisions had place.

This sounds well; and no doubt many so far impose upon themselves, as to think it all correct. But it is false notwithstanding, and injurious to Christ. Our various sects, as they actually exist, are an immense evil in the Church. Whatever may be said of the possibility of their standing in friendly correspondence, and only stimulating the whole body to a more vigorous life, it is certain that they mar the unity of this body in fact, and deprive it of its proper beauty and strength. The evil may indeed in a certain sense be *necessary*; but the necessity is like that which exists for the rise of heresies, itself the presence of a deep seated evil, in which the Church has no right quietly to acquiesce. Our sects, as they actually stand at this time, are a vast reproach to the Christian cause. By no possibility could they be countenanced and approved as good, by the Lord Jesus Christ, if he should appear again in the world as the visible head of his people. This all must feel.

We do not suppose indeed that the visible unity of the Church demands a single visible head, like the pope of Rome, who is justly styled Antichrist for this very pretension. We do not suppose that it can hold only under a given organization, stretching its arms from one end of the earth to the other, according to the dreams of the High Church Episcopalians. But this much most certainly it does require, that the middle walls of partition as they now divide sect from sect should be broken down, and the whole Christian world brought not only to acknowledge and feel, but also to show itself evidently one. How far it is from this at the present time, it is not necessary to say. Now what is wanted, first of all, is a clear perception on the part of the Church, that is, on the part of Christians generally, that the want of such visible unity is wrong, and such a wrong as calls aloud continually for redress. Without this most assuredly, the captivity of Zion will never come to an end. The heart of the Church must be filled with an earnest sense of her own calamity, as thus torn and rent with such vast division, before she can be engaged successfully to follow after union and peace. It needs to be deeply pondered upon, that the spirit of sect and party as such, is contrary to Christ. The present state of the Church involves the sin of schism, to a most serious extent. Denominations are not indeed necessarily sects, and every separate ecclesiastical position is not to be denounced at once as schismatic. But to whatever extent particular denominations may stand justified before God in occupying such positions, it is certain that in some quarter a schismatic spirit must be at work to create and maintain the necessity by which this is supposed to be right. Take it altogether, there is schism in our divisions. The unity of Christ's body is not maintained. This it is that challenges our attention. This we are called upon to consider and lay to heart.

Nor should it relieve the case at all to our feelings, that we may not be able to see how it is possible to bring this state of things to an end. An evil does not cease to be such, simply because it may seem to exclude all hope of correction. Those who seek to reconcile us to the system of sects in the Church, by insisting on the impossibility of reducing them to the same communion, presume greatly either upon our ignorance or our apathy as it regards the claims of the whole subject. If we know that the Church is called by her very constitution to be visibly, as well as invisibly one, we are not likely to believe that any difficulties which stand in the way of this are absolutely insuperable in their own nature. And if we have come to feel the weight of the interest itself, as exhibited in the last prayer of the Savior, we are not likely to be soothed and quieted over the general surrender of it by a view which cuts off all hope of its ever being recovered. Let it be admitted, that there is no way open, by which, we have any prospect of seeing these walls of partition broken down; still it is none the less the duty of all who love Christ, to take to heart the presence of the evil itself, and to be humbled before God on account of it, and to desire earnestly that it might come to an end. What is most deplorable in the case, is that so many should be willing to acquiesce in it, as something necessary and never to be changed. And what is most needed in these circumstances, therefore, is that anxiety and concern should take the place of such indifference, and that men should be brought to acknowledge openly the reigning wrong of these divisions in the Church, and to inquire earnestly after some way of escape.

To such earnest interest the subject is well entitled; for it includes, as already said, one of the very deepest necessities of the Church. Can any one suppose, that the order of things which now prevails in the Christian world, in the view before us, is destined to be perpetual and final? Does it not lie in the very conception of the Church, that these divisions should pass away, and make room for the reign at last of catholic unity and love? If sects as they now appear have been the necessary fruit of the Reformation, then must we say that the Reformation, being as we hold it to be from God, has not yet been conducted forward to its last legitimate result, in this respect. What it has divided, it must have power again in due time to bring together and unite. Our protestant Christianity cannot continue to stand in its present form. A Church without unity can neither conquer the world, nor sustain itself. We are bound therefore to expect, that this unity will not always be wanting. The hour is coming, though it be not now, when the prayer of Christ that his Church may be one, will appear gloriously fulfilled in its actual character and state, throughout the whole world. But before this great change shall be effected, it will be the object first of much earnest desire and expectation. Not while Christians continue to rest contentedly in the present system, as either sufficiently good in itself or at least fatally incapable of remedy, can any such new order come forward to occupy its place. The result will be reached, only after it shall have come to be generally felt that the present construction of the Church is false and wrong; and when with such conviction, the hearts of men shall have been prepared earnestly to seek, and cordially to welcome a more excellent way.

It is not by might and by power, we know, not by outward urging and driving in the common radical style, but only by the Spirit of the Lord, that any such revolution as this can ever be accomplished. A crusade against sects, or a society to put down sects; movements and efforts of every kind, that address themselves to the overthrow of sects, simply in a negative way, can answer no good purpose here in the end. If the evil is ever to be effectually surmounted, it must be by the growth of Christian charity in the bosom of the Church itself. No union can be of any account at last, that is not produced by inward sympathy and agreement between the parties it brings together. But this preparation of the heart is itself something to be sought and cultivated; and we may say that the very first step towards it, consists in just that consideration and concern which is now represented to be due in the case of Christians to the whole subject. In vain may we look for any such deep inward action in the Church as is needed to make room for a closer external union, if it begin not at least in this form.

Christians then are bound to consider and lay to heart the evil state of the Church, in the view now contemplated. This might seem to be indeed the most they have it in their power immediately to do in the circumstances. It is that therefore which is mainly and primarily required. Nor may it be regarded as of only small account. An immense object would be gained, if simply the conviction of deep and radical defect here were made to fasten itself upon the general consciousness of the Church. Without this it is in vain to hope for deliverance from any other quarter. But this is not the entire duty created by the case. There is a call not merely for reflection and concern, but also for action.

2. It has already been admitted, that the interest in question is not to be secured by any attempts towards a simply outward reform. A no-sect party in the Church, bent only on pulling down and having no power to reconstruct, must ever be found itself one of the worst forms of separatism, aggravating the mischief it proposes to heal. It is not by renouncing their allegiance to particular denominations, and affecting to hold themselves independent of all, that men may expect to promote the cause of Christian unity. The union of the Church in any case, is not to be established by stratagem or force. To be valid, it must be free, the spontaneous product of Christian knowledge and Christian love. It can never hold externally, till it is made necessary by the pressure of inward want, refusing to be satisfied on any other terms. But all this does not involve the consequence, that there is nothing to be done on the part of Christians, to hasten this consummation in its time. It is by inward and spiritual

action precisely that the way of the Lord is to be prepared, for any such deliverance; and to such action all who love the prosperity of Zion are solemnly bound. Every Christian in his place is required to "keep the unity of the Spirit in the bond of peace." All are under obligation to cultivate the spirit of Christian charity in their own hearts and to exemplify the power of it in their own lives. All are bound to pray for the peace of Jerusalem; and to "bow their knees unto the Father of our Lord Jesus Christ, of whom the whole family in heaven and earth is named," that he would grant us all, even his whole Church Catholic, "according to the riches of his glory, to be strengthened with might by his Spirit in the inner man; that Christ may dwell in our hearts by faith; that we, being rooted and grounded in love, may be able to comprehend with all saints what is the breadth and length and depth and height, and to know the love of Christ which passeth knowledge, that we might be filled with all the fulness of God." Unto this glorious object all are required to labor, "striving according to his working, which worketh in his people mightily." It is demanded of all that they should at least endeavor, more and more, to descend into the heart of Jesus, and take the measure of this great interest, as unfolded there, in what might seem to be the main burden of his last priestly prayer. It is the duty of all to follow after the things that make for holiness and peace; and to seek in every way the coming of God's kingdom, with new power and glory, in the hearts of his people, that they may be brought to understand and feel, continually more and more, the force of that common life, by which they are all one in Christ Jesus.

All this would be in the most important sense, to "prepare the way of the Lord and to make straight in the desert a high way for our God;" and the result of it would soon be, that the glory of the Lord shall be revealed, and all flesh made to see it together. When it shall have come to this, that by such inward and spiritual action the Church shall be fully ripe for union, the difficulties that now stand in the way will be soon found crumbling and dissolving into thin air. "Every valley shall be exalted, and every mountain and hill shall be made low; and the crooked shall be made straight, and the rough places plain." It may be utterly impossible for us to anticipate before hand, the way in which this shall take place, or the form under which it shall appear. But in the circumstances supposed, the want will provide for itself. The life that is at work will find room and scope, in some way, for its own free action. With reference to every such case, it is written: "Behold I will do a new thing; now it shall spring forth; shall ye not know it? I will even make a way in the wilderness, and rivers in the desert. The beast of the field shall honor me, the dragons and the owls; because I give waters in the wilderness, and rivers in the desert, to give drink to my people, my chosen." That which is impossible with men, is easily accomplished by God.

3. Then it is the duty of the Church, in the third place, to observe and improve all opportunities, by which it is made possible in any measure, from time to time, to advance in a visible way the interest of catholic unity. The reformation that is needed must indeed spring spontaneously from within; but the process can go forward notwithstanding only in the exercise of intelligence and will, and by the help of counsel, forethought, and wise calculation, at every point. We are not at liberty in the case to run before the Lord, presumptuously taking the whole work into our own hands; but we are bound, at the same time, to follow promptly where he leads. Just so soon, and so far, as the way may be open in any direction for advancing the outward and visible oneness of the Church, without prejudice to its true inward integrity, it is our solemn duty to turn the occasion to that high account. It is not to be imagined of course that the general reconciliation of the divisions that now prevail in the Christian world, in whatever form it may at last appear, will be effected suddenly and at once. It must come, if it come at all, as a process, gradually ripening into this glorious result. Every instance then in which the open correspondence and communion of particular sections of the Church, is made to assume in a free way, a more intimate character than it had before, deserves to be hailed as being to some extent at least an approximation towards the unity, which the whole body is destined finally to reach. No movement of this sort can be regarded as indifferent. The interest just named, is the highest that can occupy the heart of the Church. Whatever can serve in any way to bring together the moral dispersions of the house of Israel, must be counted worthy of the most earnest regard. All Christians then, in their various denominational capacities, are required, as they love the Church and seek the salvation of the world, to encourage with all their might a closer visible connection between the different parts of Christ's body, in every case in which the way is found to be open for the purpose. It is terrible to be concerned, however remotely, in dividing the Church; but a high and glorious privilege, to take part, even to the smallest extent, in the work of restoring these divisions, where they already exist. I would not for the world be the founder of a new sect, though assured that millions would at last range themselves beneath its shadow; but if I might be instrumental with the humblest agency in helping only to pull down a single one of all those walls of partition, that now mock the idea of catholic unity in the visible Church, I should feel that I had not lived in vain, nor labored without the most ample and enduring reward.

IN VIEW of all that has thus far been said, we may now be prepared, respected and beloved brethren in the ministry and eldership of the Reformed Church, to estimate aright the weight of the occasion, by which we are brought together this day. The very object of this Convention is to bring into closer visible union, the two denominations we have been appointed to represent. Apart altogether from the counsels and actions of the Convention itself, the simple fact that these bodies have been engaged to enter into the friendly arrangement, by which it is called to meet, deserves to be regarded with special interest. In the midst of the religious divisions and dissensions that are abroad in the land, it is cheering to find in any quarter, an active movement in favor of the opposite interest. May we not trust that the measure will be owned and blessed of God, and that through his blessing it may be followed in time to come with consequences of good, far more vast than we have power now to imagine.

It is true indeed, that the Reformed Dutch and German Reformed Churches in this country, can hardly be regarded as different denominations, and certainly not as different *sects*, in any right sense of the term. They have been from the beginning substantially the same Church; different national branches only of the one great communion of the *Reformed*, as gloriously represented in the ever memorable Synod of Dort. The faith of Switzerland, the faith of the Palatinate and the faith of Holland, in the Sixteenth Century, were emphatically one faith. Transplanted to this country too, the same Churches have been closely related from the first; in a certain sense borne upon the knees, and nourished from the breast, of the same compassionate mother. For the fostering care of the Synod of Holland was never more active in favor of the scion taken from its own trunk, than it showed itself to be in planting and rearing the kindred vine brought over from Germany. Nor has the sense of this relationship been lost since. Still the two bodies have stood separate and apart as distinct religious organizations, with comparatively little knowledge of each other's circumstances, and nearly as much apparent estrangement as is seen to characterize the relations of sects generally. It is well therefore that now in the end, we should be permitted to rejoice in the prospect of a communion, from this time forward, more intimate and full. It is well that the claims of our kindred life have come to make themselves so felt on both sides, that we are brought thus openly to recognize their force, and give visible expression to the one spirit by which we are consciously bound together. The Church at large have reason to rejoice, in this union. It is something won for the cause of catholic unity, in the broadest sense, that these two divisions of the Reformed Church, should thus embrace each other in the presence of the whole world, and proclaim themselves outwardly as well as inwardly the same; "one body, and one Spirit, even as we are called in one hope of our calling."

Nor should it be allowed to impair the force of this declaration, that no such union has been contemplated in this case, as might involve a formal ecclesiastical amalgamation of the two Churches concerned. All are agreed that nothing of this sort, is for the present at least, to be attempted or desired. Both Churches would only be embarrassed by the measure, if it could possibly be carried into effect. But happily no such amalgamation is needed in our circumstances, to realize the fullest unity the Church is called to seek. A merely territorial separation, where different religious bodies not only hold the same faith, but are openly identified as one interest, cannot be said in any fair sense, to involve ecclesiastical disunion. The Presbyterian Church of this country, for instance, resolved according to the recommendation of some into separate independent Synods, would be one Church still, if only there might be the presence of one Spirit always, sufficiently active to proclaim this unity and cause it to be felt, in a public way. And in the same manner the Reformed Dutch and German Churches may be as closely bound together as the honor of religion requires, forming in fact but one communion, while yet they continue denominationally distinct, as before. No closer connection than this in fact has yet come to hold, between the two Synods of the German Reformed Church itself, as here represented at this time. The only visible bond by which they are held together, is the present Convention.

In these circumstances it is plain enough, that no great amount of action, in the common sense, can reasonably be expected from this body. We must not allow ourselves however to estimate the importance of the arrangement by this measure. The simple fact of the Convention itself, as an open public demonstration of the mutual confidence and good will of the Churches to which we belong, carries in it a moral value, in all respects worthy of the occasion. But the correspondence thus established can hardly fail besides, to open the way directly for a more friendly state of feeling between the two Churches, by bringing them to know each other better, and to feel more extensively the force of that spiritual relationship by which they are united. If this Triennial Meeting should serve no other purpose, than to maintain and strengthen such right feeling, it would well deserve to be perpetuated on this account only. But it may be expected in the end to do more than this. It is the want of mutual familiar knowledge of each other's circumstances, and mutual familiar confidence in each other's feelings, on the part of the two Churches, which now more than anything else is likely to circumscribe the range of the Convention's action at this time; by creating delicacy, and caution, and restraint, when under different circumstances no call for any such feeling might be supposed to exist. In the course of time, it may be trusted, the connection which is now established, will itself serve to bring each Church more clearly before the eye, and thus more near to the heart, of the other. Points of common interest will be multiplied and room for common action extended. The relation of the two bodies may be expected to become more free, as it becomes more familiar. In this way, it is quite possible at least, that a much wider field for counsel and action may ultimately be opened for the Triennial Convention, than any have yet been led to anticipate.

It would seem to lie in the very nature of the case, that Churches so related, historically, ecclesiastically, and geographically, as the Reformed Dutch and German Reformed Churches in this country, should find occasion for common counsel and common action, in many respects. By wise co-operation, they may surely expect to make themselves felt with more effect in the land at large, than they are likely to be by standing wholly separate and apart. The interests represented in the two Churches are in all material respects the same; and this itself would seem to require, that they should regard them as a common cause, and combine their strength in carrying them forward. In the great work particularly of Home Missions in the broad valley of the West, it should be seriously considered at least whether such conjunction of counsels and efforts be not called for at their hands. I shall not pretend however to say, in what several directions or in what several forms, occasion may be found for the two bodies thus to join in carrying forward the same general work. That is a question, which as yet none of us can be rightly prepared to answer. Only we may take it for granted that opportunities for such co-operation will not fail to exist; while we trust to the hallowed influences that shall spring from this union itself to bring them in due time to light.

I may be permitted in conclusion to say, that the time has come, when the Churches of the Reformation generally have need to seek among themselves a closer correspondence and alliance, than has hitherto prevailed. The work of the Reformation is not yet complete. In every great movement of this kind, the direction taken by the general mind is liable in the end to become more or less extreme; and the consequence is then a reaction toward the abandoned error, which is often more dangerous to the cause of truth, than all the opposition it had to surmount in the beginning. To such extreme the tendencies taken by the Christian world in the religious revolution of the Sixteenth Century, have been unfortunately carried; not of course through the force of the principles which constituted the soul of that revolution at the first, but by reason of the gradual paralysis of these principles, where they previously prevailed. The most distressing phase of this bastard protestantism, the liberty of the Reformation run mad, has been presented in the modern rationalism of Germany, and the Continent of Europe generally. A different form of it we have in the religious radicalism, with its infidel and semi-infidel affinities, into which the dissenting interest of Great Britain has been to some extent too plainly betrayed. And finally it is the same evil substantially which stares us in the face, in the unbridled licentiousness of private judgment, as it appears in the endless multiplication of sects, on our own side of the Atlantic. All this may be considered the action of a general force which has been at work for three centuries, but has only come to reveal itself fully in these startling consequences, within a comparatively recent period. And now, by a necessity which holds in the inmost constitution of our nature, a wide-spread reaction has begun to show itself, which may well cause the friends of truth to tremble. This it seems to me is the true secret of the mysterious charm which popery is found of late to be exercising again over men's minds, where its power appeared once to be effectually destroyed; and the true secret at the same time of the remarkable success, which has attended thus far the progress of the Oxford doctrines in the Episcopal Church, both in England and in this country. In this view, the movement must be regarded as specially serious. For it is in no sense the result of accident or caprice. It springs from the deepest and most general ground, in the character of the age. It belongs to the inmost history of the Church. It is the grand rebounding movement of the Reformation itself, by which more fully than ever before is to be tried the truth and stability of the principles, from which the Reformation sprang, and by which it triumphed in the beginning.

The contest of the Sixteenth Century then is again challenging the strength of the whole Christian world. The work of the Reformation, is still to be made complete. It is not enough now simply to cry out against popery and puseyism, as a return to exploded errors. The truth as it wrought mightily in the souls of the reformers, must be understood as well as felt. There is an opposition to the errors of Rome and Oxford, sometimes displayed in our own country, which may be said to wrong the cause it affects to defend almost as seriously as this is done by these errors themselves. In its blind zeal, and shallow knowledge, it sinks the Church to the level of a temperance society, strips the ministry of its divine commission and so of its divine authority, reduces the sacraments to mere signs, turns all that is mystical into the most trivial worldly sense, and so exalts what is individual above what is general and catholic, as in fact to throw open the door to the most rampant sectarian license, in the name of the gospel, that any may choose to demand. Opposition to Oxford and Rome in this form, can never prevail. If the cause of the Reformation is to be successfully maintained in the present crisis, I repeat it, it must be, not simply by holding fast stubbornly to the forms in which the faith of the Reformation was originally expressed, but by entering with free and profound insight into that faith itself. What is wanted is a republication of the principles of the Reformation, not in the letter merely that killeth, but in the living spirit of the men, who wielded them with such vast effect in the Sixteenth Century. Never was there a more solemn call upon the Reformed Churches, to clothe themselves fully with the power of the life that is enshrined in their ancient symbols. And surely, in these circumstances, when the very foundations of their common faith are threatened, not by a casual and transient danger, but by a force that is lodged deep in the very constitution of the age, and may be said to carry in itself the gathered strength of centuries; when questions of vital import, which were supposed to have been settled long ago are again to be encountered and resolved, on an issue that involves the very existence of these Churches themselves; when in one word the vast struggle of the Reformation is to be taken up in its original spirit and carried forward, through a crisis that may be considered final and decisive, to its proper consummation; surely, I say, in circumstances like these, the Churches in question should feel themselves engaged to narrow as much as possible the measure of their separation, and strengthen the consciousness of their unity. The interests by which they are divided are few and small, as compared with those that should bind them together. The glory of God and the honor of his truth, as well as their own common safety, require that they should stand out to the view of the world, not as many but as one, *the Church* (not Churches,) of the Reformation, the body of Christ, "the pillar and ground of the truth," one body and one Spirit, even as they are called in one hope of their calling. May the great Head of the Church himself interpose, in ways that to his own wisdom shall seem best, to conduct the hearts and counsels of his people to this result; and in the mean time bestow richly upon us who are here present the glorious power of his grace, that we may be enabled to be faithful to this high interest especially in the exercise of the trust now committed to our hands, maintaining the unity of the Spirit in the bonds of peace.

www.ingramcontent.com/pod-product-compliance
Lightning Source LLC
Chambersburg PA
CBHW072134160426
43197CB00012B/2106